WITHDRAWN

Books by JOSEPH DUNNER

Author of:

If I Forget Thee . . .

Editor and Coauthor of:

Major Aspects of International Politics

Coauthor of:

American Experiences in Military Government in World War II

Internationalism and Democracy

THE REPUBLIC OF ISRAEL

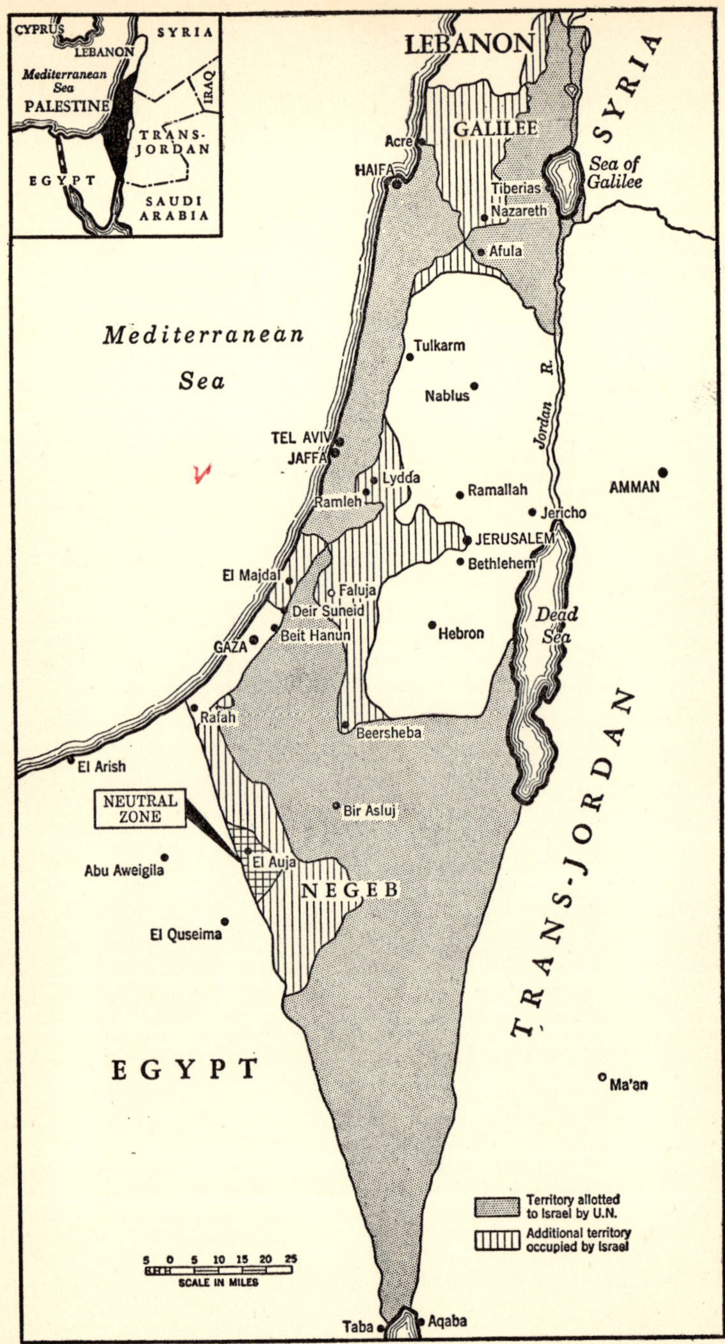

Areas of control in Palestine: the State of Israel and the Arab-administered sections of the country as of winter, 1949. *Courtesy of The New York Times.*

THE REPUBLIC OF ISRAEL

Its History and Its Promise

JOSEPH DUNNER, Ph.D.

WHITTLESEY HOUSE

McGraw-Hill Book Company, Inc.

NEW YORK LONDON TORONTO

95330

50-7653

THE REPUBLIC OF ISRAEL

Copyright, 1950, by the McGraw-Hill Book Company, Inc. All rights in this book are reserved. It may not be used for dramatic, motion-, or talking-picture purposes without written authorization from the holder of these rights. Nor may the book or parts thereof be reproduced in any manner whatsoever without permission in writing, except in the case of brief quotations embodied in critical articles and reviews. For information, address Whittlesey House, 330 West 42d Street, New York 18, New York.

PUBLISHED BY WHITTLESEY HOUSE

A division of the McGraw-Hill Book Company, Inc.

Printed in the United States of America

DS
126.4
D85

To my wife, Ada Dunner, and to
the builders of the Republic of Israel

PREFACE

On January 17, 1943, I received the following note:

THE WHITE HOUSE
WASHINGTON

January 16, 1943

DEAR DR. DUNNER:

I fear Palestine could never support all the Jews and the Arabs would start a constant war if all of them came. Why can't Jews be members of a religious body but natives of the lands in which they live?

VERY SINCERELY YOURS,
ELEANOR ROOSEVELT

A few days later I answered Mrs. Roosevelt, giving her in outline form the first four chapters of this book. Since then I have had the opportunity of observing how this great American woman has devoted much of her time and energy to help bring about the establishment of the State of Israel. I can but dedicate to the same cause this volume, begun in May, 1949, Israel's first anniversary and completed as of December 29, 1949.

There is no doubt that the emergence of the first Jewish Commonwealth in nineteen hundred years has changed the course of Jewish and world history. That a people, bitterly abused, oppressed and pogromized, could rise again, must give courage and hope to all who believe in the forward march of the human race. It is proof of what the human spirit and dedication to a noble purpose can do in spite of heavily weighted odds. No one who has visited the Middle East, no one who has met with the Jewish pioneers in the valley of Jezreel, in Galilee, or in the Negev can come away without a profound respect for the moral achievement of the Jewish people.

The building of Israel with her agricultural cooperatives, her beautiful, modern cities, her great university on Mount Scopus was at the same time a political achievement. The Palestine picture has always been a complex one. The thirty-year period from the Balfour Declaration on November 2, 1917, to the decision of the United Nations on November 29, 1947, was shrouded by a veil of confusion and distortion. The very validity of the Balfour Declaration and the British Mandate over Palestine was challenged by the ex-Mufti of Jerusalem and the governments of the seven Arab States surrounding Palestine. The British Government implemented the mandate entrusted to Great Britain by the League of Nations in accordance with varying and often contradictory interpretations of its duties. The Jews fought a relentless struggle against both the British administration and an intransigent Arab leadership to bring the remnants of their people into the Land of Promise, to rebuild its swamps and wastes and to reconstruct the fabric of their national life.

I shall endeavor to record the objections of the Arabs to the Jewish National Home, the policies of the British mandatory, and the Jewish pioneering effort in an area in which the need for the modern technological powers of the West literally cries out to heaven. I shall try to present an analysis of the various plans for the solution of the Palestine problem by the United Nations, of its decision to partition the country into an Arab and a Jewish state, and of the mediation efforts of the United Nations Security Council.

To place the picture in its true perspective, I shall not neglect to depict the role which the United States of America, the greatest and most powerful democracy in the world, has played in the establishment of the youngest democracy of our time—the State of Israel.

I shall show how the Israelis govern themselves. A critical review of the draft constitution will be followed by chapters on Israel's political parties, on her social and economic institutions, her schools, and her press. A special part of the book will deal with the Arabs in the State of Israel, with the Arab refugee problem, and with the politics of the main Arab states.

Thanks to the heroism of Haganah, the Jewish army, thanks to the wonderful spirit of its people, the State of Israel exists. But its battle for survival has only begun. An uneasy armistice has brought a temporary end to bloodshed but no genuine reconciliation between the Arab States and the Jewish State. No state has ever been called upon to absorb so many immigrants as Israel must absorb within the next few years. No state has ever faced such a wide front of economic, social, political, and diplomatic problems clamoring for solution at the same time.

Israel, as this volume will demonstrate, is not only the concern of the

Jews. The Jewish Commonwealth is the symbol of the few successful accomplishments by the United Nations. Its continued progress is essential to world peace.

One of the foremost obligations of the political scientist and indeed of any scientist is to be objective. But objectivity cannot be had by shunning expressions of preference. Some people try to win a reputation for "intellectual integrity" by refusing to take sides in a controversy, even when there does happen to be a right and a wrong in it. By vague generalizations like "The other person has a case, too," one caters to the mental laziness of those who will not bother to investigate a problem. In fact, behind this "honest, objective" front there hides quite often a dishonest purpose.

I have written against the Nazis before they rose to power. I refused to see "their side, too." But I also refused to identify the German people as a whole with a gangster clique. I have written against the Communists. But here too I refuse to identify the great Russian nation and innocent idealists with the terroristic, power-thirsty men of the Politburo. I have criticized our State Department in a number of articles, published in 1946 and 1947, for not having realized in time the Stalinist character of Chinese communism and for a policy of "too little and too late" with respect to China's National Government. Within the scope of my studies I have always taken sides.

I believe that the Jews are entitled to their own commonwealth on the ancient soil of Israel. While I have great admiration for the teachers of the Arab universities and for much in the Arab way of life, I just as firmly believe that the Arabs have had no good case in Palestine and that it is high time for them to realize that the State of Israel is there to stay. But I do not want my judgments accepted uncritically. These chapters will serve the quest for truth only insofar as they promote active discussion and further study.

Meanwhile, I shall try to follow the advice of Baruch Spinoza, the great Portuguese-Dutch-Jewish philosopher: "When I have applied my mind to politics so that I might examine what belongs to politics with the same freedom of mind as we use for mathematics, I have taken my best pains not to laugh at the actions of mankind, not to groan over them, not to be angry with them, but to understand them."

JOSEPH DUNNER

ACKNOWLEDGMENTS

The preparation of this book has been facilitated by the generous cooperation of several publishers and by the sympathetic interest of friends and associates.

I wish to thank The Macmillan Company for permission to quote from Mordecai Kaplan's *The Future of the American Jew;* Harper & Brothers for permission to quote from Richard Crossman's *Palestine Mission* and Chaim Weizmann's *Trial and Error;* and J. B. Lippincott Company for permission to quote from Walter Bedell Smith's *My Three Years in Moscow.*

I wish to express my appreciation particularly to Dr. Benjamin Schwadran, editor of *Palestine Affairs,* and Miss Sulamith Schwartz, of the American Zionist Council, for helpful advice and for tracking down elusive materials. *Palestine Affairs,* a monthly research journal published by the Research Department of the American Zionist Emergency Council from February, 1946, to December, 1949, has been particularly helpful as source material and an impartial, excellently documented guide.

I am greatly indebted to Miss Harriet Smith and Mr. Charles Ransom, of the *Des Moines Register,* for reading the first two parts of the book; to Dr. Herman Salinger, of Grinnell College, for reading the third part.

Invaluable has been the encouragement of Dr. Samuel N. Stevens, president of Grinnell College; Dr. Carl J. Friedrich, of Harvard University; Mrs. Lane Malsin, Vice-president of Lane Bryant; Mr. A. J. Savin; and the inspiration of two splendid men who passed away during the last year, Rabbi Stephen S. Wise, and my father, Samuel Dunner, one of the pioneers of European Zionism and collaborator of Theodor Herzl's *Die Welt.*

CONTENTS

I will even gather ye from the peoples, and assemble ye out of the countries where ye have been scattered; and I will give ye the land of Israel

—Ezekiel

I

HISTORICAL DEVELOPMENT

Chapter One: THE DIASPORA

ROME · JESUS OF NAZARETH · FLIGHT FROM THE WEST · FLIGHT FROM THE EAST · THE DREYFUS CASE

After three years of continuous warfare, on the ninth day of the month of Ab in the Jewish calendar, August 29 of the year 70 of the Christian calendar, the Roman legions set fire to the Temple in Jerusalem. Many Jews who could not bear to witness the destruction of their sacred citadel flung themselves into the flames. Others continued a fanatical resistance for every inch of the soil of their national home. It took 60,000 Roman soldiers under Titus another three years to clear Galilee and Judea of the last remnants of Jewish insurgents and to capture the fortresses of Herodeion, Machaerus, and Masada. In commemoration of their victory the Romans minted special coins with the inscription, *Judaea devicta, Judaea capta* (Judea conquered, Judea captured). Apparently they grasped only the external significance of the events that had taken place. Rome had been able—at least temporarily—to destroy the statehood of the Jews. Rome had made of the Jews a people in mourning, hearthless, driven from shore to shore, nowhere finding peace. But Rome had not been able to impair the spirit of the Jews, their will to live, their hope to redeem the land that yielded prophets and Maccabees, the dream of every Jewish generation that "out of Zion shall go forth the law, and the word of the Lord from Jerusalem."

Once before the Jews had been exiled from the Holy Land. When in the sixth century B.C. Jerusalem and the Kingdom of Judah were laid waste by Nebuchadrezzar, King of Babylonia, the captive Jews might have shared the fate of most of the other nations of antiquity: disintegration and oblivion. But for the Jews the Babylonian captivity proved the great trial period during which all that had been absorbed into their culture was tested and confirmed. Enjoying the freedom of settling wherever they liked, they constituted self-contained communities which preserved their native customs. They had taken with them the Torah, the Mosaic Laws, and the writings of the Prophets, the loftiest record of their history. While they could no longer gather in devotional exercises before the altar of the Temple in Jerusalem, they learned to come face to face with God in individual prayer and in those makeshift "schools" in which they spent a few hours a day to read and comment on the Holy Scriptures and to teach their offspring to go through life as Jews. When Cyrus, King of Persia, conquered Babylonia in 540–539 B.C. and allowed the Jews to return to their desolated country, many, under Ezra's leadership, availed themselves of the opportunity to rebuild the Temple and the Jewish State.

But there were also numerous Jews who preferred to stay in what was now the Persian Empire. Having been permitted to live their own cultural life, having gradually sunk roots into the new land, they had come to feel at home in the country of their exile.

With few exceptions all of them continued to observe the laws under which Israel lived in its own land as part of a religious ritual. They attributed to the festivals, which had been largely of a bucolic and local character, a transposed spiritual meaning, and in prayer they turned toward Jerusalem. Forced to rationalize their voluntary integration into a land which they had first entered as captives and foreigners, the Jews who remained evolved a new concept of their Jewishness—the idea that Israel's duty was to impart religious enlightenment to other nations, that Israel was chosen among the nations to be God's messenger in order to bring about the Kingdom of God on earth among men. Together with an undying love for the land of Israel it was this concept of Israel's mission which after the destruction of the Second Jewish Commonwealth provided the Jews with a moral justification in their continued existence as a separate entity, with a safe anchorage in the vicissitudes of life and an abiding faith.

In the Greco-Roman world, just as in Babylonia, the Jews made no effort to conceal their particularity in folkways, in ethical motivation, and direction. Although they learned to employ Latin and Greek in commerce and in letters, although they adopted the etiquette of their environment, they remained deeply conscious of their identity and solidarity. Notwithstanding the prejudiced judgments of some historians of the Roman Empire, the Jews showed no special interest in racial purity. They knew that Amorites, Hittites, Idumaeans, and other groups had been absorbed into the family of Israel, that not a few of the great leaders of their people, foremost among them Rabbi Akiba, were of non-Jewish descent; and it would not have pained them greatly had a Sigmund Freud arisen at that time to tell them that Moses was an

Egyptian prince and not a Hebrew. But they did not compromise their austere monotheism. The idolatries of the Romans and their Greek teachers could not be squared with Israel's idea of the fatherhood of the one God and the brotherhood of all men.

Frequently enough there were, even in those remote days, accusations and libels against the Jews. Seneca turned against their Sabbath day because it was responsible for the loss of one-seventh of the working life of men. "The customs of this criminal nation are gaining ground so rapidly," he wailed, "that they already have adherents in every country; and thus the conquered force their laws upon the conqueror." The Roman thinkers rightly appreciated the danger menacing their world of fundamental social inequalities, of untrammeled militarism, of petrified forms of thought and belief. They took recourse to the last weapon of those in fear and dread—slander. In the clash between a declining Roman civilization and the Mosaic ethics of the Jewish minority, anti-Semitism raised its ugly head, assuming at once all those features which it was to have to this very day—the demagogic fomentation of popular passions, the accusations that Jews kill non-Jewish children for their feast of the Passover, that Jews poison wells and the like, ad nauseam. The Jews fought back, determined to maintain their religious and cultural autonomy. The ancient world protested and scoffed but did not altogether fail to admire their stubbornness.

The Middle Ages in Western civilization was a church. From Augustine in the fifth century to the Protestant Reformation all thinking bears its stamp. Theology permeated philosophical, social, and political questions. Even the natural sciences, mathematics, and physics had to submit to the doctrines of the Church. The Jews were not members of this most influential and predominantly European association. Their membership was solicited. Yet, with few exceptions, they refused to join. At a very early stage of their history, probably even during their migration from the Arabian peninsula to the Fertile Crescent, they had learned to connect God with every act of earthly life, the humblest as well as the highest. Man created in the image of God must strive to resemble his Creator. By spiritualizing even eating and drinking, by sanctifying work, rest, and procreation, the Jews had endeavored to lift their daily existence to a spiritual plane centuries before the rise of Christianity.

Why did they refuse to accept the new religion? Why did the Jews reject Jesus? It is a very earnest question from the point of view of the Christian who has been taught that the best in Judaism came to its full realization in Christendom. Young Jews in the Western world, unfamiliar with Jewish history, often raise the same question.

Jesus (the Hebrew word is *Jehoshua,* meaning he was helped by

God) was a Jew. He was born of Jewish parents. He endeavored to be faithful to his Jewish heritage; and he ministered almost exclusively to Jews. In the Gospel of Matthew we read: "These twelve Jesus sent forth, then commanded them, saying, Go not into the way of the Gentiles, and into the city of the Samaritans enter ye not. But go rather to the lost sheep of the house of Israel." Luke reports that Jesus entered the house of the centurion at Capernaum and healed his servant only after the elders of the town had assured him that the man "loveth our nation, and he hath built us a synagogue." There is a definite bias in favor of his people, even a note of extreme chauvinism, as in Matthew's account of Jesus' visit to the coastal cities of Tyre and Sidon.

Jesus came to fulfill the Mosaic legislation, not to abrogate it. He had probably no intention of starting a religion different from that of his people. "Think not that I am come to destroy, but to fulfill. For verily I say unto you, till heaven and earth pass, not one jot or one tittle shall in no wise pass from the law till all be fulfilled." From the Christian point of view Jesus was the noblest embodiment of the Jewish prophetic promises and ideals. Why, then, did Israel reject him? Furthermore, if the Jews of Jesus' time made a mistake not to accept him—and they did from the standpoint of the Church—why do they persist in this error? Why do not the Jews accept Jesus today?

It should be borne in mind that the word "reject" implies that Jesus himself made a formal bid for acceptance and that the Jewish people as a whole either said yes or no. That never occurred. We must also remember that the sources for the life of Jesus are few and ambiguous. Jesus did not leave any writings, relying entirely upon his followers to perpetuate his teachings. All we know—or, rather, believe we know—of him comes from the Gospels of Matthew, Mark, Luke, and John, from reports, testimonies, and records which were made long after his death, when he had become the center of numerous legends. In his own lifetime, as the lack of references in Hebrew literature tends to demonstrate, Jesus apparently made only a slight impression. He was probably one of many rabbis who roamed Galilee. He would come to a village, preach a sermon, tell a parable, meet with favor or disfavor on the part of his listeners, and go his way. With the example of the ascetic Jewish sect of the Essenes before his eyes, Jesus' ideals were slightly more unworldly than general Jewish tradition had sponsored. Rabbi Abba Hillel Silver in his *Messianic Speculations in Israel* interprets the ministry of Jesus in terms of the apocalyptic thoughts of the time, the belief that the millennium was near, that men must repent, distribute their possessions among the poor, and follow those who proclaimed the Kingdom of God if they wished to escape "the wrath that is to come." But Jesus was not alone in preaching such an end-of-the-world morality. John the Baptist and other Jews had done the same before him.

Jesus was certainly in the great tradition of Israel's teachers when he insisted that clean living was more important than the keeping of every religious rite, when he answered those who criticized his association with sinners and publicans: "They that be whole need not a physician but they that are sick." To love one's enemy, to return good for evil, were essentially Jewish doctrines. There may have been "scribes and pharisees" who distorted the meaning of Judaism and clung to the form rather than its content. That type had been denounced by other rabbis throughout the centuries long before the Nazarene was born. But there was a note in Jesus' teachings which was difficult for the most truly religious Jews to accept. Always provided that he was correctly quoted by his disciples, Jesus assumed an attitude of extraordinary impatience whenever he met with criticism and opposition. Although he preached gentleness and love, he often abused his opponents, calling them "hypocrites," "a generation of vipers and serpents." He referred to the heathen as dogs; and he unreservedly condemned those who refused to do him homage.

Jewish hopes in the days of Jesus were quite naturally concentrated on liberation from Roman militarism and oppression. When Jesus commanded his fellow Jews: "Render unto Caesar the things which are Caesar's," he curiously enough expressed an attitude which had been adopted for reasons of political expediency by many pharisees and the Jewish aristocracy. But the man in the street who listened to his sermons must have jumped to the conclusion that this rabbi of Nazareth could not be the real Messiah who, in his understanding, was supposed to save his people not only from all spiritual oppression, but first of all from physical enslavement. This, incidentally, may explain the figure of Judas Iscariot, who, as the Gospels tell us, had at first been passionately convinced that Jesus was the Messiah and then was bitterly disillusioned when he found a man entangled in ambiguities and apparently unable to give direction to the people from whom he sprang.

It is very likely that Jesus had many heated arguments with the leaders of Jewish orthodoxy, as did Spinoza and others in later centuries. Quite possibly his bold behavior in the outer court of the Temple aroused the high priests who were responsible to the Romans for the peace of the community. What happened after he drove the money-changers and vendors out of the court has been the subject of more controversy than any other aspect of Jesus' career. Was he tried by the Sanhedrin and turned over to the Romans as a troublemaker to avoid the sudden descent of the Roman legions on Jerusalem? Or was he not tried at all by the religious supreme court of the Jews, which actually had no right to condemn a person to the death penalty? If Jesus admitted his messianic claims in public, he condemned himself before the Roman authorities to die as a rebel against Rome. The derisive words over his head on the cross at Golgotha, INRI (*Jesus Nazarenus Rex Judorum,* Jesus of Nazareth, King of the Jews), indicate that it was Rome which punished him for high treason as it had crucified thousands of other Jewish rebels, many rabbis among them.

Jesus' death went rather unnoticed probably. His was a typical Jewish fate in a time that was out of joint. Even the Gospel accounts show that he had died as nameless as many other sons of Israel who cried aloud to God reproaching Him with having forsaken them in their moment of greatest agony. It was but three hundred years later that Jesus became the challenging religious figure which he has been ever since; and by this time the Rabbi of Nazareth was the legend of a church with a theology and a way of life hostile to Jews and Judaism.*

Three hundred years after the death of the Nazarene, the God of Israel had suddenly become—in the literature of the Church—an abusive God of vengeance who demanded an eye for an eye and a tooth for a tooth, while Christianity was depicted as a religion of love and forgiveness. Suppressed was the Jewish belief that God forgives to the thousandth generation, that His justice is mingled with mercy, and that a contrite heart is more pleasing in His sight than all the offerings of the earth. Unmentioned and obscured was the admonition of the Old Testament, "And thou shalt love thy neighbor as thyself."

In the teachings of the Church, Israel's God-idea, the God of the universe, had retrogressed to the very beginnings of Jewish history. It was depicted as a belief in a tribal Jehovah, a sort of idol of an arrogant race that claimed to be the chosen people. No mention was made that the God of the Old Testament called the Egyptians His people and the Assyrians the work of His hands; that the Talmud, the foundations of which antedate the Christian Era, forbids Jews to interrupt idolaters in

* The following lines are not altogether favorable to the Catholic Church and Christianity as a whole. I wish sincerely that I did not have to put them into this account. But they are a matter of record, and to leave them out would prevent a real understanding of the Jewish position in the Christian-Western world. On the other hand, I want to emphasize that I am dealing with the past. I hope it will be clear that it is not to reopen old sores but rather to impart to Christians a better understanding of the Jew and to Jews a better understanding of their own history that I write this chapter.

prayer before their idols, "for it is God whom they are addressing without knowing it." No mention was made that the Talmud says: "Why did God, at the time of creation, make only one man? For the sake of peace; so that no man could ever after say to another, I am of older race than you."

The Lord's Prayer, so beautiful in its simplicity and humility, had suddenly become an exclusively Christian possession. "Our Father which art in heaven, Hallowed be Thy name. Thy kingdom come. Thy will be done in earth, as *it is* in heaven. Give us this day our daily bread. And forgive us our debts. . . . And lead us not into temptation . . . For Thine is the kingdom . . . the glory. . . ." Every one of these phrases attributed to Jesus is a Jewish phrase out of Hebrew prayers. But the Fathers of the Church neglected to remind their followers of this fact. Rather they would set aside established Judaism as a perversion of the prophetic ideals, asking the Jews to surrender their own sacred convictions and embrace the Jesus figure as the Son of God. Naïvely or deliberately, the impression was created that all Jews were groaning under the burden of the Mosaic Law and that most, if not all of them, were hypocrites and completely void of spirituality.

How is it that Jesus' love for his people—apparent in at least some of the Gospels—had so completely vanished in later Christian writings? The answer must be sought in the fact that the Church Fathers were Greeks and Romans, for whom the Jews constituted an alien and hateful minority. There were and there are, of course, other minorities in the world. Since fear of the unfamiliar, a potent legacy from the jungle days of the human race, has never completely left even so-called civilized man, minorities throughout history and everywhere on earth have been scapegoats for the majority groups—especially in times of economic, political, and psychological crisis. The position of the Jew in the Christian world can be best understood by giving heed to this simple truth. The Jew, banned from his national home, a stranger without a land, has suffered throughout the ages because he represented the most conspicuous and most ubiquitous minority.

It was certainly not from the Jewish writers of the New Testament that the Church Fathers learned to speak of the Jews as a "miserable nationality." It was certainly not the author of Romans who taught Tertullian and Chrysostom to despise the people of Israel. These Christian writers inherited their prejudices from their pagan forebears, from Hecataeus of Abdera who taught the ancient world to believe that Moses divided the Jews into twelve tribes because he attributed particular holiness to numbers; from Plutarch, who insisted that the Jews worshiped the head of an ass. It was the Greek Apion who seriously asserted that the Jews annually sacrificed a non-Jew, and it was a Christian world that into the nineteenth century shamelessly reiterated this foulest of all slanders.

For Paul the Jews were neither strangers nor a minority. Need one remind any reader of the New Testament how proud the great apostle was of his Jewish origin? "I say then, hath God cast away his people? God forbid. For I also am an Israelite, of the seed of Abraham, of the tribe of Benjamin." The writers of the New Testament bitterly resented the rejection of their Messiah. But they did not know of a gilded ass or of human sacrifices. To hope that conversion to Christianity would cause the former pagans to forget these lies was to hope for the impossible. They saw in the Jew first of all the unlike, the different, the stranger, and they were prepared to believe and say the worst about him.

To Christians of all denominations Jesus is the symbol of all that is pure, sacred, and lovely. To Jews from the fourth century on, Jesus became the symbol of anti-Semitism, of libel, of cruelty, of violent death. A few historic data must suffice.

In 1096 all the Jews of Rouen, Speyer, Worms, Cologne, Regensburg, and Prague, with the exception of a few who consented to be baptized, were massacred by the Christian Crusaders, who, laden with spoils from their victims, continued their journey to Jerusalem. Charges of ritual murder—the sacrifice of Christian children—led to the slaughter of most of the Jews of England on September 3, 1189, the day of the departure of Richard the Lion-hearted on the Third Crusade. About a hundred years later, on July 8, 1290, all the descendants of those Jews who had survived the massacre were ordered out of the country. The ejection of the Jews from England in the thirteenth century was followed by the ejection of the Jews from France in the fourteenth century.

In Spain, under the Inquisition, the charge of Judaizing, the secret practice of Judaism, was sufficient cause to condemn men, women, and children to lifelong imprisonment in a dungeon or to burning at the stake. A special square, the Quemadero, was reserved in the Spanish cities for carrying out the death sentence. It was decorated with caricatures of the Hebrew Prophets. These "acts of faith," or *autos-da-fé*, were attended by all strata of Spanish society from the Court and the Church dignitaries to the masses. The executioner was provided by the state. The Church abhorred bloodshed. The sentences were therefore carried out *sine effusione sanguinis* (without bloodshed) by burning the victims alive. In 1492, 300,000 Jews who had survived massacre and inquisition were forced to leave Spain and Portugal. They left their homes, their synagogues, their graves, and their hopes. The memory of a thousand years of persecution had destroyed in them the innocent, naïve pleasure of living. They survived, they lived; but always they glanced suspiciously into the future, fearing the next blow.

In the Middle Ages, in the name of Jesus Christ, hundreds of thousands of Jews—men, women, and children—were systematically hunted down, murdered, or driven to suicide. How could the Jew feel any impulse to respect an ecclesiastical teaching which would not prevent murder and the desecration of corpses in the name of a religion of love? How could the Jew be called upon to understand a Christian faith which proclaimed the death of Jesus as a necessary act of redemption by which the whole edifice of Christian doctrine stood or fell but whose followers continued to murder Jews as "Christ killers"?

The claim made for Jesus as the Son of God was beyond debate from the Jewish point of view. Judaism rests on the eternal rock of the one and only God, incorporeal, spiritual, before whom all human beings are equal. From the Jewish point of view any claim to a special sonship of God was blasphemous. Theologically, it is as unthinkable for the modern Jew as it was for the Jews of former ages to compromise the central watchword of his faith: "Hear, O Israel, the Lord our God, the Lord is One." Whether orthodox, conservative, or reformed, all Jews find the Son-of-God dogma simply incomprehensible.

If Jews cannot accept Jesus in the traditional interpretation, why do they not accept him from the liberal Christian point of view, seeing in him a supremely great human personality but not a uniquely divine being? The answer again is that the martyred Nazarene who toiled to enrich the spirit of his people was never known to Jews on the basis of what the Gospel writers said about him. Jews knew and know Jesus by the conduct of the Christian community. And the Christian community throughout the centuries has branded the Jew as the "Christ killer," the Judas of history, the infidel, and has placed a curse upon him and his children.

The traditional Christian version of the crucifixion, demonstrated in Passion plays all over the Western world and taught to this day, attempts to make out of Pontius Pilate, the Roman oppressor of Judea, a merciful and tender judge, eager to save Jesus, and to throw the responsibility for the execution of Jesus on the whole of the Jewish people. But this is a poisoned well and the most persistent source of anti-Semitism. To Jews, the Christian community, despite its many truly noble men and women in history and in present-day life, has been a persecuting community. Jesus is its symbol. Can it be surprising that the Jews have recoiled from Jesus?

The acid test of a man's religious convictions is his attitude toward those not of his own faith, toward the stranger in his midst. A Jew could well accept Jesus as one of the great teachers and martyrs of the human race, as a supremely gifted human being like Mahatma Gandhi, who also taught mankind much precious truth. A Jew could and should accept the fact that the nations of the West, with a tradition different from his, would walk in different religious paths, that they have their own expression of God's revelation, their own discovery of the truth about His world. Christians and Jews should learn to admit one another as partners in a divine scheme. Christians should be taught that Judaism with its interpretation of the Sinaitic revelation does not need any further "fulfillment" in the Gospels. Jews, on the other hand, should cease to regard Christianity as a less perfect form of monotheism, a sort of halfway house between paganism and Judaism. Judaism without Christianity is a perfect and complete religion in itself. Christianity without Judaism is also a perfect and complete religion in itself. Christianity and Judaism, in spite of a number of common elements, are simply different religious conceptions based on different cultural backgrounds.

The Eternal submitting to death, the Unlimited limited by human form, the visible Son of the Invisible God—these Christian axioms have their origin in Greece, not in Judea. The Greeks proceeded by subtle reasoning. Tired of Olympus, desirous of a pattern of life that would make for fulfillment in this world and, even more important, in the beyond, they smashed the images of their little gods and accepted the Son of God as the great mediator between them and the Invisible. The power of Christianity lay in its capacity to bring the activity of God into the lives of men and women who as lonely individuals felt compelled to rise above their immediate pagan environment. To recreate and sustain themselves, they needed the theophany of Bethlehem and Calvary, the symbol of the suffering Christ.

The Hebrews, emphasizing God's message to the community as a whole, followed massive religious intuition. They felt chosen as a people of priestly servants to proclaim the name of the one God. Belief in the progress of mankind, creating by its progress the Kingdom of God—this was and is the faith of Israel. According to Christians the Messiah has already come. The Jews looking around them, seeing injustice, war, and hate, experiencing persecution and discrimination in their own flesh, must await the Messiah still.

Banished from the west of Europe, the Jews fled eastward. Some went to Italy, some to the Greek Islands, some to North Africa. Many settled in the Ottoman Empire, which gave them peace, an active share in the economic life and—temporarily—some cultural autonomy. Many, lured by special invitations of the Polish kings to build up trade and commerce, went to Poland. There had been Jewish settlements in Poland since the middle of the ninth century. With every wave of persecution on German territory, a greater influx of Jewish immigrants sought refuge in these settlements. They were accompanied by German Christians who were anxious to escape the bonds of feudalism and the constant wars among the numerous German principalities. But whereas the Germans, although a national minority like the Jews, quickly adapted themselves to the economic and social conditions of the land, the Jews were confronted with the same intolerance and enmity which had been their fate in western Europe. Neighborly relations between Jews and Poles were considered dangerous by the Church. At a conference of the Polish Synod at Breslau (then a Polish city) in 1267, a resolution was adopted: "Inasmuch as Poland represents a new field in the domain of Christianity, it is to be feared that the Christian population of this country, in which Christianity has not yet laid a firm hold on the hearts of men, may be all the more easily influenced by the erroneous beliefs and corrupt morals of the Jews living in their midst."

Three centuries later, in 1542, the Polish Synod declared: "The Church tolerates the Jews only because by their presence they remind us of the martyrdom of our Saviour." No one can say that the enmity which arose in Poland between non-Jews and Jews was the result of Jewish "clannishness." It was a history of oppression which made the Jews cling together and retain their identity.

The first trial for "desecration of the Host" took place in Posen as early as 1399. As a result one rabbi and thirteen other Jews were burned at the stake. Their cries of agony did not disturb the sleep of those who demanded "vengeance for the death of Jesus." To avenge one man, but one of many martyred Jews, year after year at Easter time mobs led by pupils of the Jesuit seminaries marched into the Jewish quarters of the cities and villages of Poland to murder and to pillage. When at the end of the eighteenth century the Russian Bear gobbled up most of Poland with nearly a million Jews, czarist despotism could do little to worsen the conditions under which the Jews had lived in that country since their migration from the west.

Pogroms, wholesale murder, and plunder of Jews took place in the spring of 1881 all over southern Russia, in particular in the districts of Kiev and Odessa. In the fall of the same year 15,000 Jews were killed in Warsaw and the Ukraine. In Kishinev circulars were distributed before Easter in 1903 announcing that Czar Nicholas II had personally consented to a pogrom and that the signal for the massacre of Jews would be given by the ringing of the church bells on April 6. On April 6, as soon as dawn broke, the bells rang, and murder began. Young Jews who had organized a "self-defense" were disarmed by czarist troops. Yet the very fact that the Jews resisted cooled the ardor of the murder gangs. On April 7 the pogrom stopped. The Jewish casualties were 45 dead, 586 wounded, over a thousand homes and shops looted and destroyed.

In 1905 the "Black Hundred," one of the weapons of the czarist regime against Jews, liberals, and radicals, arranged pogroms all over the Russian Empire. In October, 1905, when the Russian government under the pressure of a general strike in the northern cities had promised to establish a parliament, the "Black Hundred" with the help of czarist troops proceeded to an indiscriminate slaughter of Jews in hundreds of Russian and Polish cities and villages. Even World War I did not put an end to the persecution of the Jews in the east of Europe. Between December, 1918 and April, 1921, 60,000 Jews were killed in the Ukraine. General Petliura, who was chiefly responsible for these massacres, was shot in Paris in May, 1926, by a Russian Jew, Schalom Schwarzbart—one of the few Jews who has ever taken justice in his own hands and avenged the martyrdom of his people.

Pogroms, civil disabilities, legal and economic restrictions, seclusion behind ghetto walls and in the pale of settlement, coupled with the attempt to lure the Jews away from their religious faith by promising an end of persecution and discrimination to those who were willing to accept baptism—this was the fate of the Jews of eastern Europe. Small wonder that hundreds of thousands of them had no other wish but to leave this hell on earth and seek refuge in America. Small wonder indeed that the proudest among them passionately longed for the restoration of a Jewish state in that land which had given birth to Jewish civilization—in Palestine.

In America the Declaration of Independence of 1776 had given legal equality to Jews. The first Article of Amendment to the Constitution of the United States, "Congress shall make no law respecting an establishment of religion, or prohibiting the free exercise thereof . . . ," was the initial instance of the political and legal emancipation of a Jewish minority in a non-Jewish world.

For a while it seemed as if the bell of freedom which had rung in America would elicit a ready echo in western and central Europe. In England both Charles II and William III had encouraged Jewish re-

Beneath the portrait of Theodore Herzl, whose fifty-year-old dream became reality on May 14, 1948, Prime Minister David Ben Gurion reads the Declaration of Independence of the State of Israel. *Courtesy of United Palestine Appeal.*

Headquarters of the Jewish Agency, Jerusalem. *Courtesy of United Palestine Appeal.*

Dr. Chaim Weizmann, Israel's first president, meets with President Truman in Washington in 1948. *Courtesy of United Palestine Appeal.*

immigration, promising a new state of freedom, though not equal rights of citizenship. In 1776 Louis XVI gave the Jews the right of domicile in France, although he imposed special taxes on them and endeavored to reduce their number by the legal limitation of Jewish marriages. In the Papal States Jews were tolerated only if they were willing to live under the old medieval ghetto conditions, paying exorbitant taxes and allowing their children to be brought up as Catholics. Of Spain and of Portugal, De Montesquieu said in 1748, in *The Spirit of Laws:* "If anyone in days to come should ever dare to say that the people of Europe were civilized in the century in which we are now living, you (the Inquisitors of Spain and Portugal) will be referred to as proof that they were barbarians." In Germany Gotthold Ephraim Lessing, the famous writer, asked the Christian princes to renounce the idea that godliness prevented them from treating the Jews as equals as long as they failed to embrace Christianity.

Suddenly in the night of August 4, 1789, the National Assembly of France abolished the ancien régime in the west of Europe. A few weeks later the Declaration of the Rights of Man was adopted. Under the influence of the French Revolution and the Napoleonic victories the walls of the ghettos fell first in Holland, then in Germany, in Austria, and in Italy. Liberal ideas, so long bubbling in the hearts of the free spirits of European society, suddenly surged out in all directions. Freed from their legal shackles, Jews participated wholeheartedly in the movement against political and religious reaction. Within a generation after the emancipation of the Jews of Italy, Ernesto Nathan was elected mayor of Rome, while Luigi Luzzatti was appointed Secretary of the Treasury of the new and unified Italian Kingdom. In England Disraeli had still to pay the price of baptism in order to rise to the post of Prime Minister. But Lionel Rothschild, a descendant of the German-Jewish banking family of Frankfurt am Main, sat in the House of Commons without being forced to renounce his faith; and in the twentieth century the Jew, Lord Reading, became Viceroy of India.

But emancipation is not a gift. It cannot be presented on a silver platter. Napoleon had already restricted the emancipation of the Jews to those who were willing to renounce Jewish nationalism, give up their group life, and become Frenchmen of a diluted Mosaic faith. *Sa Majesté veut que vous soyez Français,* Napoleon decreed, and the Jews of France obeyed. The Jews of western Europe were to be granted civic equality not as Jews, not as conscious members of one of the greatest races and cultural units that the world had ever seen, but as Frenchmen, as Englishmen, as Germans, as Italians, who, it was hoped, would either make of Judaism some sort of abstract religious doctrine or

—even better—give up the memory of their Jewishness altogether and embrace Catholicism and Protestantism, the religious beliefs of the majority. Even in the Western Hemisphere, where dissident Englishmen and immigrants from other parts of Europe were creating an American nation based on the ideal of cultural pluralism, a partly deliberate, partly unconscious, imperialism on the part of the majority group expected to devour the Jewish minority—by way of assimilation. As Reinhold Niebuhr, the great Protestant thinker, once observed, "This is a painless death, but it is death nevertheless."

Adaptation and assimilation are natural processes which come into play wherever minority and majority groups live together. As such these processes broaden and enrich the spiritual treasures of all concerned. As such they are vital for the progress of humanity. Assimilation can, however, also mean the sacrifice, the wanton destruction of one's identity and with it the falsification of one's character. There is a difference, after all, between a free give-and-take among the various groups of the human race and the one-sided demand on the part of the majority that the members of the minority group give up their identity while the members of the majority group are encouraged to cling to theirs. It was this demand which caused the personal tragedy of Heinrich Heine, who was asked to become a Protestant in order to secure a position in German university life. It was this demand which crushed the personality of many a gifted Jew. It was this demand which in England, France, and especially in Germany made Judaism a burden deeply resented by those who were too proud to renounce their Jewish heritage and yet eager to leave the state of mental and physical isolation imposed on them by the non-Jewish community.

Gabriel Riesser once made a statement which was rather characteristic of the German Jew who had left the ghetto and lost all contact with his past: "We did not immigrate here. We were born here, and, because we were born here, we lay no claim to a home anywhere else. We are either Germans, or else we are homeless." The premise of this statement was certainly correct. But the conclusion was sentimentally distorted and of little interest to those who had grudgingly and more as a by-product of their own new freedoms granted emancipation to the Jews.

The "enlightened" European remained suspicious of the Jew, particularly of the Jew who turned Christian. He never failed to see in this new Christian the descendant of Abraham, Isaac, and Jacob, of Moses and the Prophets. Whether he composed an *Elijah* or "Du bist wie eine Blume," whether he founded the Hamburg-American Line or the Red Army, he remained a Jew in the eyes of the non-Jewish majority. Worse than isolation was the fact that the converted Jew lost the dignified bearing which arises from a sense of individuality. Exchanging what was great for something which was only useful, forced to misrepresent his past and to hide his identity, the converted Jew, the new Catholic or new Protestant, was driven to overemphasize his new loyalties, to be 110 per cent for everything he did. He could not help becoming a caricature of himself.

The whole tragedy of the new Christian-Jewish relationship came to light in the very land that had given birth to the Declaration of the Rights of Man. In Germany the philosopher Duehring, in his treatise *The Jewish Question as a Problem of Race, Morals and Culture,* had inaugurated that type of modern anti-Jewish literature which describes the whole history of culture as a conflict between a "superior Aryan race" and "an inferior Jewish race" which was trying to corrupt the noble standards of the Homo Europeus.

Very soon Duehring and his followers had the satisfaction of being echoed on the other side of the Rhine. Edouard Drumont in his book, *La France Juive,* undertook to prove that the Jews were in the pay of Germany in order to keep France down. France had lost the War of 1870–71 against Prussia-Germany. A stab-in-the-back theory was highly welcome to the General Staff of the French Army. Why admit one's own shortcomings? There was the ideal scapegoat of eighteen hundred years of Western civilization—the Jew. Forgotten were the high sounding words of Equality, Fraternity, and Liberty. Most of the French generals had never liked these words anyhow. The Jews, of course, and not they, were responsible for the defeat of the Empire, for the downfall of France, for the Third Republic which they stigmatized as the "Jew Republic."

It was in this atmosphere that the Dreyfus trial occurred, the trial of a Jew who had dared to become a member of the French General Staff. It was a wintry day in December, 1894, when Alfred Dreyfus was led into the court of the École Militaire in Paris. Four men brought the Jewish officer before a general on horseback surrounded by five thousand soldiers in square formation. The general said: "Alfred Dreyfus, you are unworthy to bear arms. In the name of France I degrade you from your rank." Dreyfus lifted his right arm and called out: "I declare and solemnly swear that you are degrading an innocent man." The drums were beaten. The officer in charge tore from the condemned man's uniform the buttons and the cords. As Dreyfus was marched around the square, his fellow officers, officers of the Army of France, cried, "Jew! Judas! Traitor!" The mob of Paris swarming outside the courtyard added, *À bas les Juifs!* (Down with the Jews!)

That Dreyfus, an extremely well-to-do Jew who had been prompted to a military career by pure ambition, should have sold military secrets to the Germans was a psychological impossibility. But even the more liberal minds of France were at first convinced that a court-martial of high-ranking French officers would not condemn a fellow officer without overwhelming proof of his guilt. They overlooked the fact that this officer was a Jew. In republican, modern, civilized France, a hundred years after the Declaration of the Rights of Man, a very large portion of the French people refused to extend the rights of man to Jews.

Typical of their attitude was the article which appeared on November 3, 1894, in *Libre Parole* (which means the frank word):

> What a terrible lesson is this miserable treason committed by the Jew Dreyfus. A wealthy man, son of a rich trader, occupying one of the most coveted positions in our army, sells to a foreign country our plans of mobilization and the names of his comrades entrusted with secret missions abroad. The affair of Captain Dreyfus is but a chapter in Jewish history. Judas sold the God of love and mercy. Captain Dreyfus has sold our plans and the names of those officers who serve our country in foreign lands.

In 1896 Colonel Picquart, chief of the intelligence service of the French Army, discovered the real culprit in the person of a Major Esterhazy. He asked for an interview with his superior, General Gonse. He told the General of his investigations and demanded a retrial for Dreyfus.

"Why are you so interested in getting Dreyfus released from Devil's Island?" asked the General, obviously annoyed.

"The man is innocent," replied Picquart.

"This affair must not be stirred up again," warned the General. "Two generals, Mercier and Saussier, are too deeply involved in it."

"No revision? But Dreyfus is innocent," insisted Picquart.

"Even though he is innocent," answered Gonse sharply, "it makes no difference."

"And his family? Imagine the position of the General Staff if his family should be able to establish the true facts."

"Colonel Picquart, if you do not talk, no one will ever hear the truth."

The French Army refused a review of the case, kept the degraded Dreyfus in his cell on Devil's Island, and ordered Picquart to leave France for a "secret mission in the East." But Picquart was not silent. Thanks to him and the pressure of his friends the Ministry of War in 1898 was at last forced to put Esterhazy on trial. He was acquitted because the Army authorities refused to produce the proof of his guilt.

Against this verdict the great French novelist, Émile Zola, protested in his famous *J'Accuse.* As a reward he was sentenced to a year's imprisonment. Colonel Picquart, having dared to continue to struggle in behalf of Dreyfus, was sent to prison. Then Georges Clemenceau, the Tiger of later days, took up the cause for Dreyfus. Because of his and Zola's efforts, Colonel Henri, an accomplice of Esterhazy, finally confessed the truth and committed suicide. Esterhazy himself fled to London. In 1900—at last—Dreyfus was granted a retrial. But the Army of France could not be wrong. In spite of all revelations Dreyfus was again condemned, this time to ten years' imprisonment in a fortress, though he was immediately pardoned. Zola died in 1902. It took another four years until the untiring efforts of Clemenceau, now joined by Jaurès, the French Socialist leader, led to the complete exoneration of Dreyfus.

In 1931, when the Théâtre de l'Ambigu in Paris dared to produce a dramatized version of the Dreyfus affair, members of Action Française, Croix de Feu, and Camelots du Roi stormed the theater and compelled the management to stop all further performances. After that they marched through the streets of Paris with the battle cry, *A bas les Juifs!*

Chapter Two: THE JEWISH RENAISSANCE

THEODOR HERZL · THE BASEL CONGRESS · THE ZIONIST ORGANIZATION · DAVID WOLFFSOHN

The ghastly spectacle of Dreyfus's public degradation in the court of the École Militaire in Paris was witnessed by the representatives of the international press, among them the correspondent of the Vienna *Neue Freie Presse.* The name of this man was Theodor Herzl, or, to give him his Hebrew name, Benjamin Zeev Herzl. His Jewish education was fragmentary. His attachment to the Jewish people, in spite of occasional spurts of sentimentalism, was rather cool. Born on May 2, 1860, in the city of Budapest, educated in German law and literature at the University of Vienna, described by his non-Jewish fraternity brothers as a tall, good-looking young man who towered above his comrades and dressed with unobtrusive elegance, Herzl appeared to be especially gifted for a career as a playwright and journalist. His dramas and sketches were enthusiastically received by producers and public in Berlin, in Prague, in the Hofburg Theater of Vienna. In 1892 his reviews and short stories caused the Vienna *Neue Freie Presse,* the most distinguished newspaper in the Austro-Hungarian Empire, to offer Herzl an assignment "to furnish the paper with everything of interest to be found in Paris."

Herzl wrote ably and charmingly. Those who knew him predicted quite a future for him in the world of letters. Then, out of a clear sky, history beckoned. The Dreyfus affair shook him to the core. "Until that time," he wrote, "most of us believed that the solution of the Jewish question was to be patiently waited for as part of the general development of mankind. But when a people which in every other respect is so progressive and so highly civilized can take such a turn, what are we to expect from other peoples, which have not even attained the level which France attained a hundred years ago?"

Herzl realized that anti-Semitism is not propagated by ignoramuses, that it was rather the minority fate of the Jews which rendered them so vulnerable whenever unscrupulous but by no means illiterate demagogues wished to exploit the deep-rooted intolerance for the unlike in the masses. In the early days of May, 1895, Herzl addressed a letter to Baron de Hirsch, the great German-Jewish philanthropist. The opening paragraph contained the words, "I want to discuss with you a Jewish political plan the effects of which will perhaps extend to days when you and I are no longer here." Within a few days he outlined this plan in a 65-page pamphlet. It was the first draft of his famous book entitled *Der Judenstaat* (*The Jewish State*).

The writer became the maker of history. The more he wrote about the Jewish problem, the clearer grew the picture which he had of his own part in the destiny of his people. This is an entry in Herzl's diary:

> I pick up once again the torn thread of the tradition of our people. I shall lead it into the promised land . . . where we can live at last as free men on our own soil, and where we can die peacefully in our own fatherland. Where we can expect the award of honor for great deeds—so that the offensive cry of "Jew" may become an honorable appellation, like "German," "Englishman," "Frenchman," in brief, like all civilized peoples. So that we may be able to form our state to educate our people for the tasks which at present still lie beyond our vision. For surely God would not have kept us alive so long if there were not assigned to us a specific role in the history of mankind.

Herzl has often been referred to as the founder of political Zionism. If political Zionism means the effort to solve the problem of the geographic homelessness of the Jewish people by the creation of a Jewish homeland, the concept existed before Herzl's time. There was Moses Hess, the German-Jewish Socialist, who already in 1840 had written:

> We shall always remain strangers among the nations; these, it is true, will grant us rights from feelings of humanity and justice; but they will never respect us so long as we place our great memories in the second rank but in the first the principle, *ubi bene ibi patria* (where my wealth is, there is my fatherland).

There was Leo Pinsker, the Russian-Jewish physician, who in his *Auto-Emancipation,* published in 1882, diagnosed the Jewish problem of modern times as the tragic illusion of the Jews of Europe to hope for identification with the life of the nations in which they lived. There were the *Bilu* (*beth yaakov l'chu v'nelcha,* which means House of Jacob, come, let us go), Russian-Jewish students who felt that life was not tolerable for the Jewish people in the European East, that migration to any country but Palestine would only perpetuate the old cycle of a wandering, homeless people, that it was time for the Jews to return to their ancient homeland. They were children of the ghetto, these Bilu. They came of merchants, peddlers, scholars, rabbis. There were no farmers in their ancestry, but with iron stubbornness they founded the first agricultural cooperatives in Palestine.

There were the *Hoveve Zion* (the lovers of Zion). These were isolated groups of young Russian-Jewish enthusiasts, among them Dr. Chaim Weizmann, who went from house to house collecting funds for the colonization of Jews in Palestine. These were those Jewish men and women who with the generous assistance of Baron Edmond de Rothschild of Paris settled in *Rishon le Zion* (First in Zion), *Petach Tikvah* (Gate of Hope), and other struggling colonies.

But it was Theodor Herzl who gave the Zionist movement organization, form, direction. It was Herzl who more than any other Zionist called forth a tremendous agitation in world Jewry and who crowned his ceaseless efforts by setting up the first Jewish parliament in the history of the exile, the Zionist Congress. The idea of a world Jewish assembly had been first proposed by the German-Jewish writer, Nathan Birnbaum, who had also coined the very term "Zionism." When the wealthy Jews of Europe, foremost among them Hirsch, rejected Herzl's plan of a mass settlement of Jews in a new Jewish state, Herzl wrote to one of his main followers in England, Jacob de Haas (later one of his biographers), in 1896: "There is only one reply to this situation. Let us organize the Jewish masses immediately."

Herzl's political genius led him to realize that the fate of the Jewish people could not be left in the hands of those few rich Jews in England, France, and Germany who had arrogated to themselves the role of Jewish spokesmen and who would intercede with the non-Jewish authorities in behalf of their poorer coreligionists.

"The direction of Jewish affairs must not be left to the will of individuals, no matter how well intentioned they may be. A forum must be created, before which each one may be made to account for what he does or fails to do in Jewry," Herzl wrote in a message calling for the first Zionist Congress to be held in Munich, the capital city of Bavaria. But the leaders of German Jewry—just a few decades before Hitler—protested openly against the holding of a Zionist congress in a German city. In their opinion the aims of the Zionists contradicted the prophetic message of Israel and the "duty of every Jew to belong without reservation to the Fatherland in which he lives." Herzl replied that those who did not feel that they belonged to the Jewish people had no business to interfere in its affairs. "When they speak of Zion," he added sarcastically, "they mean, in God's name, anything but Zion. Their Jewish mission is something sated, comfortable and well-to-do. For years now I have been observing the people who retort with Israel's Mission whenever I come to talk to them about the wretchedness of the Jewish poor. These missionaries are excellently situated."

The First Zionist Congress assembled on August 29, 1897, in the beautiful old Swiss Rhine city of Basel, instead of in Munich.

The Basel Casino was the meeting place of the first world assembly of Jews since the destruction of their statehood in the year 70. A large sign displayed the Star of Zion over the portals. At one side hung a flag—a white field with two blue stripes and a star in the center. David Wolffsohn, a merchant from Cologne, one of Herzl's closest coworkers, had chosen the colors of the Jewish prayer shawl, and most of the delegates took it for granted that this was the old Jewish flag.

Herzl was thirty-seven years of age when he opened the Congress and asked the oldest member in the assembly, Dr. Lippe of Jassy, a follower of Hoveve Zion, to offer a benediction. Not a few eyes filled with tears when Dr. Lippe rose, covered his head, and said the ancient Hebrew prayer: "Blessed art Thou, O Lord, King of the Universe, who has kept us alive to witness this day." In a few words Herzl described the task of the Congress:

> We are here to lay the foundation stone of the house which is to shelter the Jewish nation. . . . The world has always been badly informed about us. The feeling of unity among us, which the world so often and so bitterly throws up to us, was in process of dissolution when the tide of anti-Semitism rose about us. Anti-Semitism has given us our strength again. . . . Zionism is the return of the Jews to Judaism even before their return to the Jewish land. . . . We Zionists seek to awaken the Jewish people everywhere to self help. We must create here and now an organ, a permanent organ, which the Jewish people has lacked till now. . . .

After Herzl, Max Nordau, the famous Parisian writer, spoke. His address was a brilliant epigrammatic picture of Jewish suffering throughout the world. But there was a ray of hope. "For the first time since the struggle of Bar Kochba (in 133) does there exist among the Jews an inclination to show themselves, and to show to the world how much vitality they still possess." After Nordau's address came the reports from the various countries. There was a large delegation from Russia. But the Russian Jews, fearing severe repercussions at home, were silent. That silence was more significant than any report.

The First Zionist Congress adopted the Basel Program which has become the official expression of Zionist efforts: "The aim of Zionism is to create for the Jewish people a publicly-recognized and legally-secured home in Palestine." To realize this aim, the Zionist Congress proposed the following measures:

1. To promote through effective means the settlement of Palestine by Jewish agricultural and industrial workers.
2. To organize the whole Jewish people by means of local and international institutions suitable for the purpose and conforming with the laws of the countries in which Jews live.
3. To strengthen Jewish national sentiment and consciousness.
4. To take the proper steps toward securing the concurrence of the Powers, insofar as their assent might be necessary for the achievement of the Zionist goal.

Any Jew or Jewess over eighteen years of age was eligible for membership in the Zionist organization provided that he or she subscribed to the Basel Program and paid the nominal contribution of a so-called shekel (after an ancient Hebrew coin) equivalent to about a half dollar in United States currency. For the purpose of representation the Jews of the world were divided into territorial shekel-unions. As a rule each country constituted such a union. Every 1,500 shekel-payers were entitled to one delegate. An exception was made in favor of the Jewish community of Palestine, where 750 Zionists were sufficient to elect one delegate. For the period between one Congress and the next, a general council, or Actions Committee, of seventy members was to administer the organization and to determine its policy. This committee was headed by the World Zionist Executive which was to carry on the day-to-day affairs and which in the course of time moved from its first seat in Vienna to Cologne, Berlin, London, and finally to Jerusalem. As the supreme legislative body, the Zionist Congress decided on the general program and the budget for the coming administration. Hermann Schapira in the Zionist monthly, *Die Welt,* had proposed the creation of a national fund for the purchase of land in Palestine. Amid general approval, plans for the Jewish National Fund and a bank were adopted by the first Congress. One of the delegates, Marcus Ehrenpreis, delivered an address on the necessity of the rejuvenation of the Hebrew language.* Professor Schapira demanded the creation of a Hebrew university in Palestine. Virtually everything that was to unfold in the Zionist movement of later years was already discernible in this first Congress in Basel.

Herzl, in the few years that were left to him, devoted most of his energies to negotiations with the powers of Europe. A Christian friend

* Hebrew was the language spoken by the first Israelites or Jews, or Hebrews. (Hebrew means those who crossed over—probably over the Euphrates River.)

of his, a Reverend Mr. Hechler, who was chaplain to the English Embassy in Vienna, had interested the Grand Duke of Baden in Zionism. The Grand Duke obtained an audience for the Zionist leader with Emperor Wilhelm II. Palestine was a province of Turkey. Despite his pronounced pro-British leanings Herzl determined that the German Kaiser was the central figure and therefore the most practicable medium for influencing the Sultan. On the soil of the ancient Jewish homeland Wilhelm II received Herzl. During the interview the Kaiser, speaking of the French, incidentally alluded to the Dreyfus affair. "Do they really think I am so crazy a fellow," he exclaimed, "that I write such letters to every first comer? Hanotaux put 27,000 francs on the table for these forgeries." The forged imperial letters were part of the case against the Jewish captain of artillery, Alfred Dreyfus.

At a mass meeting organized by the British Zionist Federation in London, Herzl made known his chief objective: "We want to obtain a charter from the Turkish government in order to colonize Palestine under the sovereignty of the Sultan." The charter—as Herzl called it—was to guarantee Jewish autonomy and self-defense in Palestine—the beginnings of a Jewish state.

There were many Zionist critics of this charter idea. Foremost among them was Ahad Haam, whose writings had profoundly influenced a younger Russian Zionist generation. He put his opposition to Herzl's activities in this nutshell: "The salvation of Israel will come through prophets, not through diplomats."

Dr. Weizmann expressed the feeling of many of the Russian Jews in his autobiography, *Trial and Error:*

> To me Zionism was something organic, which had to grow like a plant, had to be watched, watered and nursed, if it was to reach maturity. . . . Herzl was an organizer; he was also an inspiring personality; but he was not of the people, and did not grasp the nature of the forces which it harbored.

It may be true that Herzl, a Western European Jew, lacked the intimate contact with the Jewish masses of the East which men like Ahad Haam and Dr. Weizmann undoubtedly possessed. Perhaps it was because "he was not of the people" that he had a broader vision in a crucial moment of Jewish history. For almost two thousand years the idea of Jewish statehood had wept forlorn. Here and there a man appeared, proclaiming himself the Messiah, plunging his eager and credulous adherents into even deeper despair. There was a David Reubeni. There was Solomon Molcho—there were others. Then came

Herzl, who did not wait for the prophet. It may be that in a very real sense he was the Jewish prophet of modern times, the dreamer and architect of the Jewish fate.

Like Moses, Herzl was not allowed to finish his task. A number of Zionist Congresses had followed the first memorable Congress in Basel. Zionism under Herzl's direction had become a firmly established mass movement. But Herzl had not been able to secure the desired charter. He died of sheer exhaustion on July 3, 1904, when he was only forty-four. Ben Ami, the Hebrew writer, describes the reaction of the delegates of the first Zionist Congress to Herzl's personality:

> Before us rose a marvelous and exalted figure, kingly in bearing and stature, with deep eyes in which could be read quiet majesty and unuttered sorrow. . . . The dream of 2,000 years was at the point of realization. It was as if the Messiah, son of David, confronted us; and I was seized by an overpowering desire, in the midst of this storm of joy, to cry out, loudly, for all to hear, *Yehi hamelech!* Hail to the king!

With these words Ben Ami had expressed what was in the mass mind. For although Herzl was perhaps "not of the people," his fascinating personality, his self-sacrificing labors had transmuted him into a veritable prophet who in his march through life mirrored the longing of the Jewish people.

In his will Herzl had expressed the wish to be laid next to the metal coffin of his father in the Vienna Jewish cemetery "and to remain there until the Jewish people shall transport my remains to Palestine." He had asked for a burial "such as is customary among the poorest classes, no speeches, no flowers." Over six thousand men and women followed the funeral cortege to the Doeblinger cemetery. Among them were the leading figures from the political and literary world and Zionist delegations from every country of Europe. In two thousand years no Jew had been thus accompanied to his grave.

Under Herzl's influence the British Colonial Secretary, Joseph Chamberlain, had conceived the idea that the more attractive highlands of Uganda in British East Africa might serve as a Jewish homeland. The scheme was to comprise "the grant of a considerable area of land, the appointment of a Jewish official as the chief of the local administration, and permission to the colony to have a free hand in regard to municipal legislation as to the management of religious and purely domestic matters." Britain's Foreign Office had officially made this offer to the Zionist organization. Herzl's reaction had been rather cautious. "East Africa," he said, "is not Zion and can never become it." Nordau termed Uganda a *Nachtasyl* (a night shelter), a sort of halfway station on the road to Palestine. Some members of the Sixth Zionist

Congress, which assembled after the Kishinev pogrom, reflected that there was nothing to lose by accepting it. But most of the delegates, especially the men and women who were most exposed to the fury of Russian anti-Semitism, were against the project. Speaking for the Russian Zionists, Dr. Weizmann closed with these words: "If the British government and people are what I think they are, they will make us a better offer." Nothing ever came of the Uganda affair. A year after Herzl's death, at the Seventh Zionist Congress, in 1905, it was definitely rejected. However, a few delegates, the so-called territorialists, led by the famous British-Jewish novelist, Israel Zangwill, seceded from the Zionist movement. No longer emphasizing the return to Palestine, they looked for a territory—any territory—on which to settle large numbers of Jews. Needless to say, they never found one.

At Herzl's grave David Wolffsohn had spoken these words:

> You did not want us to make speeches at your coffin. But we want to vow that we shall continue the work and that we shall keep your name sacred as long as there will be a single Jew on earth. In this hour we repeat the oath, "If I forget thee, O Jerusalem, may my right hand lose its cunning."

It was Wolffsohn to whom fell the task of providing for Herzl's three children, since the founder of the Zionist Organization had given not only every ounce of energy but also all his material belongings to the Jewish people. It was Wolffsohn who was elected to follow Herzl as president of the movement.

During Wolffsohn's presidency the "practicals," those in the Zionist ranks who counseled a quiet but active penetration of Palestine, had gained the upper hand over the "politicals," who emphasized the idea of a charter and who clung to state-building on the basis of a victory in the diplomatic arena. Both "practicals" and "politicals" were reminded from time to time by Ahad Haam that man does not live by bread alone, that they should not neglect the spiritual needs of the Jewish people. When Wolffsohn died shortly after the outbreak of World War I, on September 15, 1914, there were close to fifty thousand Jewish pioneers in Palestine, struggling hard but persevering. In Palestine, as well as in the Diaspora, where young men and women gathered under the blue-and-white flag with the Star of David, Zionism had created a new and proud race of Jews.

Chapter Three: BRITAIN OPENS A DOOR

THE BALFOUR DECLARATION · THE PALESTINE MANDATE · COMMISSIONS AND WHITE PAPERS · A MUNICH PACT FOR PALESTINE

After the dispersal of the Jews from Palestine by the Romans, the country changed its masters a number of times. The Romans were followed by the Byzantines, and the Byzantines by the Persians. Subsequently, about A.D. 634, came the conquest by Moslem Arabs from the hinterland of Arabia, who demolished the Persian Empire and shook the Byzantine power to its very foundation. Damascus, from whose walls the Apostle Paul was let down in a basket on the memorable night of his flight, and Baghdad, but not Jerusalem, became the centers of the Islamic Empire. Arab overlordship of Palestine terminated in 1071 when the Seljuk Turks took over. These were succeeded by the Crusaders, who represented the reaction of Christian Europe to Moslem Asia and Moslem Spain. The Crusaders in turn were—temporarily—swept out of Palestine by the Kurdish Sultan, Saladin. Then Frederick Barbarossa, Emperor of Germany, Richard the Lion-hearted, King of England, and Philip Augustus, King of France—the most powerful sovereigns of Europe—took the Cross. Richard, full of romantic ideas, proposed that his sister marry Saladin's brother and that the two should receive Jerusalem as a wedding present. Thus, in 1192, the war between the Crusaders and the Kurds came to an end. The final blow to the cause of the Crusaders was dealt by the strange slave dynasty of the Mamelukes, who ruled Egypt and the eastern Mediterranean areas for about two and three-quarters centuries. They were overthrown by the Turk Salim in 1517. From then on until the end of World War I, Palestine was a domain of the Ottoman Empire, which held together—mainly by the sword—a heterogeneous mass of alien nationalities and different religious groupings. In recent years Arab spokesmen have claimed that the Palestine Arabs enjoyed a large measure of autonomy under Turkish rule and that the Turks promised them actual home rule, until the idea of establishing a Jewish national home in Palestine, supported by the Allies of World War I, shattered these hopes.

Actually the Palestine of Jewish days no longer existed as a separate and distinctive unit within the Ottoman Empire. Part of former Palestine belonged to the vilayet (administrative district) of Beirut, part to the vilayet of Syria, part to the sanjak (smaller administrative unit) of Jerusalem. Arabs, like the rest of the alien populations, had no autonomy in any of these parts; the coup d'état of the young Turks in 1908, far from opening a new age of freedom throughout the Ottoman Empire, stood for centralization and not local home rule, for Turcification rather than for a fuller development of Arab cultural and political life.

The truth is that what was Palestine before the year 70 never had acquired an Arab character. The only result of the Arab advent to power in 634 was that large numbers of Palestine's inhabitants sought safety from persecution by conversion to Islam. Palestine was an independent sovereign state only during three periods: when it was a Jewish state prior to the Babylonian captivity, when it was again a Jewish state after the return of the Jews under Ezra until the end of the Maccabean Dynasty, and, lastly, when it was governed by the Crusaders. At all other times Palestine was only part of another state and was not a separate, distinct entity. It did not become such a separate and distinct entity again until after the end of World War I, when the League of Nations accorded Great Britain the mandate for Palestine.

During World War I various negotiations, which were based on the assumption of an Allied victory, were carried on among the principal Allied powers as to the future of the Turkish Empire. In March, 1915, the French government suggested that it might claim control of Syria, including (as the term "Syria" had long included) Palestine. The British answer in June, 1915, was that the French claim to northern Syria should be considered but that, owing to the world-wide importance of the Holy Land, Jerusalem and the area around Jerusalem should be reserved for some form of international administration.

Husein, Sherif and Emir of Mecca and hereditary guardian of the Moslem holy places of Mecca and Medina, had long cherished the idea of throwing off the Turkish yoke. He addressed a letter, dated July 14, 1915, to Sir Henry McMahon, then British High Commissioner in

Egypt, explaining the terms on which he was prepared to cooperate with Great Britain against the Turks. He demanded independence for the Arabian peninsula and the whole Arab world in western Asia, indicating the exact boundaries. Sir Henry McMahon at first replied that the discussion of boundaries was premature. Following a second letter from Sherif Husein, dated September 9, Sir Henry McMahon wrote, on October 24, that Great Britain was prepared to recognize and support the independence of the Arabs within the territories included in the limits and boundaries proposed by the Sherif of Mecca "in regard to those portions . . . in which Great Britain is free to act without detriment to the interest of her ally, France . . ." and that "the districts of Mersina and Alexandretta and the portions of Syria lying to the west of the districts of Damascus, Homs, Hama and Aleppo cannot be said to be purely Arab, and should be excluded from the proposed limits and boundaries."

In contrast to the insistence of Arab leadership of later years, in particular the Arab Higher Committee of Palestine, that Palestine was included in the area in which Sir Henry McMahon promised British recognition of Arab independence, the British Government through Winston Churchill, then Secretary of State for the Colonies, stated in 1922:

> That letter (Sir Henry McMahon's letter of October 24, 1915) is quoted as conveying the promise to the Sherif of Mecca to recognize and support the independence of the Arabs within the territories proposed by him. But this promise was given subject to a reservation made in the same letter, which excluded from its scope, among other territories, the portions of Syria lying to the west of the district of Damascus. This reservation has always been regarded by His Majesty's Government as covering the vilayet of Beirut and the independent sanjak of Jerusalem. The whole of Palestine west of the Jordan was thus excluded from Sir Henry McMahon's pledge.

In a letter to the London *Times* on July 23, 1947, Sir Henry McMahon himself wrote:

> I feel it my duty to state, and I do so definitely and emphatically, that it was not intended by me in giving this pledge to King Husein to include Palestine in the area in which Arab independence was promised. I had also every reason to believe at the time that the fact that Palestine was not included in my pledge was well understood by King Husein.

Meanwhile, in the spring of 1916, Great Britain, Russia, and France concluded an agreement which provided that "with a view to securing the religious interests of the Entente Powers, Palestine, with the Holy Places, is separated from Turkish territory and subjected to a special regime to be determined by agreement between Russia, France and

Squadron of Israeli pilots march to their outmoded fighter planes on a field at the outskirts of Haifa during the Arab-Israeli War. *Courtesy of United Palestine Appeal.*

Israel's young women enlist in Chen, the women's army (*chen* also means "charm" in Hebrew), and drill for their country's defense. *Courtesy of United Palestine Appeal.*

Somewhere in the Negev an Israeli machine gun rakes enemy positions. *Courtesy of United Palestine Appeal.*

Jewish newcomers aboard the vessel *Jewish State* eagerly await debarkation. They were shipped to Cyprus and evacuated to Israel only after the State had been established. *Courtesy of United Palestine Appeal.*

The white and blue flag of Israel waves its greeting to the thousands of newcomers now entering the Jewish State every week. *Courtesy of United Palestine Appeal.*

Great Britain." This agreement was kept secret until November, 1917, when the Soviet government published a copy of it which had been found in the archives of the Russian Foreign Office in Petrograd (now Leningrad).

The entry of the Turkish Empire into World War I had excited the hopes of Jewish as well as Arab nationalism. Fortunately for the Zionist cause, some of its ablest and most devoted protagonists, including Dr. Chaim Weizmann, happened to be in Britain during the war. In March, 1916, Dr. Weizmann, as one of the world's outstanding chemists, was invited by the British Admiralty to help produce certain critical chemicals. His work brought him in touch with a great many British political figures, among them Churchill, First Lord of the Admiralty, Balfour, who succeeded Churchill in the Admiralty, and Lloyd George, who was Minister of Munitions. In his autobiography Dr. Weizmann, with the modesty so characteristic of him, writes:

> When the first period of experiment and construction was over, I had a certain amount of leisure, as well as more opportunity to see British statesmen. . . . The center of gravity of my life shifted once again toward my Zionist interests, and from this point on the tide of events moved rapidly toward one of the climactic points in the history of the movement and, I believe, in the history of the Jewish people, the issuance of the Balfour Declaration.

In the middle of 1916, when the British advance on Palestine was imminent, formal negotiations were opened between the Zionist leaders and the British Government. Similar negotiations ensued with the French and Italian governments. The Zionists had drawn up a document which was called "Outline of Program for the Jewish Resettlement of Palestine in Accordance with the Aspirations of the Zionist Movement." It was Herzl's charter idea translated into modern conditions; and the spadework was done by Dr. Weizmann and Nahum Sokolow, members of the World Zionist Executive, Joseph Cowan, Israel Sieff, Simon Marks, and others representing the British Zionist Federation. Significantly, Ahad Haam, who in former years had criticized Herzl for his predominantly diplomatic activities, was now among those who had a full share in the diplomatic game which led to the issuance of the Balfour Declaration.

On November 2, 1917, after a decision of the War Cabinet, the British Government published the statement of policy which became known as the Balfour Declaration. It took the form of a letter from Mr. Balfour, then Secretary of State for Foreign Affairs, to Lord Rothschild, whom Dr. Weizmann had suggested as the addressee. The text read:

I have much pleasure in conveying to you on behalf of His Majesty's Government the following declaration of sympathy with Jewish Zionist aspirations, which has been submitted to and approved by the Cabinet:

His Majesty's Government view with favor the establishment in Palestine of a National Home for the Jewish people, and will use their best endeavors to facilitate the achievement of this object, it being clearly understood that nothing shall be done which may prejudice the civil and religious rights of existing non-Jewish communities in Palestine, or the rights and political status enjoyed by Jews in any other country.

I should be grateful if you would bring this declaration to the knowledge of the Zionist Federation.

Like the McMahon letters, the Balfour Declaration was not an expression of a wholly new sentiment. Just as British public opinion had sympathized before World War I with the Arabs and other victims of the old Ottoman regime, it had on numerous occasions expressed its sympathy with the victims of anti-Jewish persecution, especially in eastern Europe. Influential British newspapers, first among them the *Manchester Guardian,* had consistently favored the Zionist solution of the Jewish problem. Since the days of Joseph Chamberlain, British statesmen, most of them genuinely religious men, had time and again expressed their intense interest in a Jewish national home. An important reason for the timing of the Balfour Declaration was, however, the development of the Allied cause in the war. Lloyd George, in his testimony before the Palestine Royal Commission in 1936, stated that while the Zionist cause had been widely supported in Britain before November, 1917, the launching of the declaration at that particular time was due "to propagandist reasons." The Rumanians had been crushingly defeated. The Russian army was utterly demoralized; the Bolshevists under Lenin and Trotsky were about to seize power in Russia and to conclude a separate peace treaty with the German Reich. The Italians had lost the decisive battle of Caporetto. Millions of tons of British shipping had been destroyed by German submarines. American divisions were not yet available on the European Continent. In this critical situation the British Government believed that Jewish sympathy or the reverse would make a substantial difference one way or the other to the Allied cause. In particular, Jewish sympathy would confirm the support of American Jewry led by such outstanding Zionist personalities as Supreme Court Justice Louis D. Brandeis, Professor Felix Frankfurter, Rabbi Stephen S. Wise, and Louis Lipsky, later the first American nominated to the World Zionist Executive. "The Zionist leaders," Lloyd George concluded his testimony, "gave us a definite promise that, if the Allies committed themselves to giving facilities for the establishment of a national home for the Jews in Palestine, they would do their best to rally Jewish sentiment and support throughout the world to the Allied cause. They kept their word."

It should be mentioned here that the Central Powers, not unaware of the war value of Jewish sympathy, at the time of the Balfour Declaration were also doing all they could to win the world Zionist movement over to their side. After the Balfour Declaration was finally issued, the German government, in conjunction with its Turkish ally, formulated a rival proposition, a chartered company which was to be under the leadership of German Zionists and which would have a limited form of self-government and the right of free immigration into Palestine.

It should also be mentioned that Arab leadership was duly informed of the Balfour Declaration. In his book *The Truth About the Peace Treaties,* Lloyd George states:

> Through Sir Mark Sykes and Colonel Lawrence we informed the Arab leaders, King Husein and his son Faisal, of our proposals (regarding the Balfour Declaration). We could not get in touch with the Palestine Arabs *as they were fighting against us*. . . .
>
> The Arab leaders did not offer any objections to the declaration so long as the rights of the Arabs of Palestine were respected. Pledges were given to the non-Jewish population of Palestine who constituted the great majority of its inhabitants, as well as to the Jews. These were the results of conversations which we had with such Arab leaders as we could get in touch with. There was a two-fold understanding given to them, that the establishment of a Jewish National Home would not in any way, firstly, affect the civil or religious rights of the general population of Palestine; secondly, would not diminish the general prosperity of that population. Those were the only pledges we gave to the Arabs.

During the course of 1917 and 1918 the Allied forces, composed almost entirely of British troops but including also French and Italian units and a special Jewish legion founded by Vladimir Jabotinsky, completed the defeat of the Turkish armies and occupied the whole of the territory comprising Palestine. On January 30, 1919, the Supreme Council of the Allies at the Versailles Peace Conference decided officially that Palestine should not be restored to Turkish rule. The representatives of the Arabs at the time of the peace conference were Husein, Sherif of Mecca, and his son, Emir Faisal, later King of Iraq. At his camp east of the Jordan Faisal in the previous summer had met Dr. Weizmann, who had apparently been able to convince the Emir of the benefits which a Jewish national home would bring not only to the Jews but the Arabs as well. Emir Faisal submitted the following memorandum to the peace conference:

In Palestine the enormous majority of the people are Arabs. The Jews are very close to the Arabs in blood, and there is no conflict of character between the two races. In principles we are absolutely at one. Nevertheless, the Arabs cannot risk assuming the responsibility of holding level the scales in the clash of races and religions that have, in this one province, so often involved the world in difficulties. They would wish for the effective superposition of a great trustee, so long as a representative local administration commended itself by actively promoting the material prosperity of the country.

This statement certainly constitutes an unequivocal refutation of the contention later made by Arab leaders and their American and European friends that the Arabs had claimed Palestine as an independent Arab country at the time of the Versailles Conference. Still weightier evidence was the agreement signed on January 3, 1919, by Emir Faisal and Dr. Weizmann. It pledged the parties to cordial cooperation, to the acceptance of the Balfour Declaration, and to the encouragement of the immigration of Jews into Palestine on a large scale and their rapid settlement on the land. Emir Faisal, in concluding this agreement in his father's name, was not, it is true, directly representing the Arabs of Palestine. But the Arabs, like the Turks, regarded Palestine as a part of Syria, and in Syria the leadership of the Emir had been accepted.

On March 3, 1919, Emir Faisal addressed to Professor Felix Frankfurter a letter which not only demonstrates his full agreement with Zionist aspirations but also reveals his concept of the term "Syria."

Hejaz Delegation
Paris
March 3, 1919

DEAR MR. FRANKFURTER:

I want to take this opportunity of my first contact with American Zionists, to tell you what I have often been able to say to Dr. Weizmann in Arabia and Europe.

We feel that the Arabs and Jews are cousins in race, suffering similar oppressions at the hands of powers stronger than ourselves, and by a happy coincidence have been able to take the first step toward the attainment of their national ideals together.

We Arabs, especially the educated among us, look with the deepest sympathy on the Zionist movement. Our deputation in Paris is fully acquainted with the proposals submitted by the Zionist Organization to the Peace Conference, and we regard them as moderate and proper. We will do our best, insofar as we are concerned, to help them through; and we will wish the Jews a most hearty welcome home.

With the chiefs of your movement, especially with Dr. Weizmann, we have had, and continue to have, the closest relations. He has been a great helper of our cause, and I hope the Arabs may soon be in a position to make the Jews some return for their kindness. We are working together for a reformed and revived Near East, and our two movements complete one another. The Jewish movement is national and not imperialistic. Our movement is national and not imperialistic; and there is room in Syria for us both. Indeed, I think that neither can be a real success without the other.

People less informed and less responsible than our leaders, ignoring the need for cooperation of the Arabs and the Zionists, have been trying to exploit the local differences that must necessarily arise in Palestine in the early stages of our movements. Some of them have, I am afraid, misrepresented your aims to the Arab peasantry, and our aims to the Jewish peasantry, with the result that interested parties have been able to make capital out of what they call our differences.

I wish to give you my firm conviction that these differences are not on questions of principle, but on matters of detail, such as must inevitably occur in every contact with neighboring peoples, and as are easily dissipated by mutual good will. Indeed, nearly all of them will disappear with fuller knowledge.

I look forward, and my people with me look forward, to a future in which we will help you and you will help us, so that the countries in which we are mutually interested may once again take their place in the community of civilized peoples of the world.

YOURS SINCERELY,
FAISAL

It was never doubted that the experiment would initially have to be controlled by "a great trustee." To that end Palestine was placed under the mandate system.

The constructive spirit which had brought about the creation of the League of Nations was also responsible for this new system of administration of the territories conquered by the Allied powers. In view of the fact that it was the British Government which had pledged itself to assist the Jewish people in the recreation of their national life, the Zionist organization, on February 3, 1919, submitted to the Allied Supreme Council this request:

The selection of Great Britain as Mandatory is urged on the ground that this is the wish of the Jews of the world, and the League of Nations in selecting a Mandatory will follow, as far as possible, the popular wish of the people concerned.

On April 25, 1920, the Supreme Council at San Remo allotted the mandate for Syria to France and the mandates for Iraq and Palestine to Great Britain, which was to be responsible for giving effect to the Balfour Declaration. Over two years lapsed after San Remo before the final draft of the Palestine Mandate was submitted to the Council of the League of Nations. The delay was largely due to the intervention of the United States government, which took a special interest in the plan for a Jewish homeland.

Great Britain sought the approval of the United States for the Balfour Declaration before it was framed. While on a visit to America in the spring of 1917, Lord Balfour himself discussed with leading Americans, notably President Wilson and Justice Brandeis, the plan of establishing a Jewish state in Palestine. On September 4, 1917, Colonel House, Wilson's personal representative in Europe, informed the President that Lord Robert Cecil, then Undersecretary of State for Foreign Affairs, had cabled him as follows:

> We are being pressed here for a declaration of sympathy with the Zionist movement, and I should be very grateful if you felt able to ascertain unofficially if the President favors such a declaration.

Unlike President Wilson, who for many years was known as a champion of Zionist aspirations, Colonel House appeared to be skeptical of any concrete commitment, for he added: "Have you made up your mind regarding what answer you will make to Cecil concerning the Zionist movement? It seems to me that there are many dangers lurking in it, and if I were British I would be chary about going too definitely into that question." Wilson answered a month later: "I find in my pocket the memorandum you gave me about the Zionist movement. I am afraid I did not say to you that I concurred in the formula suggested by the other side. I do, and would be obliged if you would let them know it."

The section of Territorial, Economic, and Political Intelligence of the American Delegation to the Peace Conference, in accordance with instructions, had prepared the following recommendations regarding Palestine for President Wilson and the plenipotentiaries:

January 21, 1919
26. Palestine

It is recommended:

1. That there be established a separate State of Palestine.
2. That the State be placed under Great Britain as a mandatory of the League of Nations.
3. That the Jews be invited to return to Palestine and settle there, being assured by the Conference of all proper assistance in so doing that may be consistent with the protection of the personal (especially the religious) and the property rights of the non-Jewish population, and being further assured that it will be the policy of the League of Na-

tions to recognize Palestine as a Jewish state as soon as it is a Jewish state in fact.

4. That the holy places and religious rights of all creeds in Palestine be placed under the protection of the League of Nations and its Mandatory.

On March 3, 1919, President Wilson again stated that "the Allied nations, with the fullest concurrence of our own government and people, are agreed that in Palestine shall be laid the foundations of a Jewish Commonwealth." In a note of November 20, 1920, the United States government claimed that the participation of the United States in the war entitled it to be consulted as to the terms of the mandates. The draft of the Palestine Mandate, together with those of the other British mandates, was submitted to the United States government, and at its request a number of alterations were made in it. The final outcome of the negotiations was a "Convention between the United Kingdom and the United States of America respecting the rights of the governments of the two countries and their respective nationals in Palestine," which was signed on December 3, 1924, and ratified in due course.

This Convention recited the whole text of the Palestine Mandate (see Appendix) as it had meanwhile, on July 24, 1922, been confirmed by the Council of the League of Nations. The Treaty added in Article Seven:

Nothing contained in the present convention shall be affected by any modification which may be made in the terms of the mandate, as recited above, unless such modification shall have been assented to by the United States.

With Article Seven the United States government reserved for itself the right to be heard in future development of the Palestine affair—at least, so far as American nationals were concerned.*

The preamble of the mandate for Palestine clearly recognized the obligation of the mandatory to translate the Balfour Declaration into practice:

Whereas the Principal Allied Powers have also agreed that the Mandatory should be responsible for putting into effect the declaration originally made on November 2nd, 1917, by the Government of His Britannic Majesty, and adopted by the said Powers, in favour of this establishment in Palestine of a national home for the Jewish people, it being clearly understood that nothing should be done which might prejudice the civil and religious rights of existing non-Jewish communities in Palestine, or the rights and political status enjoyed by Jews in any other country; and

* See Carl J. Friedrich, *American Policy Toward Palestine,* Public Affairs Press.

Whereas recognition has thereby been given to the historical connection of the Jewish people with Palestine and to the grounds for reconstituting their national home in that country; and

Whereas the Principal Allied Powers have selected His Britannic Majesty as the Mandatory for Palestine . . .

To give the Jewish people as a whole legitimate representation in the establishment of the Jewish National Home, Article Four of the mandate charged the administration of Palestine with the task of cooperating with "an appropriate Jewish agency." Articles Two and Six described the primary duties of the British administration: the encouragement of Jewish immigration and the "close settlement by Jews on the land, including state lands and waste lands not required for public purposes."

But even before September 29, 1923, when the Palestine Mandate formally came into force, Great Britain asked the Council of the League that, pursuant to Article Twenty-five of the mandate, the provisions referring to the Jewish National Home should not apply to the territories lying between the Jordan River and the eastern boundary of Palestine, subsequently known as Trans-Jordan.

As early as July, 1920, the French had upset the British plan to assure a British hegemony in the Near East by making Husein of Mecca King of Arabia, his oldest son Ali Crown Prince of Arabia, Abdullah, the middle son, King of Iraq, and Faisal, the youngest and most ambitious of the three, King of Syria. French troops drove Faisal out of Damascus, where the previous February he had been declared King by the Syrian notables. To pacify Faisal, he was given Iraq, leaving Abdullah without a throne.

In March, 1921, Winston Churchill, then Colonial Secretary, convened a Middle Eastern conference in Cairo with the objective of reorganizing British imperial defenses in that area. During the sessions word came that Abdullah had entered Amman, later capital of Trans-Jordan, with an Arab guerrilla force, supposedly on the way to liberate Syria from the French and to avenge his brother Faisal. On the advice of Colonel T. E. Lawrence, Britain's famous intelligence officer in the Near East, Churchill at once appointed Abdullah chief administrator of Trans-Jordan, to repair the dent in the "Sherifian Solution" caused by the French in Syria. It was then that Britain inserted Article Twenty-five in the Palestine Mandate, which had not existed in former drafts, and asked the League of Nations to recognize a special status for Trans-Jordan.

Trans-Jordan is the territory stretching east of the river Jordan to the Arabian Desert. It covers 34,000 square miles, roughly three times the area of Palestine west of the Jordan. Since its population in 1918 was estimated at less than 200,000, of whom a considerable percentage were nomads, the Zionists naturally had hoped to concentrate a substantial part of their colonization efforts in that region.

When Trans-Jordan was lopped off, the British Government made the point that it did not declare itself in favor of the establishment of Palestine as a national home for the Jewish people but rather the establishment of the national home of the Jewish people in Palestine. This interpretation, which could easily lead to the imposition of a permanent minority status on the Jews in Palestine, was obviously a departure from the meaning of the Balfour Declaration. What England had proposed to do for the Jews and what the Jewish people represented by the Zionist organization sought at the hands of Great Britain and the Allied Powers, was to establish the Jewish National Home in the traditional boundaries of Palestine on both sides of the Jordan. Zionists had never confined their requests to a restricted area or to limited immigration. They had published their demands for the whole world to see, and the spokesmen of the Allied Powers, foremost among them Wilson, Clemenceau, Lloyd George, General Smuts, Robert Cecil, Churchill, Balfour—great Christian names that will be enshrined in the hearts of Jews forever—had answered in the affirmative. The very term "Jewish National Home" would have been nothing but a rhetorical phrase and the Balfour Declaration an empty statement if the Jews or the Allied Powers had in mind to build in Palestine some small spiritual and physical center of Jews like Vilna, Frankfurt, New York, and similar Jewish centers outside Palestine.

Since the wording of the Balfour Declaration—thanks to the insistence of some Jewish "assimilationists" in Britain and other parts of the world—had not been too succinct, its authors explained its implications in more certain terms. Lloyd George, who had been Prime Minister at the time of the Balfour Declaration, appeared before the British Royal Commission in 1936 and stated:

> It was contemplated that when the time arrived for according representative institutions to Palestine, if the Jews had meanwhile responded to the opportunity afforded them by the idea of a national home and had become a definite majority of the inhabitants, then Palestine would thus become a Jewish Commonwealth.

In a newspaper article which appeared on February 8, 1920, Winston Churchill said:

> If, as may well be, there should be created in our own lifetime, by the banks of the Jordan, a Jewish state under the protection of the British Crown, which might comprise three or four millions of Jews, an event will have oc-

curred in the history of the world which would from every point of view be beneficial, and would be especially in harmony with the truest interests of the British Empire.

Churchill could hardly have contemplated such a large population in only a part of Palestine.

The British Labor party, at its conference in Brighton, England, in 1921, resolved:

> The Conference regrets that the economic and administrative unity of Palestine has been sacrificed because of the imperialistic rivalries between Britain and France, and that the territory has been wantonly reduced and the opportunities of its colonization seriously endangered by the cutting off of Hauran and nearly the whole of Upper Galilee. The Conference calls upon the government to put an end to the unnatural and harmful division of the British Mandate territory and to effect the unity of Eastern and Western Palestine.

But Trans-Jordan, a large underpopulated area of fertile land with no cities and only the Jordan as frontier to the west, was gone. The "whittling down" of the original mandate had begun.

Actually it began at San Remo, with the appointment of one the Jews naïvely considered a second Ezra. But Sir Herbert Samuel was a British Jew who, in order to keep his office as High Commissioner of Palestine, felt compelled to lean over backward. The era of public covenants, openly arrived at, was at an end. The military under General Allenby, the conqueror of Palestine, and General Mooney, who for a while was in direct control of Palestine, objected to the partition of Syria and to the Palestine Mandate from the beginning. They did not want Haifa to be under the guns of Beirut. They hated to see the French in the north, and they calmly ignored the Jews in Palestine. Now that the military prelude was over, the silent bureaucracy of the Colonial Office obtained possession of Palestine. It appointed and employed men trained in its service. The London *Times* in its advertising columns from time to time announced vacancies in the Palestine administration. Nothing could be more legal and more correct than these announcements. Nothing could be less objectionable except this—Palestine was no British possession. Palestine was to be developed into a Jewish state, and the men selected had neither training nor disposition for such a task. It would have been a miracle if the men of the Colonial Office, taught to rule "natives," had thought of Palestine other than as a British crown colony. As they thought, they acted. When the Jews from time to time reminded them that they were not "natives," that they were culturally at least their equals, the Colonial officials in

Palestine came to hate both the Jews and the mandate. One illustration may suffice. From 1918 to 1922 the Civil Adviser to the city of Jerusalem was C. R. Ashbee. A few excerpts from Mr. Ashbee's book, *A Palestine Notebook,* published in 1923, illuminate his attitude toward the Jewish National Home:

JULY 24, 1918—Today the Zionists inaugurated their new University . . . but it's we Protestants with our dear old English Bible who really remember Ezra, not they.

JANUARY, 1919—The Jew is unthinkable without the bargain; he bears the brand of that mean fellow Jacob upon his brow.

DECEMBER, 1919—Your Zionist does not realize that Islam has accomplished what Judaism failed to do—to establish in the peoples of Western Asia the idea of the unity of God.

This was the sum total of Mr. Ashbee's philosophy, written in conclusion of his diary: "The policy of the Balfour Declaration is an unjust policy. . . ."

Ashbee's views were shared by most of the civil servants who served England in Palestine. The majority were less educated than Mr. Ashbee, but they probably disliked the Jews even more, although they were reticent about their feelings. It was not in the blood of the Colonial Office men to cooperate with a proud lot of Jewish pioneers in the task of home-building. They liked the Arabs better. The Arabs at least behaved as "natives" were supposed to behave. Their jeunesse dorée, trained in European and American universities, knew how to play tennis and to drink tea at five o'clock. The lower classes were simply repressed. From the point of view of the Colonial official the Jew, who had less time for tea and tennis, was an undesirable intruder.

I believe that this elementary interpersonal relationship more than anything else created the growing friction between Britain and the Jews. Those Jews who came to Zionism after it had "arrived" and had become a successful cause, those Jews who do not know of the days when a British government—prompted by perfectly good faith—offered sanctuary in Palestine to the Jewish people, have come to see in British policy a deliberate, monstrous scheme to defeat every effort to create a Jewish state. They even see an anti-Semite in every Englishman. This view is unjust. It must be emphasized that the United Kingdom is after all a great political democracy whose government can be called to account by every citizen; that from the moment the Colonial officials began their policy of sabotaging the Balfour Declaration they were exposed and denounced in and out of Parliament by adherents of all three British political parties. One man in particular, a British Protestant, could always be counted upon to rise in defense of the Jewish

National Home. This was Lord Wedgwood. He never hesitated to condemn the anti-Jewish elements in the Palestine administration. "The whole trouble in Palestine," he said in Parliament during World War II, "is that the administration does not like Jews. We have had twenty-two years of this policy of continued bias against the Jews."

There can be little doubt that it was British officialdom in Palestine, mindful of the old imperialistic formula of "divide and rule," which encouraged the obstructionist tactics of the British-appointed Grand Mufti of Jerusalem and other Arab leaders. Had the administration there been willing to carry out the mandate given to Great Britain by the League of Nations, had it defined the position between Arabs and Jews in Palestine in the terms of the mandate, the outbreak of riots in 1920, in 1921, in 1929, and again in 1936 could probably have been avoided. I shall discuss Arab-Jewish relations at greater length in a later chapter. At this point I want to confine myself to the statement that a land cannot be built up systematically and consistently as the Jews were building Palestine, in the face of a deep-seated, organic resentment on the part of the majority of the population, without constant explosions and the use of force. Clearly, this was not the case in Palestine. From 1921 to 1929 the Arabs outnumbered the Jews in Palestine ten to one. In those years Jewish pioneers created cities, industries, and agricultural settlements all over Palestine west of the Jordan River. In those years the British maintained only a token force in Palestine while the Jews were virtually without arms. In Syria, under the French Mandate, the land was in perpetual turmoil. Palestine was at peace. Arab workers who worked eight hours a day in the Jewish colonies, Arab farmers who sold their fruit, vegetables, and fish in the streets of Tel Aviv and the Jewish sections of Haifa and Jerusalem, only knew that for the first time in their memory they were making a decent living. From the time of World War I the Arab Nationalist Movement in Palestine was the preoccupation of British Middle Eastern officials and a top layer of Arab moneylenders, priests, professional men, and absentee landowners. They aspired to rule and exploit the fellahin, the great majority of the Arab population, even more thoroughly than the Turks had exploited them. Since, for the most part, Arab villagers and workers maintained cordial relations with the Jews, there was only one hope of success for the Nationalists—to unloose a religious frenzy among the Arab masses.

On April 4, 1920, the annual Arab parade in Jerusalem honoring Nevi Musa (Moses the Prophet) ended with an attack by the participants on Jewish homes in the old part of the city. In 1921, while a Jewish May Day parade was being held in Tel Aviv, Arab riots broke out in Jaffa and spread to other sections of the country. Arab agitators had reported that the Jewish demonstrators planned to attack the Mosque el Akzah, which Moslems believe to be the halting place of the winged horse on which the prophet of Islam journeyed heavenward.

In 1929 the same unscrupulous accusations led to disturbances which cost 249 lives—133 Jewish and 116 Arab. Shortly before the riots, the Young Moslem Association of Haifa in a published statement had warned their coreligionists that "the Jews have ancient aspirations regarding our Mosque el Akzah in Jerusalem." Agitators all over Palestine spread the word that the Jews had killed thousands of Arabs in Jerusalem, cursed Mohammed, and destroyed the mosque. In spite of frantic appeals from the responsible Jewish leaders of Palestine to the British administration, no effort was made to check the flood of inflammatory rumors. Nothing would have been simpler than to bring to Jerusalem leading Arabs from various parts of the country to prove beyond doubt that the mosque was unscarred. British troops were brought in from Egypt when the riots were over. It was then that the Arab Higher Committee issued this statement: "The Mosque is with God's help intact, and will forever remain intact in Moslem hands." It was then that Haj Amin el Husseini, the Grand Mufti of Jerusalem, declared, "Jewish ambition and greed are responsible for provoking the Arab attack," anticipating with these words of stupefying impudence the propaganda note of Hitler, who also thought "the bigger and more fantastic a lie, the more easily it will be accepted."

Following the riots of 1920 a distinct pattern of British policy emerged. While the Colonial officials in Palestine did little or nothing to prevent actual violence committed by the henchmen of the Grand Mufti against a (for many years) defenseless Jewish community, the British Government back home in London would appoint a commission of inquiry to investigate the causes of the disturbances. Invariably the commission would exceed its specific terms of reference by drawing conclusions and offering recommendations. Those recommendations which suited the British Government at the time were accepted. The others were ignored. Probably the best description of the function of these commissions was given by Winston Churchill in the House of Commons on November 24, 1938:

> When the troubles arose in Palestine three years ago . . . what was the remedy of the national government? Their remedy was to appoint a Royal Commission. What a happy, hopeful emergency exit that provided from the immediate difficulty. A Royal Commission, a body of important gentlemen were assembled, headed by the late Lord Peel, and sent to Palestine to find out exactly what the government ought to do after hearing all persons

and parties concerned. There was no need to send such a commission to Palestine. All the facts were evident and even obvious. Having sat at the Colonial Office on these sort of matters about Palestine, I can assure the House that there was nothing that the Royal Commission, headed by Lord Peel, could possibly have discovered in Palestine that was not already known to the Middle Eastern Department of the Colonial Office—nothing. But the formation of a Royal Commission, with imposing names, the gratifying leading articles in the newspapers, all this was a device to save the Cabinet from making up its mind.

In 1921 the British Government appointed a Commission of Inquiry under the chairmanship of Sir Thomas Haycraft. Its report was published in the same year under the title, "Palestine Disturbances in May 1921." It concluded that the riots had been precipitated by the Arab leaders; but that the underlying cause of the riots was Arab opposition to the Zionist program. Although the Commission warned that Jewish immigration would result in a permanent Arab revolt in Palestine, the next eight years of accelerated Jewish settlement were completely tranquil.

After the riots in 1929, Lord Passfield, Secretary of State for the Colonies, appointed a commission with Sir Walter Shaw as chairman. It also blamed Zionist activity for the disturbances. It alleged specifically that the Jewish purchases of land in Palestine were resulting in the creation of a landless and discontented class of Arabs. The best solution of the problem, it maintained, would be to curtail the development of the Jewish National Home. One member of the commission, Mr. Harry Snell, signed the report but added a note of reservation in which he attributed to "religious propaganda" of the Grand Mufti a lion's share of the responsibility for the disturbances. The British Government adopted the recommendations of the report and appointed Sir John Hope Simpson to investigate further the questions raised by the Shaw Commission. Sir John arrived in Palestine in May, 1930. His report was published in October, and once more it was clear that the Arab rather than the Jewish point of view had prevailed. The Hope Simpson Report cut at the very roots of the National Home. Until then it had been taken for granted that a substantial amount of cultivable land was still available for the expansion of Jewish colonization without injury to Arab interests. Zionists spoke of 16,000,000 dunam of land (4,000,000 acres), the British Land Commissioner estimated the cultivable land that was still available for colonization to 10,592,000 dunam. Sir John Hope Simpson arrived at only 6,544,000 dunam. From that basic calculation he drew these two startling conclusions:

1. If all the cultivable land in Palestine were divided up among the

Arab agricultural population, there would not be enough to provide every family with a decent livelihood.

2. Until further development of the lands "there is no room for a single additional settler if the standard of life of the fellahin is to remain at its present level."

The inquiries arising from the outbreak of 1929 were now complete, and the British Government lost no time in acting on them. In October, 1930, concurrently with the Hope Simpson Report, appeared a "Statement of Policy by His Majesty's Government in the United Kingdom," soon to be known as the "White Paper," which repeated all the negative arguments in Hope Simpson's Report. There was a definite inclination toward the Arabs and a fundamental change in attitude toward the Zionists. Dr. Weizmann, who for years had worked for better understanding of Britain's difficulties with respect to Palestine, resigned his joint office as President of the Jewish Agency for Palestine and of the World Zionist Organization. Subsequent events, however, refuted the conclusions of both the Hope Simpson Report and the White Paper.

Accused by both Jewish and non-Jewish observers of having tailored the facts to suit a new policy, the British Government, in June, 1931, appointed Mr. Lewis French as Director of Development for Agriculture and Land Settlement in Palestine. His assignment was to ascertain the actual number of landless Arabs, to find methods for an increase in the standards of living of the fellahin, and to give a new and possibly exact estimate as to state and other lands that could be made available for settlement by Jewish immigrants. Mr. French defined landless Arabs as those "who were shown to have been displaced from the lands which they occupied in consequence of the lands falling into Jewish hands and who have not obtained other holdings on which they can establish themselves or other equally satisfactory occupation." Mr. French estimated that the number of landless Arabs would fall between 1,000 and 2,000 family heads.

When the British administration of Palestine finally called on all landless Arabs to register, only 664 heads of families qualified, and of these exactly 347 took advantage of the government's offer of resettlement. At last it was proved beyond doubt that Jewish purchases of land had not led to the displacement of Arab agriculturists. The Palestine Royal Commission later declared: "The Arab charge that the Jews have obtained too large a proportion of good land cannot be maintained. Much of the land now carrying orange groves was sand dunes or swamp and uncultivated when it was purchased." Significantly, Arab spokesmen since that time have rarely reiterated their charge of Arab landlessness. Rather, they start their arguments by saying, "In spite of the fact that Arabs have profited economically from Jewish immigration. . . ."

From 1930 to 1936—in sharp contrast to the pessimistic forecasts of the various commission reports and the White Paper of 1930—Palestine witnessed a period of unprecedented growth. If the Arab leaders had hoped for a Jewish exodus from Palestine, they were certainly disappointed. If those British officials in Palestine who had done everything in their power to liquidate the original policy laid down in the mandate expected a stoppage of Jewish immigration, they too were soon disillusioned. The reaction of the Jews to the riots of 1929 was this: "More immigration and defense of our lives and of our work."

By the end of 1929 Palestine had 190,000 Jews. By the end of 1935 Palestine had 375,000 Jews, the larger mass of them immigrants from eastern Europe. These were the recorded figures. But there were two kinds of immigration, Aleph and Beth. Aleph was immigration with sanction of the mandatory. Beth was "illegal" refugee immigration. But—and this should be emphasized—during those years thousands of Arabs from Trans-Jordan, Syria, and even Egypt came to Palestine, all of them likewise illegally, to participate in the better life which Jewish pioneers had created there for the entire population.

On April 15, 1936, riots broke out again. They were followed by an Arab general strike ordered by the Arab Higher Committee under the leadership of the Grand Mufti of Jerusalem. Nineteen thirty-six was a propitious year for fascist counterrevolutions against the forward march of world humanity. The great depression, driving most nations to the economic wall, had brought about a new aggressive policy on the part of a number of states and led to the conquest of Manchuria by Japanese militarism, the replacement of the Weimar Republic in Germany by the Hitlerian dictatorship, Mussolini's invasion of Ethiopia, and the general deterioration of the League of Nations.

On March 7, 1936, the Nazis staged their dramatic occupation of the Rhineland and the Ruhr. At about the same time General Francisco Franco with the aid of Italy and Germany attacked the liberal republican government of Spain. The 1936 disturbances in Palestine were different from those of 1920, 1921, and 1929. The Grand Mufti in Jerusalem and his collaborators were publicly committed to the fascist cause. This time the Arab leaders had behind them the encouragement, in money and directives, of two European powers. This time their terrorism was directed as much against Arabs who were disinclined to participate in bloodshed and the general strike as it was directed against the Jews. This time it lasted six months before it collapsed, but this time the Jews were on guard. They were determined on two lines of action: self-restraint—the refusal to be provoked into indiscriminate reprisals—and self-defense.

On May 18, 1936, the Secretary of State for the Colonies announced that a Royal Commission of Inquiry would be sent to Palestine to investigate the causes of unrest and the alleged grievances of either Arabs or Jews "without bringing into question the terms of the mandate."

The Royal Commission, headed by Earl Peel, arrived in Palestine in the fall of 1936. "The Palestine Royal Commission Report," Cmd. 5479, published in 1937, refrained from any reference, even the most tacit, to Berlin and Rome. But it nevertheless condemned the British administration in Palestine, accusing it of criminal negligence in its failure to maintain law and order and to secure the safety of all inhabitants. It upheld the charges of the Jews that many officials in the administration were hostile to the very idea of the Jewish National Home. It took the stand that a Jewish homeland had definitely been promised to the Jewish people but that despite many benefits which the Arabs derived from Jewish colonization the mandate was "unworkable." The Peel Commission, therefore, concluded that a surgical operation would be the only solution, and it demanded the partition of Palestine into an Arab state, a Jewish state and a British mandate. The Jewish State was to comprise the northeastern part of Palestine and the Mediterranean coastal belt as far south as Tel Aviv and inland from Jaffa to a point about ten miles south of Rehovoth. A narrow corridor, beginning at Jaffa and widening to include Jerusalem and Bethlehem, was to form a permanent British mandate or protectorate over the holy places in that region; the rest of the country was to be united with Trans-Jordan to form a larger Arab state.

The report concluded with the following analysis of the advantages of its proposals:

The advantages to the Arabs of Partition on the lines we have proposed may be summarized as follows:—

They obtain their national independence and can co-operate on an equal footing with the Arabs of the neighboring countries in the cause of Arab unity and progress.

They are finally delivered from the fear of being "swamped" by the Jews and from the possibility of ultimate subjection to Jewish rule.

In particular, the final limitation of the Jewish National Home within a fixed frontier and the enactment of a new Mandate for the protection of the Holy Places, solemnly guaranteed by the League of Nations, removes all anxiety lest the Holy Places should ever come under Jewish control.

As a set-off to the loss of territory the Arabs regard as theirs, the Arab State will receive a subvention from the Jewish State. It will also, in view of the backwardness of Trans-Jordan, obtain a grant of £2,000,000 from the British Treasury; and, if an arrangement can be made for the exchange of land and population, a further grant will be made for the conversion, as far as may prove possible, of uncultivable land in the Arab State into productive land from which the cultivators and the State alike will profit.

The advantages of Partition to the Jews may be summarized as follows:—

Partition secures the establishment of the Jewish National Home and relieves it from the possibility of its being subjected in the future to Arab rule.

Partition enables the Jews in the fullest sense to call their National Home their own: for it converts it into a Jewish state. Its citizens will be able to admit as many Jews into it as they themselves believe can be absorbed. They will attain the primary objective of Zionism—a Jewish nation, planted in Palestine, giving its nationals the same status in the world as other nations give theirs. They will cease at last to live a "minority life."

To both Arabs and Jews Partition offers a prospect—and we see no such prospect in any other policy—of obtaining the inestimable boon of peace. It is surely worth some sacrifice on both sides if the quarrel which the Mandate started could be ended with its termination. It is not a natural or old-standing feud. An able Arab exponent of the Arab cause told us that the Arabs throughout their history have not only been free from anti-Jewish sentiment but have also shown that the spirit of compromise is deeply rooted in their life. . . .

With the Peel Report the British Government issued another White Paper in which it expressed its agreement with the partition plan as the most hopeful solution of a deadlocked situation.

Its proposals were rejected by both the Arab Higher Committee and the Zionists. Opposition came also from many British leaders in Parliament. The Permanent Mandates Commission of the League of Nations likewise, though rather cautiously, declared its dissatisfaction with the fact that the mandatory itself had proclaimed the mandate to be unworkable.

On January 4, 1938, however, the British Government issued another White Paper which announced the appointment of the Partition Commission whose task was "to recommend boundaries for the proposed Arab and Jewish areas and the enclaves to be retained permanently or temporarily under British mandate. . . ." This commission, headed by Sir John Woodhead, came to the conclusion that no plan of partition was feasible. It challenged the view of all former commissions and declared that limitation of Jewish immigration into Palestine would be extremely shortsighted, since the growing Arab population depended for its maintenance largely upon Jewish capital and labor. Again a White Paper echoed the recommendations of the

Woodhead Report. It stated that the British Government had reached the conclusion "that the political, administrative and financial difficulties involved in the proposal to create independent Arab and Jewish states inside Palestine are so great that this solution of the problem is impracticable."

In November, 1938, the British Government proposed a round-table conference between the representatives of Palestinian Jewry and the Arab leaders of Palestine and the neighboring Arab states. The Jews, insisting that the Arabs of neighboring states had no more moral and political competence in the matter of the Jewish homeland than all other nations, requested a conference with the Palestinian Arabs alone. They felt that the invitation of the neighboring Arab states had much more to do with Britain's desire to win Arab support generally for the years to come than with the problem of Palestine itself. The Arab leaders, not a few of them already under Axis influence, were convinced that England, like the other "decadent democracies" was no longer a power to be reckoned with. They refused to meet with the Jews, and the British were obliged to conduct separate negotiations with the two groups in February and March, 1939. Anticipating the collapse of French and British power in the Mediterranean, the Arab leaders practically issued an ultimatum. They demanded the immediate stoppage of Jewish immigration into Palestine and the formal repudiation of the Balfour Declaration. It was even intimated that if they could not get all this from England, they would get it from the Rome-Berlin Axis.

It was the period of appeasement. Daladier and Neville Chamberlain had met with Hitler in Berchtesgaden in a vain effort to forestall World War II by sacrificing the democratic republic of Czechoslovakia. In May, 1939, the British Government issued the blackest of all its White Papers on Palestine, "Cmd. 6019," which violated the solemn international obligations undertaken by Great Britain in the Balfour Declaration and the mandate for Palestine. It accepted the recommendations of the Peel Commission that the mandate was unworkable. But instead of suggesting the partition of the country, the new White Paper took up the view that the promises contained in the Balfour Declaration had already been fulfilled and that the Jewish National Home was already in existence. It prohibited Jewish immigration into Palestine after a period of five years during which a maximum of 75,000 Jews were allowed to enter the land. It outlawed further Jewish land purchases in practically all Palestine. It condemned the Jewish community to the status of a permanent minority and promised the Arabs that Palestine would soon become an independent Arab state.

In pretending to be satisfied that the Jewish minority in such an Arab state could be sufficiently protected, the authors of the White Paper deliberately overlooked the question-answer period that had taken place between the members of the Peel Commission and the Grand Mufti of Jerusalem:

Q: Does His Eminence think that the country can assimilate and digest 400,000 Jews now in the country?
A: No.
Q: Some of them would have to be removed by a process kindly or painful as the case may be?
A: We must leave all this to the future.

There were a number of contradictions in the 1939 White Paper, chiefly, of course, the curious statement that the Jewish National Home was already a fact but that the people who allegedly owned that home had no rights in it, not even the right to invite their closest relatives. It was senseless to argue about the wisdom of this or that section of the 1939 White Paper. It was part of the useless retreat of the Chamberlain government before the advancing fascist powers; and those opposed to the appeasement of the fascists were naturally also opposed to the 1939 White Paper.

It was condemned by the whole of the British Labor party, most Liberals, and many members of the Conservative party—especially those who had been connected with the original creation of the Jewish National Home policy. As one of the framers of the Balfour Declaration and the Palestine Mandate, Winston Churchill said in the House of Commons on May 23, 1939:

> As one intimately and responsibly concerned in the earlier stages of our Palestine policy, I could not stand by and see solemn engagements into which Britain has entered before the world set aside for reasons of administrative convenience or—and it is a vain hope—for the sake of a quiet life. . . . I should feel personally embarrassed in the most acute manner if I lent myself by silence or inaction, to what I must regard as an act of repudiation.

Herbert Morrison, speaking for the Labor party, said on the same day:

> I think it ought to be known by the House that this breach of faith, which we regret, this breach of British honor, with its policy, with which we have no sympathy, is such that the least that can be said is that the Government must not expect that this is going to be automatically binding upon their successors. They must not expect that. I will go no further than that, but they must understand that this document will not be automatically binding upon their successors in office, whatever the circumstances of the time may be.

On the same day, speaking in the House of Lords, the Archbishop of Canterbury joined in the condemnation of the White Paper as a breach of faith with the Jews. It was heartening to those who believed in the moral stamina of Britain's leaders that at least some of them actively opposed the Munich Pact of the Chamberlain government against the Jewish people.

The White Paper was equally condemned by the Permanent Mandates Commission of the League of Nations in June, 1939. The voice of the League of Nations was no longer audible; but the record is of importance. In June, 1939, the majority of the commission stated that the policy set forth in the 1939 White Paper was incompatible with the mandate and therefore illegal.

Even so, the White Paper was adopted by the British Parliament—although with the smallest majority which the Chamberlain Cabinet had ever mustered. In September, 1939, World War II, which had engulfed the Jews since 1933, finally broke out for England and the Western world too. Appeasement had failed.

Chapter Four: WORLD WAR II

JEWISH VOLUNTEERS · WHAT IS AN ALIYAH? · THE HOME FRONT

To this day the British people are probably unaware of a fact which caused deep resentment even among Britain's best friends in world Jewry. Tens of thousands, if not hundreds of thousands, of Jews could have been rescued from torture and death in the furnaces of Hitler's concentration camps were it not for the White Paper issued by His Majesty's Government in May, 1939 and the eagerness with which Britain's officials in Palestine put the policy of that White Paper into effect. Before hostilities commenced, the Jewish Agency had asked for the immediate admission of 20,000 children from Poland and 10,000 children from the Balkan countries. The fear of impending massacres expressed by the Jewish Agency at the time was written off as groundless, and the eastern European Jewish youth went instead to Oswiescim, Maidanek, and the other Nazi extermination camps.

When World War II officially began, the Jews of Palestine could have easily argued thus: If Nazi Germany wins, we are done for. If the democracies win, we still have the White Paper to fight. Let us therefore conserve our energies. There were other peoples than the Jewish who had good reasons to fight the Axis and yet remained neutral. What freedom would have been left to Egypt, Iraq, Turkey, Syria—to name only Palestine's neighbors—if the Axis had won the war? Powerful governmental cliques in Egypt, Iraq, and Syria played the Nazi game until the tide turned. The Grand Mufti of Jerusalem drilled an Arab brigade in German army camps near Berlin under Nazi colors. It was otherwise with Jewish Palestine.

On August 25, 1939, elected representatives from almost every country assembled at the Zionist Congress in Geneva authorized Dr. Weizmann to transmit to Neville Chamberlain, then British Prime Minister, a letter, dated August 29, 1939:

DEAR MR. PRIME MINISTER:

In this hour of supreme crisis the consciousness that the Jews have a contribution to make to the defence of sacred values impels me to write this letter. I wish to confirm, in the most explicit manner, the declarations which I and my colleagues have made during the last months, and especially in the last week: that the Jews "stand by Great Britain and will fight on the side of the democracies."

Our urgent desire is to give effect to these declarations. We wish to do so in a way entirely consonant with the general scheme of British action, and therefore would place ourselves, in matters big and small, under the co-ordinating direction of His Majesty's Government. The Jewish Agency is ready to enter into immediate arrangements for utilizing Jewish man-power, technical ability, resources, etc.

The Jewish Agency has recently had differences in the political field with the Mandatory Power. We would like these differences to give way before the greater and more pressing necessities of the times. We ask you to accept this declaration in the spirit in which it is made.

WEIZMANN

Within a few weeks after the opening of hostilities, the *Yishuv* (the Jewish community of Palestine) mobilized its forces—and this must be emphasized—entirely of its own accord. Out of a total population of half a million Jews, close to 130,000 registered for war service. The offer of the Jews of Palestine to raise an army serving as a unit was rejected by the British Government. Instead only a few thousand Jews were permitted by the British authorities to form themselves into "Palestine units." They were always referred to as "Palestinians" so that the Jewish war contribution for a long time served to mask the discreditable record of the Arabs who constituted two-thirds of the population of Palestine and who had just been accorded the 1939 White Paper.

The "Palestinians" saw action at the Maginot Line in France, they were in the front lines during the capture of Tobruk, they played their part in the proud story of El Alamein. The "pipe line to victory," which brought water supplies to the desert, was a plan conceived and carried out by Brigadier General Kisch, chief engineer of the British Eighth Army and former chairman of the Jewish Agency for Palestine. Kisch, who like the other Jews from Palestine had volunteered his service, fell in action. The Palestine units fought in Greece and Crete shoulder to shoulder with New Zealanders and Australians. They fought in Syria in the days when the Vichy government decided to resist the

British advance northward from Palestine. On this occasion the reticence of the British high command on the identity of the "Palestinians" finally broke down, and General Sir Henry Maitland Wilson stated officially that he "much appreciated the assistance rendered by the Jews in this campaign." Fifteen hundred Jews from Palestine served in the Royal Air Force. Hundreds of the trainees of the Jewish Maritime Service in Palestine served in the Royal Navy. Jewish paratroopers from Palestine volunteered for special missions and were landed behind enemy lines all over Nazi Europe in order to contact the local resistance movements. By June, 1942, of the 12,000 Jewish volunteers in action outside of Palestine, 2,000 had fallen. But it was not before the last year of the war that a Jewish brigade under Brigadier General Benjamin was officially recognized by the British Government as the fighting force of the Jewish National Home. When Winston Churchill announced in the House of Commons the decision of the British Government to permit the formation of a Jewish brigade in September, 1944, he added:

> I know that there are vast numbers of Jews serving with our forces and the American forces throughout all the Allied armies. But it seems to be indeed appropriate that a special Jewish unit of that race which suffered indescribable torment from the Nazis should be represented as a distinct formation among the forces gathered for their final overthrow.

After a few weeks of intensive training, the Jewish Brigade was in action on the Italian front.

There were some 53,000 Jews in the British forces, 20,000 in the forces of Canada, South Africa, Australia, and New Zealand, over 350,000 in the armed forces of the United States, over 400,000 in the Soviet armies, and close to 17,000 in the European guerrilla forces, especially the French Maquis. For the first time since the year 70 the Jews had been spared the tragic fate of having to serve both friend and enemy. By Hitler's decree, the Jews of Axis-controlled Europe had been excluded from the armed forces of the fascist counterrevolution. It was probably the only Nazi gesture which was in harmony with the Jews' desires. Numerically, from the pure military angle, the cooperation between the Jews and the Allied Powers might perhaps be considered as not too significant. But close to one million Jewish soldiers out of a world Jewish population of (by that time) less than twelve million felt that their people had a right to be remembered around the peace table after the war.

The Jewish National Home produced the only fighting contingent the Middle East gave to the United Nations. The Yishuv stood geared for war production behind the "Palestine units" and the Jewish Brigade. From 70,000 in 1920, the Jewish population in Palestine had grown to half a million. With the help of the Jewish National Fund and private capital the Jews had bought land—mostly the land which Arabs and British officials had deemed uncultivable. They had drained the swamps and driven out malaria. They had planted vineyards and orange groves in the desert; and the dried-out, exhausted hills of Galilee and Judea had taken on fresh verdure. Jewish settlements dotted the land from Dan to Beersheba. The sons and daughters of Israel from the ghettos of eastern Europe and the far nations across the seas plowed the earth, built roads, harnessed the Jordan River, and watered the soil. Where sand dunes seemed to prohibit human settlement, they had built Tel Aviv, the Hill of Spring, which, out of a cluster of houses north of Jaffa in 1914, became the most modern city of the Middle East.

They organized their own educational system, their own press and publishing houses. They recreated Hebrew as a living language spoken today by tens of thousands as their mother tongue. They added department after department to the Hebrew University on Mount Scopus; they opened agricultural and industrial research stations like the Daniel Sieff Institute, staffed by some of the most distinguished scientists of our time. Hadassah, the women's Zionist organization of America, turned its hospital system over to the Yishuv, and concentrated on a university hospital and youth aliyah, for the rehabilitation of immigrant children. Kuppath Holim (Sick Benefit Fund) cared in particular for the workers of the National Home. In the process Jewish public hygiene brought healing to an Arab population that had hitherto been stricken with trachoma and other diseases, making the Palestine Arab the healthiest Arab in the Middle East.

The primitive port of Jaffa (Joppa at the time of Jonah) without a jetty or docking facilities, had remained unimproved for over two thousand years. The Jews built a small but modern harbor at the shore of Tel Aviv. As they had talked before of the conquest of the resources of the land, they began to talk about the conquest of the resources of the sea, and by 1939 over 1,500 Jewish fishermen were organized in the Palestine Maritime League, while the Atid Navigation Company was founded to maintain Mediterranean and coastal shipping services. Prior to World War II the Palestine administration had been under the direction of the most sympathetic High Commissioner the National Home had ever known—Sir Arthur Wauchope. Although hampered by the anti-Jewish bias of most of his subordinates, at least he made it possible for the Jews to demonstrate their skills and imagination.

To show the reader the conditions under which the Jews of Palestine built their colonies prior to the creation of the State of Israel, I quote here the newspaper *Davar's* account of the foundation of Hanita, which was settled in 1937 on the northwestern boundary of Palestine:

On Monday, March 19, at daybreak, four hundred men left Mishmar Zebulun at Kiriath Hayim and headed for Hanita where they were going to establish a new settlement on the Lebanese frontier, three kilometers from Ras-el-Nakura, on a four thousand dunam tract recently acquired by the Jewish National Fund. A train of thirty-seven lorries, loaded with tents, fence materials, tools and food. Of the four hundred men who had been scrupulously chosen from all the settlements of the Yishuv, ninety were detailed to remain at Hanita. Among them were forty supers and ten girls and the rest, three hundred men, were members of various groups who came along to lend a hand: seventy ghaffirs (Jewish policemen) from the Emek and a group of road-builders who were to lay an 800-meter road from the highway to the new settlement.

This was the most daring as well as most dangerous attempt of the past years, since the place is distant and cut off from all Jewish settlements. The hill upon which the temporary camp was pitched is surrounded by mountains, an excellent hiding place for evilly disposed persons. The environs had not been explored by the settlers.

The convoy arrived at seven that morning. The whole camp was immediately divided into two groups: workers and watchmen. The lorries could not ascend the height and so the loads were transferred to donkeys (of which 40 were brought by lorry) and so all day long they loaded donkeys. And the men themselves carried loads too.

Meanwhile, another group was busy setting up a military fence. Trenches were dug, tents were pitched on the terraces of the eastern slope looking seaward: it was all done in a single day. The same day work was begun to install pipes for water from a copious fountain 750 meters away. The road-builders made a road to the highway.

At dusk, the mobilized help returned to Haifa and there remained only the settlers, the guards and the various skilled workers.

At midnight there was a heavy attack: simultaneous fusillades from three directions, and from fifteen different points. There was an hour of heavy firing. But each and every man stood his ground, every ghaffir was at his post. The defenders replied with all their power and the aggressors went off.

There is a Hebrew song, "God will build up Galilee." But according to Jewish belief God cannot build unless man assists.

What the farmers of the Edmond de Rothschild colonies and the Bilu had started before World War I, successive waves of immigration continued and improved. Each *aliyah* (which means going up) had its own character, its own group personality. The first, from 1882 to 1904, was, as Maurice Samuel describes it, but the opening demonstration of "the will to the Return." The second, entering Palestine between 1904 and 1914, and the third, from 1919 to 1924, laid the foundations of the emerging homeland by creating the instruments of Jewish self-government, the *Assefath Hanivharim,* or the Assembly of Deputies, representing the *Knesseth Israel,* or the whole of the Jewish community. It was during this period that the Jewish Labor Movement, represented by the General Federation of Jewish Labor, or the *Histadruth,* founded its collective farms, its cooperatives in transportation and urban development, a workers' bank, a country-wide health system, and other social and economic institutions which made the National Home the most progressive commonwealth in the Middle East—and not only in the Middle East.

It was the third wave which gave birth to the word *halutz,* or *pioneer,* to describe a new Jewish type. It is as meaningful as the term "Pilgrim Father" or "frontiersman" in the American vocabulary. The third aliyah also opened the valley of Jezreel, for hundreds of years a barren swamp, to new settlers, new life, new cheerfulness—all expressed in the host of songs that have been coming from that part of the country.

The fourth wave came in 1925 from Poland, Lithuania, and Russia. Not a few of the immigrants were middlemen without adequate means of support and without proper training for a pioneering life. Their little tailor shops, shoe stores and soda fountains were too numerous even in a boom time. Many of them collapsed during the depression years.

The fifth wave came after the riots of 1929. It created industries. In 1932 the Levant Fair in Tel Aviv, an imposing exposition of goods manufactured by the National Home, with 1,300 firms participating, attracted visitors and buyers from all over the Mediterranean area. The first Maccabi Sports Festival, held at the same time, counted 3,000 contestants from the United States, Great Britain, the European Continent, Egypt, Syria, and Palestine. This was the period when German-Jewish immigrants joined their fellow Jews from eastern Europe in ever-increasing numbers.

Some German Jews, the members of the Blau Weiss and the K.I.V. (Union of Jewish University Fraternities) had participated in the upbuilding of the Jewish homeland long before the rise of Hitler. But the vast majority of German Jews had been outspokenly anti-Zionist. In no other country had the ideal of assimilation become so dogmatic and impenetrable as in Germany. Even German Jews who left Germany during the nineteenth century for the United States had been affected by it to such an extent that many of them became the spokesmen of anti-Zionism in America. Germany was par excellence the country of assimilation. Many German Jews had been settled in the Fatherland for over a thousand years. To them Germany was the be-all of their existence, while the link between them and the Jews of other lands was at best a philanthropic one. In Germany intermarriage between Jews and Gentiles had proceeded to a degree unknown anywhere else. By 1933 one-third of the Jewish marriages were actually mixed marriages. If there was one land on earth where, according to the advocates of assimilation, the Jewish question should have been on the road to final solution, it was Germany.

By the strange irony of history the Nazis singled out the assimilated elements for special persecution, just as the Spaniards had done in the fifteenth century. Intermarriage, conversions to either Catholicism or Protestantism, far from being a protective shield, brought even deeper misery and anguish to those who thought that the close kinship between them and the Germans would render them indistinguishable. Instead of being accepted as a symbol of their desire for complete Germanization, their assimilation was taken as a vicious attempt to debase the "pure German society." Most German Jews who entered Palestine after 1933 constructively and tactfully joined their fellow Jews from eastern Europe in the great attempt to overcome the homelessness of the Jewish people, but a few carried into Palestine a note of loudmouthed chauvinism which had until then been foreign to the Zionist movement, a sort of *Judea über alles* attitude which formed the exact equivalent of the pathological desire on the part of the so-called assimilationists to lose their Jewish identity at any price.

In the beginning Jews who left Germany for Palestine were able to take at least some of their possessions with them and to transfer others through a complicated exchange system. The immediate effect was noticeable in a sudden blossoming of shops and restaurants which reminded one of the Kurfürstendamm in Berlin. But many German-Jewish professors, lawyers, physicians, and journalists turned to farming and founded a number of agricultural settlements; and it was not unusual that the man who washed windows or shined shoes to start a new life was *ein Herr Doktor.*

In the summer of 1934 I was invited to give a series of lectures in the Farm School of Ben Shemen, not far from Lydda. I have written about this experience at greater length in a novelized account, *If I Forget Thee. . . .* There were a number of German-Jewish children in the school who had been brought to Palestine with the assistance of the American Hadassah. They were attractive, bright youngsters, although their natural gaiety was dampened by thought of their parents back in Nazi Germany. When I asked some of them, "*Was willst Du werden?*" (What do you plan to become?) the answer was invariably, "A lawyer, a physician, a *Herr Kommerzienrat,* like my father." After a few years of training in Ben Shemen, having learned to plow and harvest, to milk cows, and to tend orchards, they joined the other pioneers. Those whom I saw again in 1946 were the best proof of the validity of Zionism. Probably no other land, however understanding, however friendly, could have done what the National Home had done for these uprooted young human beings. Only Jewish Palestine was able to make the Jewish refugee whole again in soul and body.

While Hitler's extermination mills continued to devour their Jewish and other victims, while the remnants of the Warsaw ghetto battled, house by house, heroically but hopelessly against the Nazi liquidation squads, Jewish Palestine turned out textiles, metals, machine parts, armored cars, antitank mines, ambulances, hospital equipment, hundreds of thousands of tons of potash and critical chemicals for the Allied war effort. It must be remembered that this production was achieved without large governmental investments and special incentives of wartime industrial promotion as in Great Britain and the United States. Palestine's contribution to the war effort would have been impossible without the work of the Jewish pioneers who had laid the foundation of Palestine's industries, without Jewish engineers who, like the late Rutenberg, had built the country's electrical system. It would have been impossible without the scientists of the Hebrew University and the Haifa Technical Institute, without Hadassah hospitals, and without the expansion of Jewish farming.

Thousands of Australians and New Zealanders found in Tel Aviv and other Jewish settlements a few days of well-deserved recreation during the war. Hundreds of Allied troops were cared for in the hospitals of the Jewish National Home. While the cash value of the Jewish war effort in Palestine could not begin to compare with that of Britain and the United States, the soldiers of all democratic countries who had seen the National Home in action were no longer willing to identify "Jew" and "jew down." Since the early Middle Ages the Jewish people, to be distinguished from the Gentile population, had been deliberately exposed to an abnormal economic development. For many centuries they had been denied the right to buy land and to work on land. For centuries they had been denied entry into the basic industries, thus making the Jewish economy a main street, a small merchant, a middleman economy; or, to use Nordau's famous term, making of the Jews *Luftmenschen.* Zionism, at last, with its Jewish National Fund, its

Foundation Fund, and similar institutions, had rooted the Jew into the soil of his ancient homeland; had, step by step, opened up all branches of production for the men and women of the Return.

A new frontier of democracy had been created far away from its centers in Europe and America.

Chapter Five: NOWHERE TO LAY THEIR HEADS

DISPLACED PERSONS · THE ANGLO-AMERICAN COMMITTEE OF INQUIRY · THE END OF THE BRITISH MANDATE

As an intelligence officer of the Psychological Warfare Division, SHAEF, and later USFET, I saw Dachau and other concentration camps at the very beginning of the Allied occupation of Germany. I saw the gas chambers where every day hundreds of Jewish men, women, and children had been asphyxiated. They were brought to these chambers, naked, after having been ordered to take showers in a special huge shower room connected with the gas furnaces. Their Nazi sentries used to look through peepholes and watch the Jews writhing in their death agonies. I saw the gallows where, especially on Jewish holidays, Jews were hanged to "amuse" their non-Jewish fellow prisoners, and I saw the dog kennels in which German police dogs were bred and trained to fall upon stragglers as the Jews were driven to work in the underground ammunition factories or led to their death. I witnessed how many of the former concentration-camp inmates who were liberated by the Third United States Army died from having been given too much food too suddenly.

I saw the pitifully small remnant of European Jewry, the survivors of 6,000,000 Jews who had been tortured and butchered to death by the German Nazis and their non-German fellow travelers in Nazi-occupied Europe. I have personally talked to hundreds of so-called Displaced Persons (DP's), men and women who were liberated by the Allied armies from Dachau, Belsen, Oswiescim, and all the other death traps for the Jews of Europe. Most of the women had been raped, both men and women had been tortured and crippled; the parents among them saw their little children smashed against the walls of the camps until the blood flowed from their broken bodies. I could name

Jewish boys of seventeen and eighteen who for six months and longer periods ate nothing but the flesh of their comrades—executed or worked to death by SS guards.

Now that they had been liberated, the Jewish DP's hoped to be treated as allies and not as prisoners or parasites. The world had been largely indifferent toward their indescribable sufferings during the Hitler years. This same world, not feeling their terror and their pain, still seemed aloof and cold.

On June 11, 1945, I submitted to the headquarters of the Psychological Warfare Division a detailed account of seventeen DP centers with an aggregate of 14,000 Jewish inmates. In some of the camps the Jews lived in barbed-wire enclosures still equipped with the deadly electrical apparatus that was designed to keep the ambitious from escaping to life outside. In none of the camps were the DP's allowed or able to secure the tools which they needed to build bathrooms, kitchen, and laundry facilities. In most of the camps, in spite of the official extra ration, the food was insufficient for people who had been undernourished for years and who were suffering from various diseases. Since in the beginning the G5 sections of the United States Armies had refused to regard the Jews as Jews, they were classified as Czechs, Poles, Yugoslavs. When the National Committees of these groups recalled their DP's, it was assumed that the Jews would return with the non-Jews to their countries of origin. When the Jews refused to board the army trucks that were to take them across the borders, the army authorities were obviously annoyed. They did not realize that the Jews—unlike the non-Jewish DP's—faced peculiarly difficult problems in returning to their native countries. In spite of the fact that the non-Jews had been dragged away from their communities, they had somehow retained their connection with relatives and friends back home. The persecution of the non-Jews in the Nazi-occupied territories, barbarous and cruel as it was, could not be compared with the complete uprooting, the outright massacre of the Jewish population, the cold-blooded design to exterminate "the race." For the Jewish DP's there were no relatives and friends in Europe who could receive them with open arms and help them to rehabilitate themselves. Their relatives and friends were dead; and the ghettos from which most of the Jewish DP's hailed were utterly destroyed.

The Jewish DP's did not want to stay in Germany either. In answer to a questionnaire circulated in DP camps at the end of 1945, 97 per cent of the Jewish inmates named Palestine as the country in which they preferred to live permanently. Europe, for them, was the continent of crematoriums and gas chambers where the lives of their loved ones had been snuffed out mercilessly. As time passed the military authorities began to understand their problems and learn to deal with them more adequately. With the exception of a few sworn anti-Semites —Nazis in American uniforms—the troops and officers of the United States behaved generously and humanely toward the DP's. But the Jewish DP's expected more than sympathy. What they awaited was a clear and lucid message from the United Nations Organization telling them that they could leave Europe to join their fellow Jews in the National Home.

Moved by previous reports, President Harry S. Truman sent Earl G. Harrison, Dean of the Law School of the University of Pennsylvania, as his personal investigator to Europe to report to him on the conditions of the Jews in the American occupation zone of Germany. On the basis of Harrison's report, the President wrote to British Prime Minister Clement R. Attlee, urging that 100,000 certificates (visas) be issued immediately for Jewish immigration into Palestine. After protracted negotiations between the two governments the British made the suggestion that before any action was taken a new investigation of conditions should be conducted.

On November 13, 1945, President Truman and British Foreign Secretary Ernest Bevin announced that an Anglo-American Committee of Inquiry would be appointed to investigate the situation of the Jews in Europe and the possibilities of Jewish immigration in Palestine. On December 11 the personnel of this committee—six Americans, six Englishmen—was named, with Judge Joseph C. Hutcheson of Texas and Sir John Singleton as chairmen, to serve on a rotating basis.

The hearings of the Anglo-American Committee of Inquiry began in Washington, D.C., on January 7, 1946, where Rabbi Stephen S. Wise, Emanuel Neumann, Rabbi Wolff Gold, Mrs. Moses Epstein, Dr. Joseph Schwartz, Chaim Greenberg, Judge Joseph Proskauer for the Jewish organizations, along with such non-Jewish experts as Earl Harrison and Dr. Lowdermilk, the planner of a Jordan Valley Authority, presented the arguments for the formation of a Jewish state in Palestine. There was one dissenting voice. Lessing J. Rosenwald, president of the American Council for Judaism, testified that, in his view, Jewish nationalism was a cause of anti-Semitism.

From Washington, D.C., the committee went to London, where it sat from January 25 to February 1. In London the representatives of the Arab States appeared, headed by the Crown Prince of Saudi Arabia. The committee then broke up into subsections which visited different parts of Europe. From there the full group went to Cairo, where it held sessions from February 28 to March 5.

In Cairo, Azzam Pasha, the gifted secretary of the League of Arab States, dealing with the reasons for Arab intransigence toward the Jewish National Home idea, gave in a few sentences probably the most eloquent and most significant of all Arab arguments.

> Our brother [he said] has gone to Europe and to the West and come back something else. He has come back a Russified Jew, a Polish Jew, a German Jew, an English Jew. He has come back with a totally different conception of things, Western and not Eastern. That does not mean that we are necessarily quarreling with anyone who comes from the West. But the Jew, our old cousin, coming back with imperialistic ideas, with materialistic ideas, with reactionary or revolutionary ideas and trying to implement them first by British pressure and then by American pressure, and then by terrorism on his own part—he is not the old cousin and we do not extend to him a very good welcome. The Zionist, the new Jew, wants to dominate and he pretends that he has got a particular civilizing mission with which he returns to a backward, degenerate race in order to put the elements of progress into an area which has no progress. Well, that has been the pretension of every power that wanted to colonize and aimed at domination. The excuse has always been that the people are backward and that he has got a human mission to put them forward. . . . The Arabs simply stand and say NO. We are not reactionary and we are not backward. Even if we are ignorant, the difference between ignorance and knowledge is ten years in school. We are a living, vitally strong nation, we are in our renaissance; we are producing as many children as any nation in the world. We still have our brains. We have a heritage of civilization and of spiritual life. We are not going to allow ourselves to be controlled either by great nations or small nations or dispersed nations.

From March 6 to March 28 the committee held hearings in Palestine, the Lebanon, Syria, Saudi Arabia, and Trans-Jordan. From the Middle East it went to Lausanne to write its report. On April 24 the American chairman, Judge Hutcheson, presented the report to President Truman; and on April 30, 1946, it was released for publication.

The Anglo-American Committee of Inquiry submitted a number of recommendations, two of which were of immediate practical importance for the Jews in the European DP camps. The first was that "100,000 certificates be authorized immediately for the admission into Palestine of Jews who have been the victims of Nazi and Fascist persecution," and "that these certificates be awarded as far as possible in 1946, and that actual immigration be pushed forward as rapidly as conditions will permit." The second was that the restrictive land regulations of 1940, which were the outcome of the 1939 White Paper, be "rescinded and replaced by regulations based on a policy of freedom in the sale, lease, or use of land, irrespective of race, community, or creed."

Following the publication of the report, President Truman made this statement:

> I am very happy that the request which I made for the immediate admission of 100,000 Jews into Palestine has been unanimously endorsed by the Anglo-American Committee of Inquiry. The transference of these unfortunate people should now be accomplished with the greatest dispatch. The protection and safeguarding of the holy places in Palestine sacred to Moslem, Christian and Jew is adequately provided in the report.
>
> One of the significant features of the report is that it aims to insure a complete protection to the Arab population in Palestine by guaranteeing their civilian and religious rights, and by recommending measures for the constant improvement in their cultural, educational and economic position.
>
> I am also pleased that the committee recommends in effect the abrogation of the White Paper of 1939, including existing restrictions on immigration and land acquisition, to permit the further development of the Jewish national home. It is also gratifying that the report also envisages the carrying out of large-scale economic development projects in Palestine which would facilitate further immigration and be of benefit to the entire population.
>
> In addition to these immediate objectives, the report deals with many other questions of long-range political policies and questions of international law which require careful study and which I will take under advisement.

The British Government took an entirely different view. It was expressed by Prime Minister Attlee in the House of Commons on May 1 in these words:

> The Report must be considered as a whole in all its implications. Its execution would entail very heavy immediate and long term commitments. His Majesty's Government wish to be satisfied that they will not be called upon to implement a policy which would involve them single-handed in such commitments, and in the course of joint examination they will wish to ascertain to what extent the Government of the United States would be prepared to share in resulting additional military and financial responsibilities.
>
> The Report recommends that 100,000 certificates for the admission of Jews to Palestine should be authorized immediately, and awarded so far as possible in 1946, and that actual immigration should be pushed forward as rapidly as conditions permit. The practical difficulties involved in the immediate reception and absorption of so large a number would obviously be very great. It is clear, from the facts presented in the Report regarding the illegal armies maintained in Palestine and their recent activities, that it would not be possible for the Government of Palestine to admit so large a body of immigrants unless and until these formations have been disbanded and their

arms surrendered. As the Report points out, private armies constitute a danger to the peace of the world and ought not to exist. Jews and Arabs in Palestine alike must disarm immediately. The Committee have drawn attention to the failure of the Jewish Agency to cooperate in dealing with this evil, and have expressed the view that the Agency should at once resume active and responsible cooperation with the mandatory power. His Majesty's Government regard it as essential that the Agency should take a positive part in the suppression of these activities. They hope that both Jewish and Arab leaders will give counsels of patience and restraint. His Majesty's Government recognize that decisions must be taken as soon as possible but meanwhile the House will understand that I am unable to make any further statement.

In contrast to Truman, who made no qualifications, Attlee imposed three conditions: the acceptance of the recommendations as a unit, United States military and financial assistance for the implementation of the recommendations, and the dissolution of the Jewish illegal armies.

Richard Crossman, a member of the Anglo-American Committee, in his personal account, *Palestine Mission,* describes the first reaction to the committee report in these words:

Most of the British officials condemned it roundly as a sellout to the Americans, and reiterated their warning that British authority could only be restored by the disarming of the Haganah, and the reorganization of the Jewish Agency. The Arab Higher Committee, after long discussions, came to the conclusion that, in view of the peaceful attitude of their followers, no violent resistance was practicable. They would reject the report, call a token strike in protest and await events. They were fairly confident that the Palestine Administration, which did not disguise its dislike of the report, would provide a more effective opposition in London than they could. The first reaction of the Jews had been one of indignation at the rejection of the Jewish state and the strictures in the report on the deterioration of Jewish education and the toleration of violence. But they soon came to realize that the report at least remedied the injustices of the White Paper. This in itself was a defeat for the extremists who had wanted to boycott the committee. Dr. Weizmann's prestige rose proportionately. For the first time since 1937, the policy of moderation and cooperation with Britain had scored a victory. For a few hours after the publication of the report, a new era of sanity seemed to have begun.

Attlee's disavowal of the report destroyed the new atmosphere of conciliation and justified the prediction of Abba Hillel Silver, one of America's most vigorous Jewish leaders, that the committee was but a smoke screen and that the British Cabinet would disregard its findings and recommendations.

The third condition in Attlee's statement was particularly significant.

The vast majority of the Jews of Palestine were law-abiding, democratic citizens. Their *Haganah* (which means Self-defense), now termed by Attlee an "illegal army," was the expression of their determination to safeguard the lives and the liberty of the Jews of Palestine which the mandatory had been unable or unwilling to do. In a very real sense Haganah was the whole Jewish community in Palestine organized for the purpose of protecting itself against the lawless encroachments from any quarter on the basic Jewish rights in Palestine as laid down in the Balfour Declaration and the Palestine Mandate. During the war Haganah rescued Jews from destitution and annihilation in Hitler's Europe and transported them by every means available to Palestine. In his book, *Underground to Palestine,* I. F. Stone has graphically told of the operations of the Haganah during the immediate postwar period, of its attempts to defy the immigration decrees following the White Paper of 1939, which, I should like to remind the reader, the Permanent Mandates Commission of the League of Nations had itself declared a violation of the Palestine Mandate.

In a memorandum submitted to the Anglo-American Committee of Inquiry, on March 25, 1946, the command of Haganah had frankly stated:

> There exists in this country a secret Jewish armed force. This force has one fixed purpose—the defense of the Jewish settlement and the Jewish work of construction. This force exists because no government—formerly Turkish and latterly British—has protected or has been able to protect us properly. This force is secret because no government has been prepared to recognize it and leave its control in our hands.

Haganah's extremely efficient intelligence service had been one of the most helpful weapons in the war against the Axis; and its shock division, known as *Palmach,* consisting of close to 7,000 men, had carried out some of the most daring commando raids during the Allied campaigns in North Africa.

Haganah took its orders from the highest authorities of the Jewish community in Palestine. It never indulged in terrorism or in indiscriminate violence. In this respect it is important to differentiate between Haganah and those dissident groups like Irgun Zvai Leumi and the Sternists, who believed in terror as the main means to end the White Paper policy and to drive the British out of Palestine. While Haganah had promised to suppress the Irgun and the Sternists the moment the Jewish wrongs were righted and to cooperate loyally with the British as it had done during the war, Attlee's speech frustrated all conciliatory efforts and strengthened the position of the terrorists. To make conditions worse the British military authorities in Palestine, on order of Lieutenant General Barker, began military operations against Haganah in a number of Jewish settlements and imprisoned in the detention camps of Latrun and Rafa several hundred of the outstanding leaders of the Palestine Jewish community.

It was at this juncture, on June 11, 1946, that Mr. Truman appointed a Cabinet Committee on Palestine and Related Problems, consisting of the Secretaries of State, War, and Treasury, to deal with the Palestine problem. The President declared that "in view of the urgency of the solution of various problems relating to the displaced Jews in Europe and to Palestine," he was appointing this committee to assist him "in the early consideration of the recommendations of the Anglo-American Committee of Inquiry."

The next move came in the form of a speech by British Foreign Secretary Bevin at the British Labor Conference in Bournemouth on June 12. These are excerpts from Mr. Bevin's speech:

> Regarding the agitation in the United States, and particularly New York, for 100,000 Jews to be put into Palestine, I hope that it will not be misunderstood in America if I say, with the purest of motives, that that was because they did not want too many of them in New York. . . .
>
> Do you want a settlement of this problem? If you do, I would suggest to you that you leave the thing where it is, after I have explained what is happening.
>
> In Palestine there are illegal armed forces. If we put 100,000 Jews in Palestine tomorrow, I would have to put another division of British troops there. I am not prepared to do it. This business grew, I know, out of 1937 and the White Paper and all the agitation, but I must say to the Jews and Arabs:
>
> "Please put your guns away. Do not blow up the British Tommy, who is quite innocent in this business. You are creating another phase of anti-Semitic feeling in the British army."
>
> The commission quite rightly said that these illegal armies on both sides ought to be disarmed. I believe that if both sides do disarm, then peace and development can be much easier.
>
> Secondly, the financial issues involved in this business are tremendous, and the British Chancellor of the Exchequer cannot carry them. Taxation in this country is at such a point that we cannot take on expenditure of another £200,000,000 ($800,000,000) on Palestine, for that is really what is involved. It is not merely the taking of people and putting them there.
>
> Therefore, the Prime Minister and I have suggested to the United States that we have experts right away and consider the implications of this report (of the Inquiry Commission) together—financial, military, transport, housing, and what is probably the most vexed problem of all, the land problem.
>
> I am not committing myself, but I think I may venture a thought.
>
> The more I study the development of Palestine with the Trans-Jordan

scheme, and the possibility of fertilizing—I do not know whether it is scientifically possible—and the real development, in order to achieve this purpose, I think we shall have to come to a conclusion quickly that the land will have to be publicly owned, and that it will have to be leased out, perhaps by an arbitration tribunal, and allocated, because if you have to raise the Arab to the standard of the Jews, you cannot do it if you take away their land. . . .

I came into this Jewish problem in the 1929 government. I have been working with the Arabs and the Jews. I believe, handled properly and with patience, this can be settled, as somebody said, as a part of a Middle Eastern problem. You cannot deal with the Palestine Arabs alone. The Arab League has become a fact, and you cannot ignore it. . . .

I would tell the Jews this: "While I agree with a Palestinian state of some kind, I don't believe in the absolutely exclusively racial states, because you cannot sort the world out that way. . . ."

I say to the Arabs and Jews: "There is a great territory. There are millions of people. I beg of you not to push your particular points of view to a point perpetuating disagreement, but to strive with us to put agreement in its place, constitutionally, diplomatically and territorially, in the belief that this anguish you have suffered might be put to an end."

I cannot accept the position that the Jews in Europe or anywhere else should be excluded (from their home country). I know they have had these terrible gas chambers. I know the horrors. But when you have done all you can in Palestine, then there will still be many left. I must try for the equality of the Jews in the country of their adoption, for Jews to observe the laws of the country of their adoption, while the Jews themselves must enjoy all the rights of that country as they do in Great Britain—as everybody does in this country.

With its overtones of insult, Mr. Bevin's statement accomplished the very opposite of what he intended. The general reception given to the speech in the United States was hostile. The reaction in Jewish Palestine was one of utter defiance. The Jews remembered only too well that Bevin was the Foreign Secretary of a Labor government commanding an overwhelming majority in Parliament and elected with a clear mandate to implement the program of the Labor party. The party platform, moved at the last Labor party conference by Mr. Attlee himself, contained a resolution relating to Palestine which read:

Here we have halted half way, irresolute between conflicting policies. But there is surely neither hope nor meaning in a "Jewish National Home" unless we are prepared to let the Jews, if they wish, enter this tiny land in such numbers as to become a majority. There was a strong case for this before the war. There is an irresistible case now, after the unspeakable atrocities of the cold and calculated German Nazi plan to kill all the Jews in Europe. . . . The Arabs have many wide territories of their own; they must not claim to exclude the Jews from this small area of Palestine, less than the size of

Wales. . . . Moreover, we should seek to win the full sympathy and support of both the American and Russian governments for the execution of this policy.

Two months before the election, the Labor Party Executive unanimously reaffirmed this resolution. Two months before the Labor party took the reins of power, it called upon Churchill's government to remove the barriers to Jewish immigration which the White Paper of 1939 had erected.

There was no trace of the traditional policy of the Labor party and its resolution in Mr. Bevin's statement, which studiously avoided the terms "Jewish people" and "Jewish National Home" and only mentioned a "home" for "Jews." Unlike Mr. Bevin, the Jews of Palestine knew only too well that the survivors of the Nazi horrors were not inclined to respond to his invitation to remain in Europe. The Hebrew press reminded him of the fact that the Jewish immigrants had raised the standard of living of the Arabs in Palestine without taking "their land." His own colleague in the Cabinet, Deputy Prime Minister Herbert Morrison, speaking in the House of Commons in 1936, had this to say about the Jewish colonization of Palestine:

> I have seen these Jewish agricultural settlements. They are one of the most wonderful moral demonstrations of the human race in the whole of the civilized world. . . . Here are colonies in which people are working on a voluntary cooperative basis with no element of dictatorship or compulsion behind them, actually reclaiming soil hitherto unfertilized and untillable and making it productive. It is being done not as a mere capitalist exploiting business but directly in association with and under the control of the great Jewish Trade Union organisation, the Jewish Federation of Labor, which is one of the finest Trade Union organisations. One of the most elevating moral efforts in voluntary communism that I have ever seen is among these agricultural communities in Palestine. I have seen these fine young people coming from various countries. . . . I came back with a humble feeling that I should like to give up this game of House of Commons and politics and join them in the clean, healthy life that they are living. It is one of the most wonderful manifestations in the world. When I think of these splendid young people happily working in a cooperative and communal spirit for the building up of a National Home, subject to murders and shootings, I feel indignant about it, as if there is some crude and bloody butting into one of the finest moral efforts in the history of mankind.

At no time had the Jews asked the British taxpayer to foot the bill for their endeavors in Palestine. In fact, it was the Jewish taxpayer in the National Home and other communities, especially in the United States, who paid a substantial part of the upkeep of the British mandatory administration throughout some thirty years. At no time after Haganah had come into existence had the Jews of Palestine asked the British Government to employ its troops in Palestine. The Jews knew only too well that British warships and the air-borne divisions had been sent to Palestine not to protect Jewish immigration but to prevent it and to maintain Britain's strategic position in the Middle East. In fact, one of the most glaring instances of the mandatory's disregard of its own status in Palestine was the maintenance in Palestine of foreign troops, the so-called Trans-Jordan Arab Legion under Glubb Pasha. Since the British had publicly recognized the independence of Trans-Jordan, these troops were not entitled to be in Palestine under the mandate and could be viewed by the Jews only as a potential Arab army of invasion. Later events proved that this evaluation was correct.

At no time had the Jews planned to create a "racial" state in Palestine. Since the days of the Balfour Declaration Zionist leaders had time and again stated that Arabs and others would enjoy the same rights as Jews in a Jewish commonwealth, apart from having complete cultural autonomy.

With many of the officials of the Jewish Agency in the detention camps of Latrun and Rafa, with a Jewish population in open rebellion against what even the most moderate elements called "Britain's betrayal," the extremists had a field day. These are excerpts from my articles in the *New Leader* of August 10 and August 17, 1946. They were dispatched from Jerusalem on July 23, 1946, and from Tel Aviv on August 1.

JERUSALEM, JULY 23—Yesterday members of the Irgun Zvai Leumi, a gang of Jewish terrorists, attacked the offices of the secretariat of the Palestine Government, housed in the King David Hotel in Jerusalem, killing and injuring over a hundred innocent people—British, Jews, Arabs.

This outrage makes no sense. It is indefensible. For centuries the Jews have been known for their abhorrence of violence. It is tragic that the Jews of Palestine who have labored so fervently for the renaissance of Jewish nationhood and for the peace which is denied their brothers in the Kielces of Europe were destined to experience the evil fruits of all nationalistic fanaticism.

Jerusalem is a small city, and a deed like the bombing of the King David Hotel encompasses it. The corteges yesterday moved off from no one house and not one quarter, and the lamentations were in many tongues. But the sadness weighing upon the city in these days is not enough. . . .

Having said all this I want to state just as emphatically: England is not free of blame. Most of her officials in this country have no interest in the cause of the Jewish National Homeland. Some of them are known for their alliance with the adherents of the former Mufti of Jerusalem who played the same role among the Arabs as Hitler played among the Germans. . . . Indeed, it is my belief that certain British officials in Palestine, in order to confuse public opinion in the world, are not too anxious to suppress the extremists in the Arab and the Jewish camps.

Just a few weeks ago Glubb, the British Commander of the Arab Trans-Jordan forces stationed in Palestine, deemed it necessary to threaten Arab violence if the recommendations of the Anglo-American Commission with regard to the immigration of 100,000 Jewish DP's from Germany should be carried out. This threat by a high-ranking officer, commanding the best-trained and best-armed Arab forces in the Middle East, has a very particular significance. It is like the threat of a robber who prophesies that his victim will be shot unless he submits. . . .

TEL AVIV, AUG. 1—Like all the 200,000 residents of Tel Aviv I was under house arrest while some 20,000 British soldiers searched house by house. When at the Labor Party's Conference Bevin said, "If we put 100,000 Jews in Palestine tomorrow, I would have to put another division of British troops there," he evoked in his listeners the belief that British troops already stationed in Palestine are there for the protection of the Jews. This, however, is fallacious, as is shown by the hostile behavior of the troops during the curfew in Jerusalem and in today's curfew in Tel Aviv.

In spite of great inconvenience, and even hardships, in spite of the fact that this siege must be ruinous for the economic life of the city, in spite of the fact that the great body of soldiers, many of them obviously unseasoned troops, treat the people of Tel Aviv like an enemy population, men and women submit quietly to the search and show no open resentment. . . .

If the siege of Tel Aviv were not punitive and if the Sixth Airborne Division and all the other units under the command of Major Gen. A. J. Cassells are really out to apprehend those who caused the death of almost 100 Britons, Arabs and Jews in the King David explosion, most Jews in this country would approve of action taken to cope with the terrorists. But there are some considered doubts with regard to the whole operation.

If it is true—as has been announced by the Palestine Government—that the British troops and police know for whom they are looking and even have photographs of the members of the terrorist gangs, some of the most unpleasant features of this search could easily be avoided. A radio and press announcement that the ring leaders have been found in Jerusalem or Haifa accompanied by a temporary isolation of Tel Aviv and a number of plain clothes men actually hunting for the criminals in Tel Aviv could have done the job. In fact under the circumstances the job could have been done long before the King David Hotel affair.

If the members of the Irgun and the Stern group are not known to the authorities, the present search will most likely not achieve its objective. Each person in Tel Aviv is required to produce an identity card. The terrorists are provided with the most excellent identity cards. . . . It is safe to assume that during the next few days quite a few people will be shipped to Rafa and Latrun who as members of Haganah, the Jewish Home Guard, have assisted the British during the war and who have kept their arms, having learned during the Arab Revolt of 1936–39 that in an emergency they have to rely upon their own fighting power. Their detention in turn might quite likely be used for a new indictment of the whole Jewish community in line with the "Palestine statement relating to acts of violence" recently published by the Colonial Office.

There were a number of instances where British soldiers donned swastika arm bands and chalked anti-Jewish slogans on buildings throughout Palestine. There were scattered attacks on British troops for which the Irgun and the Sternists claimed full responsibility. There were British soldiers who ran riot in Jewish towns. British officers were flogged by members of the Irgun in retaliation for the whipping of Irgunists. At the same time the Royal Navy intercepted dozens of boats trying to discharge Jewish refugees from Europe and North Africa in the National Home and forced them to land at Cyprus or to return to their ports of origin. In the midst of this general turmoil Nimer el Hawari under orders of the Arab Higher Committee in Palestine announced that an Arab army had been formed to drive the Jews out of Palestine as soon as the British would give up their mandate.

It was a difficult time indeed for those who preached moderation. Haganah's *Voice of Israel* warned the extremists in the Jewish camp to desist from their activities. Finally on October 29 the Inner Zionist Council of Palestine published this proclamation:

> The Inner Zionist Council declares that the Zionist movement has always rejected, and continues to reject, terrorist bloodshed as an instrument of political struggle. The banner of Zionism must be kept pure and unbesmirched. The Council denounces without reservation the bloodshed caused by groups of terrorists who defy national discipline and thereby place themselves outside the ranks of the organized community. These deeds defile the struggle of the Jewish people and distort its character; they strengthen the hands of the opponents of Zionism and the enemies of the Jewish people. The Council calls upon the Yishuv to isolate these groups and deny them all encouragement, support and assistance.

A few days later, on November 5, eight Jewish leaders were released from Latrun, and a large number of Jews detained in Rafa were also freed. Both the British Government and the Jewish leaders emphasized that the release was unconditional. Nevertheless, Richard Stubbs, Palestine Government Public Information Officer, said at a news conference in Tel Aviv on November 5:

> His Majesty's Government have done the utmost to turn the clock back . . . as a gesture in return for the declaration of the Inner Zionist Council and other Jewish institutions that they are seriously determined to end ter-

rorism in this country. His Majesty's Government hope this gesture will lead to the participation of the Jews in the London Conference.

The British Government had prepared another British-Jewish-Arab round-table conference in London—this time with an American "observer." In the hope of securing Jewish participation in the conference, Bevin had come to America where he and United States Secretary of State Byrnes had held a number of meetings with Rabbi Abba Hillel Silver, Dr. Stephen S. Wise, and Nahum Goldmann of the Jewish Agency Executive. The conference, convened in September, had been adjourned October 2 since the Palestine Arabs refused to attend, while King ibn-Saud of Saudi Arabia and other members of the League of Arab States warned the United States government to retreat from its "interference." The conference convened again on January 27, 1947. This time the representatives of the Palestine Arab Higher Committee were present, while the Jews, following a resolution of the Twenty-second Zionist Congress in Basel, in December, 1946, decided to meet only "informally" with the British representatives.

The British point of view was laid down in a memorandum which proposed a British trusteeship over Palestine for the period necessary to effect the transition to complete independence. During that period a British High Commissioner was to exercise "the supreme legislative and executive authority." In conclusion the memorandum stated:

> His Majesty's Government are not prepared to continue indefinitely to govern Palestine themselves merely because the Arabs and Jews cannot agree upon the means of sharing its government between them. The proposals contained in the present memorandum are designed to give the two peoples an opportunity of demonstrating their ability to work together for the good of Palestine as a whole and so providing a stable foundation for an independent state.

The Arabs rejected the memorandum outright, declaring that they regarded any concession to Zionism as "new aggression." The Jews made it clear that if Great Britain were prepared to return to the original mandate, they would not press for immediate statehood. If, however, the British Government were unwilling to reestablish the full provisions of the mandate, the Jews would carry them out themselves by the establishment of a Jewish state.

On February 14, 1947, at the last meeting of the Palestine Conference in London, Mr. Bevin formally announced that since "no proposals put forward by His Majesty's Government had proved acceptable as a basis for further discussion, His Majesty's Government had decided to refer the whole problem to the United Nations."

Chapter Six: PALESTINE AND THE UNITED NATIONS

UNSCOP · NOVEMBER 29, 1947 · AMERICAN SIGNS OF SCHIZOPHRENIA · PROCLAMATION OF THE JEWISH STATE

In view of the urgency of the Palestine problem, the United States State Department, on March 28, 1947, informed the British Ambassador in Washington, D.C., that the United States would support a request by Great Britain for the convening of a special session of the General Assembly of the United Nations Organization to prepare recommendations for consideration by the General Assembly at its regular session in September, 1947. On April 2 the British Delegation of the United Nations asked the Secretary-General to summon a special session. In accordance with the provisions of the United Nations Charter, the Secretariat sounded out the opinion of the fifty-five member nations. Since a majority indicated approval, the special session of the United Nations on Palestine was scheduled to begin on April 28.

It opened with a decided advantage for the Arabs by virtue of the fact that five Arab states—Egypt, Iraq, Syria, Lebanon, Saudi Arabia—held official membership in the United Nations, while the Jews, having no recognized state of their own, were without representation. From the start the Arab strategy was to prevent the Jewish Agency from getting a hearing. The idea was to demote the Agency from its unique international status as spokesman for world Jewry on matters relating to Palestine. Unfortunately, the United States delegate, Ambassador Warren R. Austin, arguing that the "sacred" Charter of the United Nations must be upheld, insisted likewise that the prestige of the General Assembly would suffer should a nongovernmental organization like the Jewish Agency be permitted to appear before the General Assembly. American policy toward the National Home for domestic consumption was often pro-Zionist. But whenever actual implementation of promises and gestures became imperative, the State Department showed definite signs of schizophrenia.

Due to the pressure of the Polish and Czech delegations in the United Nations "to give careful consideration to the point of view of the Jewish people in the Palestine question," a compromise solution was finally worked out. Spokesmen of both the Jewish Agency for Palestine and the Palestine Arab Higher Committee were permitted to appear, not before the General Assembly itself, but before the Political and Security Committee of the General Assembly.

David Ben Gurion, Moshe Sharett (Shertok), and Dr. Silver presented the Jewish case. Henry Cattan and other members of the Arab Higher Committee presented the case of the Palestine Arabs. In the midst of the general debate, on May 14, much to the surprise of the entire assembly, Andrei Gromyko, the Soviet Russian delegate, revealed an attitude which marked a complete departure from Soviet Russia's well-known anti-Zionist position in the past. He pointed out that "the aspirations of an important part of the Jewish people are bound up with the question of Palestine, and with the future structure of that country. This interest is comprehensible and completely justified." Having made this statement, Gromyko suggested a binational, Arab-Jewish state, with equal rights for both sides; and if this could not be effected, partition of Palestine into two states, one Arab, one Jewish. For years British Middle Eastern officials and their counterpart in the United States State Department had insisted that Soviet Russia was playing the Arab game and that Britain, by making concessions to the Arab cause, was holding back the flood tide of communism in the Middle East. All of a sudden, in a moment of high international drama, Soviet Russia tossed a diplomatic bombshell into the deliberations of the United Nations General Assembly by supporting a partition plan which all Arab spokesmen had repudiated as "imperialism" and "Zionist aggression." If the United States, which was unofficially known to be supporting some sort of a partition, and the Soviet Union would at least this time refrain from engaging in a power struggle with the Jewish people as a pawn, the United Nations would have a fair chance of settling the issue.

On May 15 the General Assembly adopted by an affirmative vote of 46, with the five Arab states, Turkey, and Afghanistan in opposition, the following resolution:

WHEREAS the General Assembly of the United Nations has been called into special session for the purpose of constituting and instructing a special committee to prepare for the consideration at the next regular session of the Assembly a report on the question of Palestine,

The General Assembly RESOLVES that:

1. A special committee be created for the above-mentioned purpose consisting of the representatives of Australia, Canada, Czechoslovakia, Guatemala, India, Iran, Netherlands, Peru, Sweden, Uruguay and Yugoslavia;

2. The special committee shall have the widest powers to ascertain and record facts, and to investigate all questions and issues relevant to the problem of Palestine; . . .

7. The special committee's report shall be communicated to the Secretary General not later than September 1, 1947, in order that it may be circulated to the Members of the United Nations in time for consideration by the second regular session of the General Assembly.

In view of the fact that Arab interests were adequately represented within the United Nations by the delegates of five Arab states, the Arab Higher Committee could afford to boycott the United Nations Special Committee on Palestine (UNSCOP).

UNSCOP began its hearings on June 17 in Jerusalem in an atmosphere of tension. This was heightened as the British sentenced to the gallows three Jewish youths who had participated in the escape of Jewish political prisoners from the old Acre prison in the north of Palestine. It was a tragic coincidence. There had been a time, not so very long before, when Great Britain was Zionism's best friend in all the world. With their compassion for the people of the Bible, with their traditional spirit of fair play and sportsmanship, the British had been the first to grasp the inner justice of the Jewish request for the return to their ancient homeland. Now, while the death sentence for Field Marshal Kesselring, one of the top men of the Nazi high command, had just been commuted by a British military court, Jewish youngsters who had fought in World War II against the Nazis were hanged by their former allies. The British administration of Palestine refused to commute their death sentences—in spite of the pleas of several members of UNSCOP.

It was not until August 31 that UNSCOP completed its task. Although the Arab Higher Committee had refused to cooperate, UNSCOP had heard many Arab leaders inside and outside of Palestine. Some members of UNSCOP had visited the European DP camps. Others had held secret sessions with the leaders of the Jewish Resistance Movement, in particular with those of the Haganah. The two reports, majority and minority, represented a painstaking effort to do justice to all parties concerned and to eliminate the causes for further disturbances in a land holy to three great religions.

The majority report of UNSCOP can be best characterized by the words: political partition—but economic union. According to this plan, signed by the representatives of Canada, Czechoslovakia, Guatemala, the Netherlands, Peru, Sweden, and Uruguay, Palestine was to be divided into two politically independent states, one Jewish and one Arab, with special safeguards for the Holy Places. The city of Jerusalem was to be placed under a United Nations' trusteeship. During a transition period of two years, 150,000 Jewish immigrants were to be permitted to enter the Jewish state territory. If the transitional period lasted longer, 60,000 additional Jewish immigrants would be admitted each year thereafter.

The minority report, signed by the delegates of India, Iran, and Yugoslavia (Australia's delegate did not sign either report), proposed the creation of an independent federal state of Palestine with two federal legislative bodies, one elected on the basis of proportionate representation by all the inhabitants of Palestine, the other giving equal representation to Arabs and Jews. Jewish immigration into the Jewish area would be permitted during a period of three years—its size to be determined by a special agency of the United Nations. Thereafter it was to be regulated by the federal government.

On September 17, when the regular session of the General Assembly met at Lake Success, New York, United States Secretary of State George C. Marshall declared that "the United States gives great weight not only to the recommendations which have met with the unanimous approval of the Special Committee but also to those which have been approved by the majority of the Committee."

The British Government announced that it would support neither of the plans. The Soviet government stated that because it realized that the ambitions of Jews and Arabs could not be reconciled it would support the majority proposal. An ad hoc committee, composed of representatives of all the member nations in the United Nations, was created. Its function was to pass upon Great Britain's original request that the General Assembly make recommendations concerning the future government of Palestine, to deal with the proposal submitted by Saudi Arabia and Iraq that the mandate be terminated and Palestine be recognized at once as an Arab state, and to investigate the recommendations of UNSCOP.

On September 29, before the ad hoc committee launched into the general debate, it heard Jamal el Husseini, a relative of the ex-Mufti and Deputy Chairman of the Palestine Arab Higher Committee, uncompromisingly reject both the majority and the minority plans. On October 2 Rabbi Abba Hillel Silver told the committee that although the majority plan entailed "a very heavy sacrifice on the part of the Jewish people" the Jewish Agency was ready to accept the plan "subject to further discussion of the constitution and territorial provisions which we assume will take place in the course of these sessions." During the following days warnings came that the ex-Mufti had arrived in Jerusalem from his exile in Egypt and that the armies of five Arab states were about to march on Palestine. The ad hoc committee made no progress. In view of the sensational reports emanating from the Middle East, the representatives of practically all smaller states in the United Nations hesitated to commit themselves.

At this stage Herschel Johnson, on behalf of the United States government, declared that the American delegation in principle favored the majority report. He stated:

> Much has been said during the course of these debates on the desirability and necessity of presenting to the General Assembly a plan which would command the agreement of both the principal protagonists in this situation. . . . No such plan has ever been presented, and I do not believe that any such plan will ever be presented. If we are to effect through the United Nations a solution of this problem, it cannot be done without the use of the knife, partition.

Mr. Johnson was followed by Semyon K. Tsarapkin of the Soviet Union, who likewise supported the recommendations submitted by the majority of UNSCOP, adding that "such serious questions as the question of the frontier line between the two states or the measures during the transition period after the termination of the British Palestine mandate and a number of other more or less important questions . . . call for further and thorough consideration."

On October 18 Chaim Weizmann addressed the ad hoc committee. He emphasized the moral issue of the Palestine problem, referring to his treaty with Emir Faisal (later King of Iraq) and continuing:

> The condition which he then stipulated, the independence of all Arab territories outside Palestine, has now been fulfilled. The realm of Arab independence stretches far and wide. Independence is not the exclusive right of the Arabs. We Jews have an equal claim to it. This assembly cannot possibly decree that the desire of the Arabs to possess an eighth state (in addition to Egypt, Lebanon, Syria, Iraq, Trans-Jordan, Saudi Arabia, Yemen) must obliterate the right of the Jews to possess a single center of independent national life.

But there were a number of countries, represented in the General Assembly, that could not afford to incur the hostility of the Arab States and therefore, nolens volens, had to sidetrack the moral aspect of the problem. Even France, faced with a Moslem majority in Algeria, Morocco, and Tunisia, appeared to be reluctant to take a stand that might increase unrest in French North Africa. The Chinese delegates, too, were confronted with a very real difficulty. The Moslems in China had demanded from the government that it support no move opposed by their fellow Moslems in the Arab States. When the partition plan was finally introduced in the plenary meeting of the General Assembly on November 26, the outcome looked uncertain.

In the light of later events and for the sake of historic justice, it is necessary to emphasize the position which the United States government assumed in this particular moment. By special order of the President of the United States all American officials were directed to do their utmost to secure affirmative votes for the majority plan of UNSCOP. It was largely due to President Truman's courage and firmness that on November 29, 1947, a two-thirds majority, including many Latin-American nations that were known to be uncertain, voted in favor of the resolution to partition Palestine into an Arab and a Jewish state.

In 1897 Theodor Herzl had written: "In Basel I founded the Jewish state. If I said it today, it would be greeted with laughter; but in fifty years from now the truth of this assertion will be understood and universally acknowledged." Exactly fifty years had passed. When the final vote was taken in the General Assembly, everyone felt the great historic impact of the occasion. The phrase heard over and over again among the delegates and in the audience was: "I was present when the Jewish State was established. This was a historic assembly."

Needless to say, November 29, 1947, was a holiday in the Jewish DP camps in Europe. Needless to say, Jewish Palestine gave vent to a spirit of jubilation unprecedented in all of Jewish history since the beginning of the dispersion. After weeks of nerve-racking tension, with their ears close to short-wave receivers, devouring every line of news that emanated from Lake Success, the Jews of the National Home expressed their pent-up emotions in mass demonstrations of such joy that even British police and troops were infected with their spirit and joined in celebrating the rebirth of Jewish statehood.

There was, however, a serious constitutional defect in the resolution adopted by the General Assembly on November 29 (for text see Appendix). It failed completely to provide for any method of enforcing the partition plan should that prove necessary.

When the Arab League met to consider measures by which the partition plan might be stopped, there was no United Nations' organ to provide swift and effective action against a possible military intervention. True, the General Assembly had called on the Security Council of the United Nations "to term as a threat to the peace, breach of the peace, or act of aggression . . . any attempt to alter by force the settlement envisaged by this resolution." But the Security Council was paralyzed by the same deficiencies which had wrecked the League of

Nations. In particular, there were the veto right of the Big Five and the lack of an effective international police force.

The urgency of the problem was emphasized by the proclamation of the British Government on December 11 that Britain would terminate her mandate over Palestine on May 15, 1948, and complete the evacuation of her troops and civil servants by August 1. While the Arab States adjacent to Palestine openly encouraged the enlistment and arming of "volunteers" within their boundaries, the Security Council was unable even to create a temporary United Nations constabulary. Because of the inner conflict between the Soviet bloc and the Anglo-American powers, neither wanted to see the troops of the other side in such an international contingent. The idea of building up a well-equipped force from volunteers of the smaller nations only, although suggested by the Citizens Committee for United Nations Reform, did not find approval in United Nations circles.

It was a propitious moment for antipartition and anti-Jewish elements in both the State Department and the Congress of the United States to push forward their own phobias and pet theories, especially the discredited Arab propaganda rumor that United States support of a Jewish state had opened the way for Soviet Russia to drive a wedge into the Middle East.

Stories were planted in the American press through pro-Arab columnists to the effect that the military leaders of the United States were greatly disturbed over the Arab-Jewish clashes which might give the Soviet Union an excuse for sending an army to Palestine under the pretext of fulfilling her United Nations obligations and thus secure a foothold in the Mediterranean basin. "Highly placed officials in Washington, D. C." were quoted as being suspicious of this one and only case of Soviet cooperation with the United States, interpreting the Soviet declaration in favor of partition as a skillful operation to bring about a permanent break between the United States and the Arab countries, and that as a first measure King ibn-Saud would cancel the American oil concessions in his territory.

In the meantime the eyes of the world were focused upon the five members of the Palestine Commission which had been created by the General Assembly to supervise the setting up of the Arab and Jewish states in Palestine—Eduardo Morgan of Panama, Raul Diaz de Medina of Bolivia, Karl Lisicky of Czechoslovakia, Vincente Francisco of the Philippines, and Per Federspiel of Denmark. It was a complicated task. From the very beginning the British had insisted that until the mandate was terminated, they alone would be responsible for law and order in Palestine. They had opposed inclusion in the November 29 Resolution of any clause which would have granted the United Nations Commission a share of authority during the transition period. Moreover, the British had stated that they would transfer governmental authority only to the United Nations Commission, and not to the Provisional Councils of Government of the two states in Palestine, as envisaged in the November 29 Resolution. They also warned the commission that the British administration in Palestine would not be in a position to guarantee its safety.

On January 29, 1948, the Palestine Commission therefore reported to the Security Council that "all information thus far available to the Commission leads to the conclusion that the situation in Palestine as regards both security and civil authority is more likely to worsen than improve." It listed these three factors which had contributed to the deterioration of security in Palestine:

a. Organized efforts by strong Arab elements inside and outside Palestine to prevent the implementation of the Assembly's plan of partition and to thwart its objectives by threats and acts of violence, including armed incursions into Palestinian territory.
b. Certain elements of the Jewish community in Palestine continue to commit irresponsible acts of violence which worsen the security situation, although that community is generally in support of the recommendations of the Assembly.
c. The added complication created by the fact that the mandatory power, which remains responsible for law and order in Palestine until the termination of the mandate, is engaged in the liquidation of its administration and preparing for the evacuation of its troops.

On February 16 the commission added that it would be unable to establish security and maintain law and order "unless military forces in adequate strength are made available to the Commission when the responsibility for the administration of Palestine is transferred to it."

The implementation of the partition plan depended clearly on the position of the two great powers that had engineered it, the United States and the Soviet Union. Even before the meeting of the Security Council on February 24, 1948, there were definite indications that the United States Delegation in the United Nations was no longer wholeheartedly behind the Assembly resolution. While the British Government continued to send military supplies to Egypt, Iraq, and Trans-Jordan in fulfillment of "contractual obligations," while Arab "volunteers," smuggled from across the borders, were roaming Palestine completely unmolested by the British police and troops, the United States State Department on December 5, 1947—just as in the days of the Spanish Republic—clamped an embargo on armed shipments to the Middle

East, particularly to Palestine. Though supposedly aimed at neutrality, this action affected only the Jews, since the Arabs of Palestine could easily obtain arms and ammunition from the neighboring Arab countries.

The actual first shot culminating in the retreat of the United States from the partition plan was fired by Warren R. Austin in his statement before the Security Council on February 24. Reviewing the events in Palestine, he declared that "the Charter of the United Nations does not empower the Security Council to enforce a political settlement, whether it is pursuant to a recommendation of the General Assembly or of the Security Council itself." After several weeks of debate and a number of meetings of the delegates of the five major powers, on March 19 Ambassador Austin left no further doubt that the United States had reversed its policy. He declared that from the discussion in the Security Council it was clear the Council was not prepared to implement the partition plan in the existing situation. He submitted in the name of the United States the following three propositions:

1. The plan proposed by the General Assembly is an integral plan which cannot succeed unless each of its parts can be carried out. There seems to be general agreement that the plan cannot now be implemented by peaceful means.

2. We believe that further steps must be taken immediately not only to maintain the peace but also to afford a further opportunity to reach an agreement between the interested parties regarding the future government of Palestine. To this end we believe that a temporary trusteeship for Palestine should be established under the Trusteeship Council of the United Nations. Such a United Nations trusteeship would be without prejudice to the rights, claims or position of the parties concerned or to the character of the eventual political settlement, which we hope can be achieved without long delay. In our opinion, the Security Council should recommend the establishment of such a trusteeship to the General Assembly and to the mandatory power. This would require an immediate special session of the General Assembly, which the Security Council should request the Secretary-General to convoke under Article 20 of the Charter.

3. Pending the meeting of the proposed special session of the General Assembly, we believe that the Security Council should instruct the Palestine Commission to suspend its efforts to implement the proposed partition plan.

It was a new Black Friday in the calendar of Jewish history, this March 19. Reporters in Lake Success, long accustomed to double talk and cynical action, for once were stunned into a dazed silence. But the Jewish organizations of the United States spoke up. The Jewish War Veterans, through their commander, Brigadier General Julius Klein, stated: "As Hitler triumphed at Munich, so now has his criminal war partner, the Grand Mufti, triumphed at Lake Success. Power politics and the oil interests have become his allies."

The American Jewish Congress termed the "shameful tactics and duplicity to which our State Department has resorted, un-American and thoroughly dishonorable." The American Zionist Emergency Council attacked the new American policy as "nothing less than an act of betrayal." In an article in the *New York Times* I had already warned that the United States retreat from the November Resolution would disillusion all the smaller nations as to the integrity of American policy and drive them into the arms of any would-be aggressor, just as in Hitler's days. At the request of the Zionist organization of the State of Iowa I published in the *Des Moines Register* of March 25 an article to which I gave the heading, "Surrender to Terrorism." As this article summed up the Palestine issue before the United Nations, I include part of it here:

> In flat contradiction to the stand taken by the United States delegation in the United Nations five months ago, Mr. Warren R. Austin, chief American delegate to the United Nations, has now proposed to scrap the partition program and instead set up a United Nations trusteeship over Palestine when Britain, trustee of the deceased League of Nations, ends its mandate on May 15, 1948.
>
> Austin's demand has a legal basis in the charter of the United Nations, which provides for postponement and reconsideration. But the point is that responsible officials of a great country should do their thinking in advance, should know the risks involved, and should, therefore, be able to abide by their decisions.
>
> When the United Nations, upon the urgent recommendation of the United States, voted in favor of the partition of Palestine, the British had already announced their desire to relinquish the mandate. The Arab leaders, largely under the influence of the notorious war criminal, Haj Amin el Husseini, promised (in typical Nazi language) armed resistance and the extermination of the Jewish National Home. One of the steps absolutely required was the creation of an international police force strong enough to implement the decision of the Assembly. Instead, the United Nations, approaching the time for action, became stricken with paralysis.
>
> When, with the active encouragement of some of the British policy-makers in the Middle East—the same clique which is responsible for the loss of British prestige in India—well-armed Arabs from Saudi Arabia, Egypt and Syria crossed the frontier of Palestine to engage in open warfare against the Jews, when the British military began to disarm the Jewish defense forces, the United Nations did nothing except hold meetings, issue reports and pious proclamations.

It is but a few years ago that the gentlemen of the League of Nations looked on from the ramparts of a comfortable neutrality while Japan conquered Manchuria and while Mussolini overran Ethiopia. Anyone who has studied the laws of politics realized at that time that the days of the League were numbered.

If the United Nations Assembly should follow our present administration in its predilection for irresponsible vacillation and back down in the face of Arab terrorism, we need no skyscrapers to house our guardian of the peace. Some less conspicuous memorial will do to mark the grave of the United Nations.

The retreat from partition has been heralded by a number of semi-official statements pointing to Arab intransigence and Arab oil, to the British hope to leave Palestine with the blessings of the Arab leaders, and to the fear of Soviet entrenchment in the Middle East.

The Arabs have neither a legal nor a moral case in Palestine. In 634 A.D. they came as conquerors in the land, which, they knew, had never been their own. They based their own religion on Jewish traditions. They were, therefore, quite familiar with Jewish history in Palestine. Moreover, from 1071 onward the land passed into the hands of the Crusaders, the Mamelukes and Turks, until finally, in 1923, the Turkish government surrendered its rights to the Allied and Associated Powers by the Peace Treaty of Lausanne.

The Jews, on the other hand, have never renounced their rights to Palestine. Since the destruction of their statehood by the Roman Empire, over and over again they tried to return to their homeland; and, in spite of persecution and oppression, there has always been at least a small Jewish population in Palestine.

This old Jewish claim has been explicitly acknowledged in the preamble of the Palestine Mandate. . . .

Woodrow Wilson, Lloyd George, General Smuts, Lord Balfour and Winston Churchill have made it quite clear that "National Home" meant the establishment of a Jewish state and not the settlement of a Jewish minority in an Arab-dominated country.

Emir Faisal, representing the Arab principalities during the peace conference in Versailles, testified to this interpretation of the National Home by signing on Jan. 3, 1919, a treaty with Dr. Weizmann, president of the World Zionist Organization, "on the relations between the Arab state and Palestine," providing in Article I that "to this end Arab and Jewish duly accredited agents shall be established and maintained in their respective territories."

When, in 1882, modern colonization of Palestine began, there were 106,000 Arabs and 35,000 Jews in the land who could claim to have been there for more than one generation. Arab national life had its centers in Arabia, Syria and Egypt, but not in Palestine. Much of Palestine was covered by swamps, the largest part was desert. Everywhere was decline and devastation.

The Jewish settlers bought the deserted land from its absentee land owners, drained the swamps and drove out malaria. When, due to their daring and enterprise, orange groves began to blossom in the desert, Arabs came by the tens of thousands from the surrounding countries to enjoy the better life which Jewish pioneers had created in the ancient home of Israel.

Does this mean that the Arabs have now a claim to the land which the Jews have built? If Hitler was right in raping Norway, Holland and France, the Arab leaders too are entitled to the possession of Palestine. If our Iowa farmers are willing to surrender their homes and fields to anyone who lives from the work of others, then, of course, the Jews, too, might be asked to surrender Palestine to the Arab Higher Committee.

The forty million Moslem Arabs of the world have their national independence in many lands. All of these territories are underpopulated. The Jewish survivors of Hitler's war in Europe have no place to go but to Palestine. The decision of the United Nations to permit the Jews their own state in an area of 6,000 square miles, or half the size of Belgium, was not overly generous. To revoke even this meager promise constitutes a perfidy for which there are few parallels in the annals of history.

Non-Americans, particularly those who know only the "American innocent abroad," do not always have a realistic picture of the average American citizen. In fairness it should be stated that this citizen has very little traffic with those who put their vested interests over considerations of equity and justice. Americans are actually idealists in the best sense of the word and not dollar-hunters as too many foreigners assume. Americans in their vast majority stand for a square deal. Americans are very generous. They have an immense pride in the good name of the United States. Even the few political isolationists left in the United States after World War II believe that their nation must respond to a call for moral leadership. Many non-Jewish Americans felt a sense of deep personal humiliation when they witnessed the change in their government's policy toward the Palestine issue.

After a few days of bewilderment the general press of the United States, the overwhelming majority of commentators, the American Christian Palestine Committee, and many church organizations demanded the immediate return of United States policy to its stand of November 29. Just at this moment Sumner Welles, former Undersecretary of State, one of the ablest and best-informed statesmen the United States has ever had, published his book *We Need Not Fail.* He insisted that the United States government, instead of causing a defeat for the whole system of collective security, should stand squarely by its original vote in the United Nations General Assembly. When the American Zionist Emergency Council called on the Jews of New York to march down Fifth Avenue in protest against the American switch in Palestine policy, some sixty thousand Jewish war veterans in uniform were joined by official non-Jewish delegations of the American Legion, the American Veterans of World War II, and Catholic War Veterans. Close to five hundred thousand onlookers cheered Rabbi Abba Hillel Silver for many minutes when he declared:

> You need take no lessons from the oil lobbyists who have been responsible for the shocking reversal of the American position. . . . American Jewry continues to stand by the United Nations' decision and will not be intimidated by the propaganda of those who wish to scuttle it.

On March 23 the Jewish Agency for Palestine and the *Vaad Leumi*, the National Council of the Jews of Palestine, replied to the United States' proposal of March 19 in the following resolution:

> The Jewish Agency for Palestine and the Vaad Leumi have learned with regret and astonishment of the attitude adopted by the United States representative in the Security Council concerning the United Nations decisions on Palestine.
>
> The Jewish Agency and the Vaad Leumi declare:
>
> 1. The Jewish people and the Yishuv in Palestine will oppose any proposal designed to prevent or postpone the establishment of the Jewish State.
>
> 2. We categorically reject any plan to set up a trusteeship regime for Palestine, even for a short period of time. A trusteeship would necessarily entail a denial of the Jewish right to national independence. It would leave Palestine under a foreign military regime.
>
> 3. The failure and disintegration of the mandatory administration, the continuation of which was unanimously rejected by the United Nations, necessitates the early arrival in Palestine of the United Nations Palestine Commission. The Provisional Council of Government of the Jewish State should be recognized without delay by the United Nations Palestine Commission so that authority may be transferred to it as envisaged in the United Nations decisions.
>
> 4. Upon the termination of the mandatory administration and not later than 16 May next, a provisional Jewish government will commence to function in cooperation with the representatives of the United Nations then in Palestine. In the meantime, we shall do our utmost to minimize the chaos created by the present government, and we shall maintain, so far as lies in our power, the public services neglected by it.
>
> 5. The Jewish people extends the hand of peace to the Arab people and invites representatives of the Arab population of the Jewish State to take their rightful place in all its organs of government. The Jewish State will be glad to cooperate with the neighbouring Arab States and to enter into permanent treaty relations with them to strengthen world peace and to advance the development of all the countries of the Near East.

When the Security Council met on March 30, 1948, the prestige of the United Nations had reached its lowest ebb. International confidence in the ability of the United States government to offer constructive guidance in an attempt to settle the Palestine issue was painfully lacking. The general atmosphere of pessimism was not improved by Ambassador Austin's two resolutions, one calling "upon Arab and Jewish armed groups in Palestine to cease acts of violence immediately," and the other requesting "the Secretary General, in accordance with Article 20 of the United Nations Charter, to convoke a special session of the General Assembly to consider further the question of the future government of Palestine."

Andrei Gromyko took the opportunity to declare that "full responsibility for the killing of the decision on the partition of Palestine rests on the United States." He added that he could see no reason for calling a special session of the General Assembly. A departure in the British position was indicated when Sir Alexander Cadogan announced that Great Britain, which until then had consistently abstained on all issues connected with Palestine, approved Mr. Austin's resolutions. Secretary-General Trygve Lie finally announced that on April 16 the General Assembly would be convened in a special session.

When the Assembly met, a number of well-intentioned and less well-intentioned proposals came forward from unofficial sources. There was an appeal, fully justified, of course, by a number of religious leaders that Jerusalem should be declared an "open city" and guaranteed against attack. There was a proposal by a committee under the chairmanship of Dean Virginia C. Gildersleeve suggesting "some sort of compromise agreed to by both the Arabs and the Jews." James G. McDonald, now United States Ambassador to Israel, who for many years had been interested in the solution of the international refugee problem, pointed out that the proposal of the Gildersleeve Committee was tantamount to asking the Jews to surrender their hopes and their rights in Palestine:

> In view of this Arab defiance, the call of the Committee for a "compromise" agreeable to both the Jews and the Arabs must have the effect of bringing pressure to bear upon the Jews to yield to Arab intransigence. How such pressure can contribute toward peace and justice in the Holy Land is a mystery which neither the Committee's statement nor the explanation of its Chairman does anything to clear up.

The proposals offered by the United States Delegation for the consideration of the General Assembly bore a rather close resemblance to the recommendations of the Gildersleeve Committee. In the main they asked for a temporary trusteeship until Jews and Arabs had agreed on a future government of Palestine, for an elected legislature in which the Jews would naturally be a minority, and for the subordination of further Jewish immigration and land purchases to an agreement between Jews and Arabs.

It was apparently hoped that since the Soviet Union had refused to participate in the Trusteeship Council, it would have no part in a Palestine trusteeship in the event of the adoption of the American proposals by the General Assembly. But on April 25, 1948, the Soviet government again surprised United Nations circles by naming Semyon Tsarapkin its delegate to fill the seat in the Trusteeship Council to which Soviet Russia as a major power was entitled under the United Nations Charter.

Against the background of the "cold war" in which the United States and the Soviet Union were engaged, it could not be doubted for a moment that if the United States should undertake to send troops to police Palestine under the trusteeship setup, the Soviet Union would ask for the same privilege and thereby secure for the Soviet Union an equivalent access to the eastern Mediterranean and the oil resources of the Near East. The trusteeship idea of the policy makers in the United States State Department had overnight become a boomerang that threatened to undermine the very pattern of security which the State Department in collaboration with the British Foreign Office was trying to establish in the Middle East.

Furthermore, in early May it became apparent that if a trusteeship was imposed, it would mean the use of repressive force against the Jews of Palestine who were determined to abide by the decision of the General Assembly of November 29, 1947, and to establish their national independence.

The last plenary meeting of the Second Special Session of the General Assembly on Palestine was opened at five o'clock on May 14. Before it was a report which no amount of legalistic sophistry could explain away. At 4:06 P.M., on Friday, the fifth day of the Jewish month of Iyar, May 14, 1948, the sovereign Republic of Israel, the Third Jewish Commonwealth in the history of the human race, had come into existence.

II

THE GOVERNMENT OF ISRAEL

Chapter Seven: THE PANGS OF BIRTH

DECLARATION OF INDEPENDENCE · THE ARAB-JEWISH WAR · UNITED NATIONS MEDIATION

On the eve of the Sabbath day which marked the birth of the Republic of Israel, the prophecy of Amos was read in synagogues throughout the world: "On that day I will reestablish the fallen Tabernacle of David, and they shall not any more be uprooted from their land."

For over one thousand eight hundred long years millions of Jews had prayed for this promise to become reality. Now at last the Star of Zion which was imposed upon the homeless Jew of the Middle Ages and the Hitlerian Empire shone forth again as the symbol of a re-established Jewish Commonwealth. On May 14, 1948, the Provisional State Council of the government of Israel issued the following proclamation, which will probably enter history as the Jewish Declaration of Independence:

> The Land of Israel was the birthplace of the Jewish people. Here their spiritual, religious and national identity was formed. Here they achieved independence and created a culture of national and universal significance. Here they wrote and gave the Bible to the world.
>
> Exiled from Palestine, the Jewish people remained faithful to it in all the countries of their dispersion, never ceasing to pray and hope for their return and the restoration of their national freedom.
>
> Impelled by this historic association, Jews strove throughout the centuries to go back to the land of their fathers and regain their Statehood. In recent decades they returned in their masses. They reclaimed the wilderness, revived their language, built cities and villages, and established a vigorous and ever-growing community, with its own economic and cultural life. They sought peace yet were prepared to defend themselves. They brought the blessings of progress to all inhabitants of the country.
>
> In the year 1897 the First Zionist Congress, inspired by Theodor Herzl's

vision of the Jewish State, proclaimed the right of the Jewish people to national revival in their own country.

This right was acknowledged by the Balfour Declaration of November 2, 1917, and reaffirmed by the Mandate of the League of Nations, which gave explicit international recognition to the historic connection of the Jewish people with Palestine and their right to reconstitute their national home.

The Nazi holocaust, which engulfed millions of Jews in Europe, proved anew the urgency of the reestablishment of the Jewish State, which would solve the problem of Jewish homelessness by opening the gates to all Jews and lifting the Jewish people to equality in the family of nations.

The survivors of the European catastrophe, as well as Jews from other lands, proclaiming their right to a life of dignity, freedom and labor, and undeterred by hazards, hardships and obstacles, have tried unceasingly to enter Palestine.

In the Second World War the Jewish people in Palestine made a full contribution in the struggle of the freedom-loving nations against the Nazi evil. The sacrifices of their soldiers and the efforts of their workers gained them title to rank with the peoples who founded the United Nations.

On November 29, 1947, the General Assembly of the United Nations adopted a Resolution for the establishment of an independent Jewish State in Palestine, and called upon inhabitants of the country to take such steps as may be necessary on their part to put the plan into effect.

This recognition by the United Nations of the right of the Jewish people to establish their independent state may not be revoked. It is, moreover, the self-evident right of the Jewish people to be a nation, like all other nations, in its own sovereign state.

ACCORDINGLY, WE, THE MEMBERS OF THE NATIONAL COUNCIL, REPRESENTING THE JEWISH PEOPLE IN PALESTINE AND THE ZIONIST MOVEMENT OF THE WORLD, MET TOGETHER IN SOLEMN ASSEMBLY TODAY, THE DAY OF THE TERMINATION OF THE BRITISH MANDATE FOR PALESTINE, AND BY VIRTUE OF THE NATURAL AND HISTORIC RIGHT OF THE JEWISH PEOPLE AND OF THE RESOLUTION OF THE GENERAL ASSEMBLY OF THE UNITED NATIONS, HEREBY PROCLAIM THE ESTABLISHMENT OF THE JEWISH STATE IN PALESTINE, TO BE CALLED ISRAEL.

We hereby declare that as from the termination of the Mandate at midnight, this night of the 14th to 15th May 1948, and until the setting up of the duly elected bodies of the State in accordance with a Constitution, to be drawn up by a Constituent Assembly not later than the first day of October 1948, the present National Council shall act as the Provisional State Council, and its executive organ, the National Administration, shall constitute the Provisional Government of the State of Israel.

The State of Israel will be open to the immigration of Jews from all countries of their dispersion; will promote the development of the country for the benefit of all its inhabitants; will be based on the precepts of liberty, jus-

Dagania B—one of the first agricultural settlements to be founded by the Keren Hayesod, thirty years ago. *Courtesy of United Palestine Appeal.*

Nahalal was the first smallholders' settlement to be established in the western part of the valley of Jezreel. Since 1921 it has been converted from a malaria-infested swamp into one of the garden spots of Palestine. *Courtesy of United Palestine Appeal.*

Palestine's ex-G.I.'s build the new all-veterans settlement of Kfar Kisch. *Courtesy of United Palestine Appeal.*

Homecoming—this old man will be reunited with his son in Palestine. *Courtesy of United Palestine Appeal.*

This boy's forearm was tattooed by a Buchenwald guard. *Courtesy of United Palestine Appeal.*

A member of Chen, the women's army. *Courtesy of United Palestine Appeal.*

A new settler comes to Israel from Yemen, the southernmost Arabian kingdom. *Courtesy of United Palestine Appeal.*

tice and peace taught by the Hebrew Prophets; will uphold the full social and political equality of all its citizens, without distinction of race, creed or sex; will guarantee full freedom of conscience, worship, education and culture; will safeguard the sanctity and inviolability of the shrines and Holy Places of all religions; and will dedicate itself to the principles of the Charter of the United Nations.

The State of Israel will be ready to cooperate with the organs and representatives of the United Nations in the implementation of the Resolution of the Assembly of November 29, 1947, and will take steps to bring about the Economic Union over the whole of Palestine.

We appeal to the United Nations to assist the Jewish people in the building of its State and to admit Israel into the family of nations.

In the midst of wanton aggression, we yet call upon the Arab inhabitants of the State of Israel to return to the ways of peace and play their part in the development of the State, with full and equal citizenship and due representation in all its bodies and institutions, provisional or permanent.

We offer peace and amity to all the neighboring states and their peoples, and invite them to cooperate with the independent Jewish nation for the common good of all. The State of Israel is ready to contribute its full share to the peaceful progress and development of the Middle East.

Our call goes out to the Jewish people all over the world to rally to our side in the task of immigration and development and to stand by us in the great struggle for the fulfilment of the dream of generations—the redemption of Israel.

With trust in Almighty God, we set our hand to this Declaration, at this Session of the Provisional State Council, in the city of Tel Aviv, on this Sabbath eve, the fifth of Iyar, 5708, the fourteenth day of May, 1948.

On the same day, the government of the United States through President Truman recognized "the Provisional Government as the de facto authority of the new State of Israel."

To the world at large, to the United Nations, and more especially to Jews and Arabs in Palestine, the policy of the United States prior to May 14, 1948, had seemed to be full of contradictions. But in the twilight in which diplomacy usually operates, there might have been a guiding principle of United States policy that was not always discernible to the outsider. As a member of the United Nations, the United States had to cooperate with its fellow members. The prime objective of the United Nations was to maintain peace in the world. By supporting the partition plan on the strength of the recommendations made by UNSCOP, the United States had probably hoped to contribute to the tranquillity in the Holy Land. When the five-member Palestine Commission subsequently reported that the partition plan could be implemented only by force, the United States called for a truce and a temporary trusteeship. As Mr. Truman pointed out on several occasions, this was merely to afford a "cease-fire" agreement between the warring Jews and Arabs. With the lapse of the mandate and the failure of the United Nations to establish a comparable authority, a vacuum was created. Once the State of Israel presented itself as an accomplished fact, immediate United States recognition was not only logical but imperative.

It is by no means certain, however, that United States policy was as consistent as this. Only a few hours before Israel's recognition there was talk in some State Department circles about possible sanctions against the Jews should they resist the trusteeship plan. Mention was even made of an embargo on funds to Palestine from the United Jewish Appeal, the head organization for American-Jewish overseas relief, and the cancellation of its tax-exempt privileges. To those in the State Department who were prepared to follow Britain's Middle Eastern policy of appeasing the Arab ruling class at practically any cost, the de facto recognition of Israel by the President must have come as a distinct shock. On the other hand, there was the disquieting information which reached both the State Department and the armed forces of the United States that the Arab armies showed poor discipline and even poorer fighting spirit and that in a real showdown with the Jews the whole myth of Arab military superiority in the Near East might be exploded. This was the news: On April 8 the troops of the Trans-Jordan Arab Legion had opened fire on the Jews in lower Galilee. On April 22 the British had given up control of Haifa, precipitating an all-out battle between Haganah and Arab military units. The Jews seized Haifa, next to Alexandria the most important port in the eastern Mediterranean, on the same day. On April 29 Jaffa, Palestine's largest all-Arab city, fell to the Jewish forces. As April ended, Haganah took over most of Jerusalem. Meanwhile, Haganah's shock troops, the Palmach, though heavily outnumbered, decided the military campaign for eastern Galilee in successful surprise attacks on Safad and other Arab strongholds.

The Iraqi troops were defeated at Givat Napoleon, the hill near which Napoleon I was stopped on his famous march northward during his Egyptian campaign. By noon of May 14, 1948, the Jews held all the territory allotted to the Jewish State by the United Nations decision of November 29, 1947; only the airport of Lydda was in Arab hands, and this had been handed over to them by the British. There was a young generation of Jews in Palestine that went into battle with the same grin with which boys go to a ball game in the United States. It is not unlikely that the military prowess of the Jewish armies had its share in the swift move of the White House to recognize the State of Israel.

It was of extreme significance that the very first government to recognize Israel was the greatest democracy of the Western world and not the Soviet Union. On May 17 Molotov informed the Israeli Foreign Minister that "the government of the U.S.S.R. has decided to recognize officially the State of Israel and its Provisional Government." Despite its belated change of heart, Soviet Russia, which since the October Revolution in 1917 had persecuted Zionism and Zionists, hardly deserved a historic claim on the gratitude of the people of Israel. On the other hand, the United States of America, in spite of many zigzags in official policy, had consistently been a haven of refuge for the persecuted of the Jewish people and an outstanding material and spiritual center which enabled Zionists the world over to carry out their hope of the renaissance of Israel. There was an intensely dramatic quality in President Truman's step—a tiny, valiant republic arising in the face of foreign invasion and heavy odds, with the great faraway United States of America, true to the best in its tradition, leaning forward to help it stand erect.

The French National Assembly sent a "fraternal salute" to Israel. Guatemala, Uruguay, Venezuela, the Union of South Africa, Poland, Czechoslovakia, and Yugoslavia extended either de facto or de jure recognition within the first few days after the proclamation of the Jewish Republic. The British Government was stunned. While the friends of Israel in the Cabinet, especially Health Minister Aneurin Bevan, did not hide their joy, Mr. Ernest Bevin remarked in the House of Commons that the Jews "seemed to be better armed than the Arabs." The Foreign Minister of Britain, in the name of expediency, had backed the wrong horse. Now the whole British Middle Eastern policy was in danger of being shown up for the house of cards which it had always been. If the British public, however, had hoped that the departure of the High Commissioner on May 14 and the evacuation of British troops from Palestine would mark the end of Britain's concern for Palestine, it was mistaken. It must be stated for the historic record that Mr. Bevin's policy made Great Britain an accomplice in the Arab war of aggression against the Republic of Israel. The facts which bear out this charge were listed by Major Lyall Wilkes, a Member of Parliament, in the London *Times* on May 22. He wrote:

> Does public opinion at home appreciate (as it does abroad) that every tank and aeroplane now being used by the Arabs has been supplied from the United Kingdom; that the British air mission is still functioning in Iraq;

that British missions are now working, training and re-equipping Arab armies in Saudi-Arabia and Iraq; that between 1945 and 1947 we supplied Egypt alone with 40 military aircraft, 38 scout cars, and 298 carriers, apart from a great quantity of small arms and light equipment; that the Arab Legion now waging war is wholly subsidised by us with £2,000,000 a year and is commanded by 38 British officers; that Trans-Jordan under the March, 1948, treaty is bound to "undertake not to adopt in regard to foreign countries an attitude which is inconsistent with the alliance or might create difficulties for the other party thereto"; and that no word of protest has come from the British Government at the Arab invasions, but that the Jews within the boundaries given them by the United Nations partition decision (which still stands) are denied arms by the British? . . .

Will we never learn that we cannot subsidise aggression in the Middle East and oppose it in Greece or Persia—that to climb now into the grandstand and attempt to wash our hands of responsibility for the slaughter perpetrated by our Spitfires and British-trained and officered Arab troops is conduct unworthy of the traditions of a great nation and indicates a moral degeneration within the political leadership of this country far more alarming than any signs of a merely materialistic or economic decline.

The full-scale invasion of Palestine by the military forces of the Arab States started on May 15. It was conducted principally by Egypt and Trans-Jordan. Egyptian planes bombed Tel Aviv on the same day, taking forty-one lives. An estimated force of 3,000 Trans-Jordan Arab legionnaires, commanded by British Brigadier General J. B. Glubb, besieged Jerusalem. After eleven days the old walled part of Jerusalem fell into their hands. Israeli forces, on the other hand, made raids into the territories of Syria, Lebanon, and Trans-Jordan.

On March 17, 1948, in the Security Council of the United Nations, Ambassador Austin voiced his conviction that the Palestine situation was a threat to the peace and a breach of the peace within the meaning of Article 39 of the Charter. He asked that the Security Council order all governments and authorities "to cease and desist from any hostile military action." He recommended that a cease-fire and stand-still order be issued to military and para-military forces, to become effective "within 36 hours after the adoption of this resolution." Austin also suggested that a questionnaire be sent to the Arab governments, the Palestine Arab Higher Committee, and the Provisional Government of Israel, asking for information as to their further intentions. Gromyko supported Austin's resolution. But Sir Alexander Cadogan, the British representative, opposed a cease-fire order by the Security Council. He raised the issue of the legality of the State of Israel. If the State of Israel was not legal, he argued, then no act of aggression could have been committed. He questioned Austin's assertion that aggression according to Article 39 had actually taken place in Palestine. He even toyed with the idea that "any threat to the peace" meant only international peace, adding that he was doubtful whether the Palestine situation was a threat to international peace. The replies to the questionnaire, with the exception of those from Yemen and Saudi Arabia which arrived later, were presented to the Security Council on May 22. They were practically identical. The Arab States proudly asserted that their armies were in Palestine at the invitation of the Palestine Arabs to fight the "Zionist terrorist gangs."

As Austin's resolution did not secure passage, a compromise between the American-Russian and the British positions was finally accepted on May 22. It read:

> THE SECURITY COUNCIL,
>
> TAKING INTO CONSIDERATION that previous resolutions of the Security Council in respect to Palestine have not been complied with and that military operations are taking place in Palestine;
>
> CALLS UPON all Governments and authorities, without prejudice to the rights, claims or position of the parties concerned, to abstain from any hostile military action in Palestine and to that end to issue a cease-fire order to their military and para-military forces to become effective within thirty-six hours after midnight New York standard time, 22 May 1948;
>
> CALLS UPON the Truce Commission and upon all parties concerned to give the highest priority to the negotiation and maintenance of a truce in the City of Jerusalem;
>
> DIRECTS the Truce Commission established by the Security Council by its resolution of 23 April 1948 to report to the Security Council on the compliance with the two preceding paragraphs of this resolution;
>
> CALLS UPON all parties concerned to facilitate by all means in their power the task of the United Nations Mediator appointed in execution of the resolution of the General Assembly of 14 May 1948.

Two days later the Provisional Government of Israel notified the Security Council that it had accepted the cease-fire order. The Arab States had asked for an extension of time. Faris el Khouri, representative of Syria on the Security Council and spokesman for the Arab governments, reasoned that "the matter concerns the seven states of the Arab League which are distant from each other." On May 26 the Arab rejection of the cease-fire recommendation was received.

Despite the fact that the Arabs had rejected the recommendation of the United Nations Security Council, the British Government, upon the insistence of Mr. Bevin, continued to supply arms and ammunition to Iraq and Egypt, and officers, military supplies, and financial aid to Trans-Jordan. On May 27, Sir Alexander Cadogan frankly declared in the United Nations Security Council:

The responsibility which rests upon my government to maintain the flow of material constitutes an international obligation of major importance. . . . My government will continue to honor its obligations under these treaties (with Iraq, Egypt, Trans-Jordan).

Mr. Bevin was a poor gambler and a bad loser. He gambled and lost again.

Between November 29 and May 14 the Jews had demonstrated their ability to clear the Jewish area of Palestine of Arab "volunteers." In the four-week period that followed the proclamation of the Jewish State, they proved that they were strong enough to hold their country against the combined forces of the League of Arab States although the League commanded armies totaling some 250,000 men, amply supplied with British planes, tanks, and armored cars. The Egyptian air force bombed Jewish settlements daily. By June 1 the toll of their Spitfires was more than 1,400 Jewish lives. Since Abdullah's army held Latrun, the bottleneck of the Jerusalem–Tel Aviv Highway, the Jews built a Burma Road over the hills surrounding Latrun and continued to ship supplies into Jerusalem. The Egyptian army moving northward to Tel Aviv never succeeded in gaining possession of even the full length of the coastal strip which the United Nations had allotted to the Arabs in Palestine. The Iraqi forces were stopped at Tulkarm and Ras el-Ein. The Lebanese and Syrians never came closer than border territory.

For their part, the Israeli had conquered a large portion of territory originally assigned by the United Nations to the Arab State in Palestine. Their new navy controlled the ports. On June 1 the new Jewish air force bombed Abdullah's capital, Amman, and nine days later hit Damascus. It was about to visit Cairo when on June 11 the Arab governments accepted the cease-fire order issued on June 7 in the name of the United Nations Security Council by the Mediator of the United Nations, Sweden's Count Folke Bernadotte.

Bernadotte had accepted his office on May 21. Since that date he had held a number of meetings with the representatives of the Arab States and of the State of Israel. But his efforts at mediation had failed in the face of the Arab hope of conquering Israel with their combined forces and confronting the United Nations with a new fait accompli. In Israel, on the other hand, the suspicion grew that the United Nations machinery functioned well only when the Arab aggressors were about to pay the price of their aggression.

The very term "mediation" placed those who had taken up arms against the decision of the United Nations on the same footing with their intended victims. Somehow it implied willingness to conciliate the leaders of the Arab States at the expense of Israel. This implication was borne out by the character of the terms which Bernadotte had worked out for both sides. They were presented to Arabs and Jews in his headquarters on the Mediterranean island of Rhodes on June 28.

According to Bernadotte's suggestions, the whole or part of the Negev was to become Arab territory. The city of Jerusalem was to be included in Arab territory "with municipal autonomy for the Jewish community." Haifa was to become a free port, Lydda a free airport. In return the Jews were to get the whole or part of western Galilee, which was in their hands anyhow. The Jewish State was to form an economic union with the Arab State in Palestine, which Bernadotte suddenly defined in accordance with the original Palestine Mandate as including Trans-Jordan. This meant that British-supported Trans-Jordan, enlarged by the Arab area of Palestine, and with Jerusalem as the capital, would form a union with the Jewish State. The functions of this union would be to operate and maintain common services including customs and excise, to coordinate foreign policy and measures for common defense. Immigration within its own boundaries would be within the competence of each member, "provided that, following a period of two years from the establishment of the Union, either member would be entitled to request the Council of the Union to review the immigration policy of the other member and to render a ruling thereon in terms of the common interests of the Union." Should the Council of the Union be unable to reach a decision, the issue would have to be referred to the Economic and Social Council of the United Nations, "whose decision, taking into account the principle of economic absorptive capacity, would be binding on the member whose policy is at issue."

The Mediator's plan was ultimately rejected by both the Arabs and the Jews. The Jews reacted like the London *New Statesman and Nation,* which called the Bernadotte plan "the 1939 White Paper translated into 1948 language with the full approval of the Foreign Office and the State Department." It was indeed a cleverly concealed attempt to make the Jewish economy depend upon Great Britain, to coordinate Haganah under British command with the Trans-Jordan Legion, the very army that had attacked the Jews along the whole eastern border of the new State of Israel, and—finally—to exercise at least some control over Jewish immigration into the new state.

Since the time of the truce was running out, Bernadotte appealed to both sides to prolong the truce for another thirty days. Israel agreed. The Arab States refused. On July 8, a day before the expiration of the truce, the Egyptians resumed hostilities, and on July 9 Palestine was again at war.

Having at last secured arms and munitions from a number of European countries, the Israeli forces emerged from the truce with unexpectedly heavy fire power and greatly improved staff work. In a series of swift actions they took Nazareth, the key to central Galilee, from the "National Liberation Army" under the leadership of Fawzi el Kaukje. They defeated the Trans-Jordan Legion at Lydda and came into the possession of the only modern airport in Palestine. They routed the Iraqi at Ras el-Ein. In Jerusalem itself they resumed battle for the old walled part of the city. This was the only section which Abdullah's troops had managed to seize, and it was in a surprise attack after the Jews had been told by the United Nations that Jerusalem was to be part of an international zone. Curiously enough, as long as the Trans-Jordan Arab Legion seemed to have some hope of gaining Jerusalem the British Foreign Office did not hide its plan to reward Abdullah by making Jerusalem his capital. Echoing the British Foreign Office, United Nations Mediator Count Bernadotte suggested that Abdullah should become King of Jerusalem. Now that the Jews were about to take the Arab-held section of the city, both Mr. Bevin and Count Bernadotte suddenly returned to the November 29 partition scheme, according to which Jerusalem was to be internationalized.

By the middle of July the diplomatic breach between the United States and Great Britain had been completely repaired. The British Foreign Office and the American State Department coordinated their policy in the Middle East. The Soviet Union, at first in the same camp with the United States, was isolated from now on. On July 15 the Security Council by a vote of seven to one, with three abstentions, approved the following Anglo-American resolution:

THE SECURITY COUNCIL,

TAKING INTO CONSIDERATION that the Provisional Government of Israel has indicated its acceptance in principle of a prolongation of the truce in Palestine; that the States members of the Arab League have rejected successive appeals of the United Nations Mediator, and of the Security Council in its resolution of 7 July 1948, for the prolongation of the truce in Palestine; and that there has consequently developed a renewal of hostilities in Palestine;

DETERMINES that the situation in Palestine constitutes a threat to the peace within the meaning of Article 39 of the Charter;

ORDERS the Governments and authorities concerned, pursuant to Article 40 of the Charter of the United Nations, to desist from further military action and to this end to issue cease-fire orders to their military and para-military forces, to take effect at a time to be determined by the Mediator, but in any event not later than three days from the date of the adoption of this resolution;

DECLARES that failure by any of the Governments or authorities concerned to comply with the preceding paragraph of this resolution would demonstrate the existence of a breach of the peace within the meaning of Article 39 of the Charter requiring immediate consideration by the Security Council with a view to such further action under Chapter VII of the Charter as may be decided upon by the Council;

CALLS UPON all Governments and authorities concerned to continue to co-operate with the Mediator with a view to the maintenance of peace in Palestine in conformity with the resolution adopted by the Security Council on 29 May 1948;

ORDERS as a matter of special and urgent necessity an immediate and unconditional cease-fire in the City of Jerusalem to take effect 24 hours from the time of the adoption of this resolution, and instructs the Truce Commission to take any necessary steps to make this cease-fire effective;

INSTRUCTS the Mediator to continue his efforts to bring about the demilitarization of the City of Jerusalem, without prejudice to the future political status of Jerusalem, and to assure the protection of and access to the Holy Places, religious buildings and sites in Palestine;

INSTRUCTS the Mediator to supervise the observance of the truce and to establish procedures for examining alleged breaches of the truce since 11 June 1948, authorizes him to deal with breaches so far as it is within his capacity to do so by appropriate local action, and requests him to keep the Security Council currently informed concerning the operation of the truce and when necessary to take appropriate action;

DECIDES that, subject to further decision by the Security Council or the General Assembly, the truce shall remain in force, in accordance with the present resolution and with that of 29 May 1948, until a peaceful adjustment of the future situation of Palestine is reached;

REITERATES the appeal to the parties contained in the last paragraph of its resolution of 22 May and urges upon the parties that they continue conversations with the Mediator in a spirit of conciliation and mutual concession in order that all points under dispute may be settled peacefully;

REQUESTS the Secretary-General to provide the Mediator with the necessary staff and facilities to assist in carrying out the functions assigned to him under the resolution of the General Assembly of 14 May, and under this resolution; and

REQUESTS that the Secretary-General make appropriate arrangements to provide necessary funds to meet the obligations arising from this resolution.

The government of Israel again indicated promptly that it would accept the truce both for Jerusalem and for Palestine as a whole. The Arab States stipulated that their acceptance of the cease-fire order was conditional on a fixed time limit, cessation of Jewish immigration, and the return of Arab refugees to their homes in Israeli territory. The Security Council took the position that both parties had accepted the truce unconditionally and asked the Mediator to map out some permanent solution.

The truce became effective on July 18. It was a truce without peace. Sniping and military skirmishes continued. Jerusalem was entirely without water. Despite the Mediator's assurances that water would be provided from the Arab-held Latrun pumping station, Jerusalem got no water. The Arabs blew up the Latrun pumping station during the truce.

Thanks to the truce Great Britain was enabled to continue the imprisonment of some twelve thousand young Jews in Cyprus. Thanks to the truce the invading armies of Egypt, Trans-Jordan, and the other Arab states were permitted to remain on the soil of Palestine, unchallenged and undisturbed by the world community.

The Swedish Count was in no enviable position. To the Arabs he seemed to be pro-Jewish; to the Jews pro-Arab. Actually he was as undetermined as was the whole of the United Nations Organization in this Palestine affair. The Palestine truce had become a charter of procrastination and indecision.

The government of Israel hinted repeatedly that it would prefer direct negotiations with the Arabs to United Nations mediation. This suggestion was rebuffed by the League of Arab States. The League showed signs of discord and rivalry as never before. Created on March 22, 1945, upon the initiative of Anthony Eden, it had never been forced to test its unity until the Arab war against Israel. It was soon clear that the Arab armies had no chance of standing up to the Jews on Israeli home grounds. The expected Arab guerrilla warfare in Palestine, which some British Foreign Office and some American State Department "experts" had forecast would eventually wear down the Israeli, had completely failed to materialize. Far from organizing guerrilla warfare, over three hundred and fifty thousand Palestine Arabs had taken to wholesale flight, creating a serious Arab refugee problem for the neighboring Arab states.

On the diplomatic front a major source of disunity was ibn-Saud's distrust of Abdullah. Their feud went back to the end of 1924, when ibn-Saud declared war on Sherif Husein, Abdullah's father, and proclaimed himself King of the Hejaz. It influenced the entire pattern of the League campaign in Palestine. Ibn-Saud obviously did not want Abdullah to get too strong. Egypt's strategy, too, was at least partly designed to contain Abdullah and prevent Trans-Jordan's expansion toward the Egyptian frontier. The League was successful in other endeavors—largely unpolitical. It was responsible for the exchange of teachers and educational missions in the Arab world. It assisted in fighting down the cholera epidemic in Egypt in 1947. It did much for the Arab independence movement in North Africa. But in Palestine, where the Hebrew watchword *Ein b'rerah* (No alternative) inspired a Jewish heroism reminiscent of the Maccabean days, the League of Arab States failed completely.

In the conflict for the possession of Palestine the Jews had the better moral case. They were a landless people; and Palestine, their ancient home, was their salvation. The Arabs had 1,200,000 square miles of land—not counting Egypt—an area which will take many generations to cultivate. Saudi Arabia, their ancestral home, three times the size of Texas, is underpopulated and rich in oil. Yemen, the most fertile part of the Arabian peninsula, is underpopulated. Iraq, site of the Mosul oil fields, today has a population of only slightly over four million. As the seat of the empires of Assyria and Babylon it supported a population estimated at over fifteen million. Trans-Jordan, three times the size of western Palestine, is by far richer in soil and water than the Jewish territory and is virtually unpopulated. Only Syria and Lebanon, temperate in climate and better developed for both agriculture and industry, are fairly well populated.

Neither Arabs nor Jews were likely to side with Soviet Russia in the overriding world conflict. Apart from the highly important moral issue, the main question therefore was to decide which side was more deserving of support in terms of hard-boiled realistic politics. Faced with the choice between the small but modern Jewish Commonwealth and the large but unmodern Arab States, the British Government chose numbers, while the American government—at least the White House and the armed forces—backed efficiency. Events proved the United States policy to be right.

The Arab leaders did not dare to admit their failure openly. But Moslem Turkey, which at the start of the Arab-Jewish war had adopted an attitude of friendly nonbelligerence toward the Arabs, began to favor the recognition of Israel and the replacement of the League of Arab States by a closer alliance between Turkey and the Arab countries.

On September 18, 1948, Count Bernadotte's Progress Report was submitted to the Secretary-General of the United Nations. It contained these seven basic premises:

Return to Peace. Peace must return to Palestine and every feasible measure should be taken to ensure that hostilities will not be resumed and that harmonious relations between Arab and Jew will ultimately be restored.

The Jewish State. A Jewish State called Israel exists in Palestine and there are no sound reasons for assuming that it will not continue to do so.

Boundary Determination. The boundaries of this new State must finally be fixed either by formal agreement between the parties concerned or, failing that, by the United Nations.

Continuous Frontiers. Adherence to the principle of geographical homogeneity and integration, which should be the major objective of the boundary arrangements, should apply equally to Arab and Jewish territories, whose frontiers should not therefore, be rigidly controlled by the territorial arrangements envisaged in the resolution of 29 November.

Right of Repatriation. The right of innocent people, uprooted from their homes by the present terror and ravages of war, to return to their homes, should be affirmed and made effective, with assurance of adequate compensation for the property of those who may choose not to return.

Jerusalem. The City of Jerusalem, because of its religious and international significance and the complexity of interest involved, should be accorded special and separate treatment.

International Responsibility. International responsibility should be expressed where desirable and necessary in the form of international guarantees, as a means of allaying existing fears, and particularly with regard to boundaries and human rights.

These premises formed the basis of the following conclusions:

a. Since the Security Council, under pain of Chapter VII sanctions, has forbidden further employment of military action in Palestine as a means of settling the dispute, hostilities should be pronounced formally ended either by mutual agreement of the parties or, failing that, by the United Nations. The existing indefinite truce should be superseded by a formal peace, or at the minimum, an armistice which would involve either complete withdrawal and demobilization of armed forces or their wide separation by creation of broad demilitarized zones under United Nations supervision.

b. The frontiers between the Arab and Jewish territories, in the absence of agreement between Arabs and Jews, should be established by the United Nations and delimited by a technical boundaries commission appointed by and responsible to the United Nations, with the following revisions in the boundaries broadly defined in the resolution of the General Assembly of 29 November in order to make them more equitable, workable and consistent with existing realities in Palestine.

i) The area known as the Negev, south of a line running from the sea near Majdal east southeast of Faluja (both of which places would be in Arab territory), should be defined as Arab territory;

(ii) The frontier should run from Faluja north northeast to Ramleh and Lydda (both of which places would be in Arab territory), the frontier at Lydda then following the line established in the General Assembly resolution of 29 November;

(iii) Galilee should be defined as Jewish territory.

c. The disposition of the territory of Palestine not included within the boundaries of the Jewish State should be left to the Governments of the Arab States in full consultation with the Arab inhabitants of Palestine, with the recommendation, however, that in view of the historical connection and common interests of Trans-Jordan and Palestine, there would be compelling reasons for merging the Arab territory of Palestine with the territory of Trans-Jordan, subject to such frontier rectifications regarding other Arab States as may be found practicable and desirable.

d. The United Nations, by declaration or other appropriate means, should undertake to provide special assurance that the boundaries between the Arab and Jewish territories shall be respected and maintained, subject only to such modifications as may be mutually agreed upon by the parties concerned.

e. The port of Haifa, including the oil refineries and terminals, and without prejudice to their inclusion in the sovereign territory of the Jewish State or the administration of the city of Haifa, should be declared a free port, with assurances of free access for interested Arab countries and an undertaking on their part to place no obstacle in the way of oil deliveries by pipeline to the Haifa refineries, whose distribution would continue on the basis of the historical pattern.

f. The airport of Lydda should be declared a free airport with assurance of access to it and employment of its facilities for Jerusalem and interested Arab countries.

g. The City of Jerusalem, which should be understood as covering the area defined in the resolution of the General Assembly of 29 November, should be treated separately and should be placed under effective United Nations control with maximum feasible local autonomy for its Arab and Jewish communities, with full safeguards for the protection of the Holy Places and sites and free access to them, and for religious freedom.

h. The right of unimpeded access to Jerusalem, by road, rail or air, should be fully respected by all parties.

i. The right of the Arab refugees to return to their homes in Jewish-controlled territory at the earliest possible date should be affirmed by the United Nations, and their repatriation, resettlement and economic and social rehabilitation, and payment of adequate compensation for the property of those choosing not to return, should be supervised and assisted by the United Nations conciliation commission described in paragraph (*k*) below.

j. The political, economic, social and religious rights of all Arabs in the Jewish territory of Palestine and of all Jews in the Arab territory of Palestine should be fully guaranteed and respected by the authorities. The conciliation commission provided for in the following paragraph should supervise the observance of this guarantee. It should also lend its good offices, on the invitation of the parties, to any efforts toward exchanges of populations with a view to eliminating troublesome minority problems, and on the basis of adequate compensation for property owned.

k. In view of the special nature of the Palestine problem and the dangerous complexities of Arab-Jewish relationships, the United Nations should establish a Palestine conciliation commission. This commission, which should be appointed for a limited period, should be responsible to the United Nations and act under its authority. The commission, assisted by such United Nations personnel as may prove necessary, should undertake

(i) To employ its good offices to make such recommendations to the parties or to the United Nations, and to take such other steps as may be appropriate, with a view to ensuring the continuation of the peaceful adjustment of the situation in Palestine;

(ii) Such measures as it might consider appropriate in fostering the cultivation of friendly relations between Arabs and Jews;

(iii) To supervise the observance of such boundary, road, railroad, free port, free airport, minority rights and other arrangements as may be decided upon by the United Nations;

(iv) To report promptly to the United Nations any development in Palestine likely to alter the arrangements approved by the United Nations in the Palestine settlement or to threaten the peace of the area.

This report had become Bernadotte's testament. For on September 17 he was assassinated in Jerusalem by terrorists of the "Fatherland Front," evidently an offshoot of the Sternists. His death grieved the whole world. It was denounced by the government of Israel as an appalling crime, an act of treachery against the Israeli army and an attack on the authority of the United Nations. The Provisional Council published this statement:

> We will use all the force at our command to suppress this insane attempt by gunmen to wreck Israel's relations with the United Nations. The perpetrators of this crime are traitors to the people and enemies of its liberty.

Dr. Ralph J. Bunche, a former professor of political science of Howard University in Washington, D.C., was appointed Acting Mediator in Count Bernadotte's place.

One of the most striking features of the Bernadotte Report as distinguished from his earlier recommendations was its unequivocal recognition of the Jewish State. It showed that its author was deeply impressed by the Jewish war effort. There was no prospect as yet that the Arabs would recognize the State of Israel. But Bernadotte's tempered optimism was obviously based on his conviction that the more reasonable elements in the Arab world had begun to realize that Israel was there to stay.

Bernadotte himself was a realist. When he became aware that the realities had changed, he did not hesitate to change his own views. Since the Jews had won the war, he reversed the position which he had taken in his proposals of June 27 and lent his unreserved support to the Jewish State. This approach had its inherent weaknesses. It diminished the effectiveness of moral claims and of impartial international judgments. It harked back to the old and dangerous dictum that might is right. But the fault did not lie altogether with Bernadotte. His policy simply reflected the current state of world affairs and the fundamental failure of the United Nations as an objective supreme arbiter.

What Bernadotte said in his testament to this world of ours, was, in effect: "As things are, conquest and defeat in war are still the shaping forces of political reality. Everything else is but a smokescreen." I, for one, am diametrically opposed to this attitude and utterly unwilling to submit to it. I would never have supported Zionism had I not believed in its moral justification; and I would have used my pen to fight for the Arab cause had I believed that in this Palestine issue the Arabs were right. Here was, fortunately, one of the rare instances in which right and might were on the same side. The Jews were morally right, and they proved to be the superior military force. But to make military power the yardstick of international mediation and arbitration is to revert to the jungle.

As the government of Israel indicated in a memorandum to the United Nations on October 3, there were serious defects in Bernadotte's last proposals. They reduced the Jewish territory to about 2,180 square miles by adding the 420 square miles of western Galilee to the State of Israel but taking away 3,800 square miles of Negev land originally assigned to the Jews by the United Nations decision of November 29, 1947. By comparison Trans-Jordan, which was to gain all the Arab areas of Palestine, as well as the Negev, would then have a total area of approximately 42,500 square miles. The Israeli memorandum read as follows:

> . . . Trans-Jordan is already the possessor of large tracts of barren land. Its annexation of the Negev would mean nothing more than the acquisition of another item in a collection of arid and uncultivated wastes. Humanity would gain nothing from the perpetuation of sterility. But for Israel, the Negev holds out the promise of agricultural, scientific, industrial and economic development, with important benefits to the Near East as a whole.
>
> Israel has an urgent need for land upon which to settle the many hundreds of thousands of Jews who will immigrate in the next few decades. The soil of the Negev, neglected for many centuries, is itself arable. The factors for development of this area are water and the ingenuity to unite it with the soil. In 1943, the Jews successfully established three experimental settlements in the Negev. Another 15 were established toward the end of 1946. Today there are 27. Water is made available by pipeline, and by the capture and storage of winter rains in reservoirs. Thus, at Revivim, the southernmost Jewish settlement, the United Nations Special Committee on Palestine in 1947 inspected a large dam and reservoir and witnessed the fruits of this

agricultural venture. Moreover, for several years, engineers have been at work on plans for large-scale irrigation projects which will open large tracts of land for new settlement. The hydroelectric development involved in these irrigation plans will bring low-cost power to the Negev, and furnish an economic base for industrial enterprise. To put these areas of Jewish settlement under the political domination of an Arab ruler would be sowing the seeds of fresh conflict. To sever the Negev from Israel is to separate it from those whose needs guarantee its maximum use.

In previous discussion of the Palestine problem it has been argued on the Arab side that the pressure of Jewish immigration would force the Jewish State to become expansionist, and to threaten the existing territory of the Arab States. If the land reserve of the Negev were taken away from the State of Israel, and this large area ceases to be available for Jewish settlement, Arab fears would be intensified, and the prospects of pacific cooperation between Israel and its neighbors would be prejudiced. It must be emphasized that the inclusion of the Negev in the State of Israel is the population safety-valve for any partition plan, and therefore a major factor making for peace and operating against population pressure. . . .

Deprived of the Negev, the Jews would be forced to give up all access to the mineral deposits of the Red Sea. These are the only reserve of valuable minerals close to Israel, and they provide the basis for a highly specialized chemical industry. Israel would lose the use of the port of Aqaba on the Red Sea and a share in the oil deposits which are supposed to be in that region.

It was perhaps these stipulations of the report which encouraged Mr. Bevin to accept it. Another recommendation in the Bernadotte Report facilitated the turnabout of the British Foreign Office—the internationalization of Haifa. Mr. Bevin was thus able to give "wholehearted and unqualified" support to Secretary Marshall's statement that the Bernadotte plan provided a fair and sound settlement.

In the shadow of the tragic and heinous assassination of Count Bernadotte, numerous violations of the truce were disregarded. Near Latrun a Jerusalem-bound Israeli convoy under the United Nations flag was ambushed by the Trans-Jordan Legion. The second week of October was highlighted by a flare-up of fighting in the Negev. The Egyptian forces holding the east-west Majdal-Faluja-Beit Jibrin road attempted to disrupt Israeli communications with the Jewish colonies in the Negev and denied the right of passage which had been permitted the Jewish convoys by the truce authorities. In view of the failure of the United Nations to take any active measures, Israeli forces attacked the Egyptian army, split it into two camps, and gained absolute control of the road.

Foundations for reservoirs are erected in the arid Negev for Jewish pioneer settlers. *Courtesy of United Palestine Appeal.*

Pipelines extending for more than one hundred miles have been laid to bring precious water to Negev settlers. *Courtesy of United Palestine Appeal.*

Festival in an Israeli village, and harvest scene. *Courtesy of United Palestine Appeal.*

On October 16, in the name of Dr. Bunche, United States Brigadier General William E. Riley ordered both sides to stop firing and to return to their original positions. Egypt expressed willingness to comply with the request. Israel asked for guarantees that "further Egyptian attacks against Jewish settlements, positions and communications will cease." At the request of Dr. Bunche the Security Council met in emergency session on October 19. Dr. Bunche blamed Israel outright for the Negev battle. The cease-fire ultimately went into effect three days later. But the Israeli government rejected the withdrawal order. On the basis of past experience, it insisted that the withdrawal of its forces would endanger its Negev settlements. Major Aubrey S. Eban, the extremely able representative of Israel in United Nations circles, explained that the Egyptians, after all, had invaded Palestine. Any return to original positions should be to those of May 14, 1948. Forcing the Jews to return to their former lines in the Negev to enable the Egyptians to reoccupy the area, would amount to sanctioning the aggressive war of the Arabs.

On November 4 the Council adopted the following resolution:

THE SECURITY COUNCIL,

HAVING DECIDED on July 15 that subject to further decision by the Security Council or the General Assembly the truce shall remain in force in accordance with the resolution of that date and with that of May 29, 1948, until a peaceful adjustment of the future situation of Palestine is reached;

HAVING DECIDED on August 19 that no party is permitted to violate the truce on the ground it is undertaking reprisals or retaliations against the other party, and that no party is entitled to gain military or political advantage through violation of the truce; and

HAVING DECIDED on May 29 that if the truce was subsequently repudiated or violated by either party or by both, the situation in Palestine could be reconsidered with a view to action under Chapter VII of the Charter;

TAKES NOTE of the request communicated to the Government of Egypt and the Provisional Government of Israel by the acting Mediator on Oct. 26 following upon the resolution adopted by the Security Council on Oct. 19, 1948; and

CALLS UPON the interested Governments, without prejudice to their rights, claims or position with regard to a peaceful adjustment of the future situation in Palestine or to the position which members of the United Nations may wish to take in the General Assembly on such a peaceful adjustment;

1. To withdraw those of their forces which have advanced beyond positions held on Oct. 14, the acting Mediator being authorized to establish provisional lines beyond which no movement of troops shall take place;

2. To establish through negotiations conducted directly between the par-

ties, or failing that, through intermediaries in the service of the United Nations, permanent truce lines and such neutral or demilitarized zones as may appear advantageous in order to ensure, henceforth, full observance of the truce in that area. Failing an agreement, the permanent lines and neutral zones shall be established by decision of the acting Mediator; and

APPOINTS a committee of the Council consisting of the five permanent members together with Belgium and Colombia to give such advice as the acting Mediator may require with regard to his responsibilities under this resolution, and in the event that either party or both should fail to comply with subparagraphs (1) and (2) of this resolution within whatever time limits the acting Mediator may think it desirable to fix, to study as a matter of urgency, and to report to the Council on further measures it would be appropriate to take under Chapter VII of the Charter.

Meanwhile, the Negev was militarily active. The Egyptians tried to force their way through the Israeli lines in order to reunite their army. The attempt failed. Haganah reduced the Egyptian lines to the strongholds of Gaza and Faluja. Everything else in the Negev was in Israeli hands. On October 24 the "National Army of Liberation," coming from the Lebanon, had attacked Jewish settlements in northern Galilee. By November 1 the Jews swept all Arab forces out of Galilee and occupied Lebanese territory. On November 6 Brigadier General Riley, the Acting Mediator's chief of staff, finally told the Arab representatives in the United Nations Assembly in Paris that the Israeli army dominated the military situation in Palestine, that the military position of the Arabs was hopeless, and that the only course left for them was to negotiate for a permanent peace.

As soon as it became known that the Jews had forced the Arabs out of Galilee and advanced into Lebanese territory, the British representative in the Security Council proposed an amendment to the November 4 Resolution. He would order the Jews back to their original lines in the northern area of Palestine, under threat of sanctions. Both the United States and the Soviet Union failed to support Great Britain's proposal, and it did not secure passage. Finally, on November 15, an Armistice Resolution was adopted by the Security Council. It read:

THE SECURITY COUNCIL,

Reaffirming its previous resolutions concerning the establishment and implementation of the truce in Palestine, and, recalling particularly its resolution of July 15, 1948, which determined that the situation in Palestine constitutes a threat to peace within the meaning of Article 39 of the Charter;

Taking note that the General Assembly is continuing its consideration of the future government of Palestine in response to the request of the Security Council of April 1, 1948;

Without prejudice to the actions of the acting Mediator regarding implementation of the resolution of the Security Council of Nov. 4, 1948;

DECIDES that, in order to eliminate the threat to peace in Palestine and to facilitate the transition from the present truce to permanent peace in Palestine, an armistice shall be established in all sectors of Palestine;

CALLS upon the parties directly involved in the conflict in Palestine, as a further provisional measure under Article 40 of the Charter, to seek agreement forthwith, by negotiations conducted either directly or through the acting Mediator on Palestine, with a view to immediate establishment of an armistice including:

1. Delineation of permanent armistice demarcation lines beyond which the armed forces of the respective parties shall not move;

2. Such withdrawal and reduction of their armed forces as will ensure the maintenance of the armistice during the transition to permanent peace in Palestine.

After endless debates of the Bernadotte proposals and a multiplicity of rejected resolutions, the General Assembly of the United Nations on December 11, 1948, voted 35 to 15, with 8 abstentions, a resolution which follows in part:

THE GENERAL ASSEMBLY, having considered further the situation in Palestine, . . .

2. ESTABLISHES a Conciliation Commission consisting of three states members of the United Nations which shall have the following functions:

a. To assume, in so far as it considers necessary in the existing circumstances, functions given to the United Nations Mediator on Palestine by resolution of the General Assembly of 14 April, 1948.

b. To carry out specific functions and directives given to it by the present resolution and such additional functions and directives as may be given to it by the General Assembly or by the Security Council.

c. To undertake upon request of the Security Council any of the functions now assigned to the United Nations Mediator on Palestine or to the United Nations Truce Commission by resolutions of the Security Council; upon such request to the Conciliation Commission by the Security Council with respect to all remaining functions of the United Nations Mediator on Palestine under Security Council resolutions, the office of Mediator shall be terminated;

3. A committee of the Assembly consisting of China, France, U.S.S.R., United Kingdom and the United States of America shall present for approval of the Assembly a proposal concerning the names of three states who will constitute the Conciliation Commission.

4. REQUESTS the Commission to begin its functions at once, with a view to establishment of contact between the parties themselves and the Commission at the earliest possible date.

5. CALLS UPON the Governments and authorities concerned to extend the

scope of negotiations provided for in the Security Council's resolution of 16 November, 1948 and to seek agreement by negotiations conducted either with the Conciliation Commission or directly with the view to final settlement of all questions outstanding between them.

6. INSTRUCTS the Conciliation Commission to take steps to assist Governments and authorities concerned to achieve final settlement of all questions outstanding between them.

7. RESOLVES that holy places, including Nazareth, religious buildings and sites in Palestine should be protected and free access to them assured, in accordance with existing rights and historical practice; that arrangements to this end should be under effective United Nations supervision. . . .

8. INSTRUCTS the Conciliation Commission to present to fourth regular session of General Assembly detailed proposals for a permanent international regime for Jerusalem area which will provide for maximum local autonomy for distinctive groups consistent with the special international status of the Jerusalem area.

The Conciliation Commission is authorized to appoint United Nations representatives who shall cooperate with local authorities with respect to the interim administration of Jerusalem area.

9. RESOLVES that, pending agreement on more detailed arrangements among Governments and authorities concerned, the freest possible access to Jerusalem by road, rail or air should be accorded to all inhabitants of Palestine.

INSTRUCTS the Conciliation Commission to report immediately to the Security Council for appropriate action by that organ any attempt by any party to impede such access.

10. INSTRUCTS the Conciliation Commission to seek arrangements among Governments and authorities concerned which will facilitate economic development of the area, including arrangements for access to ports and airfields and use of transportation and communication facilities.

11. RESOLVES that refugees wishing to return to their homes and live at peace with their neighbors should be permitted to do so at the earliest practicable date, and that compensation should be paid for property of those choosing not to return and for loss of or damage to property which under principles of international law or in equity should be made good by Governments or authorities responsible.

INSTRUCTS the Conciliation Commission to facilitate the repatriation, resettlement and economic and social rehabilitation of refugees and payment of compensation, and to maintain close relations with the Director of the United Nations Relief for Palestine Refugees and through him with appropriate organs and agencies of the United Nations. . . .

The United Nations Conciliation Commission was composed of Turkey, the United States, and France, in order to represent the Arab viewpoint, the Israeli viewpoint, and a neutral position. But Turkey, having for years enjoyed the material and moral support of the United States, could not vigorously oppose any stand taken by the latter. For political and economic reasons, also, France would not antagonize the United States. In the final analysis the delineation of Israel's boundaries was left largely to the United States representative. The United States, of course, could not and would not disregard the British official position, which Winston Churchill called one of "sulky boycott."

As the year drew to an end, it became quite clear that the final solution of the Palestine truce ultimately lay outside the United Nations. With the dwindling of the prestige of the United Nations throughout the Middle East, in the Arab territories as well as in the State of Israel, the field was still wide open for those who wished to embark upon military and other adventures. Azzam Pasha, the Secretary-General of the Arab League, was making frantic efforts to save the League and his own position. Success on his part could well lead to a resumption of the war. One of the main problems in the Arab camp was whether Syria and Iraq would side with Egypt or with Trans-Jordan. Turkey, hostile to Syria ever since its annexation of Alexandretta, tended to favor Trans-Jordan. Syria on the other hand, herself politically unstable, was afraid of the "Greater Syria" plans of King Abdullah. War or peace depended less on the efficiency of the United Nations Commission than on the power struggle within the Arab world and the willingness of the more reasonable Arab leaders to come to terms with the government of Israel.

Chapter Eight: THE DRAFT CONSTITUTION

BILL OF RIGHTS · LEGISLATIVE POWER · EXECUTIVE POWER · JUDICIARY · A CRITICAL EVALUATION

As soon as the partition resolution, recommending the establishment of a Jewish state, was adopted by the United Nations General Assembly, a committee of legal experts headed by Dr. Leo Kohn was appointed to draft a constitution for the new state (for text see Appendix). This committee transmitted its draft to a special subcommittee of the Provisional Council of State, which in turn submitted it to the Constituent Assembly on January 25, 1949. While at the present writing the Israeli constitution has not been promulgated and while some of the stipulations of the original draft may still be tentative and experimental in character, the basic structure appears to be definitive.

The draft begins with this moving preamble:

The Jewish people,

Humbly giving thanks to the God of our fathers for having delivered us from the burden of exile and brought us back to our ancient land,

Recalling the tenacious endurance and the heroic sacrifice of countless generations for the survival of our people and the preservation of its spiritual heritage,

Gratefully remembering the faithful remnant which maintained the continuity of Jewish settlement in Palestine throughout the centuries and the inspired efforts of the national revival,

Resolved to build our commonwealth in accordance with the ideals of peace and justice of the Prophets of Israel, to open our land to every Jew who seeks entry, to maintain the rights of the strangers within our gates, and to promote the peace of the Holy Land and the security and prosperity of all who dwell therein,

Have adopted the following constitution.

Although the State of Israel is new, although its provisional government had to start under the most adverse conditions imaginable, the draftsmen of the Israeli constitution did not write in a vacuum. The Jewish community in Palestine had provided for itself a form of internal self-government which had been operative under the British Mandate and which permitted the Jewish State to take over all essential functions of government on May 14, 1948.

Under the mandate the *Assefath Hanivharim* (Jewish elective assembly) had served as the legislative body of the Jewish community. The Vaad Leumi (Jewish national council), a small administrative body arising out of the elective assembly, was divided into various departments resembling the executive branch of Western governments. They included social welfare, health, defense, education, and religious affairs. Additional functions in the fields of immigration, land purchase, agricultural colonization, building, and industry were entrusted to various agencies of the World Zionist Organization, with headquarters in Jerusalem.

From these precedents the draftsmen envisaged a simple pattern of government combining certain aspects of the United States Constitution with some of the essentials of the Continental European parliamentary system.

The legislature consists of only one house, the Chamber of Deputies, rather than two houses, as in the United States, Great Britain, and other democratic countries. As in Great Britain, the Cabinet or Executive Council, headed by the Prime Minister, is chosen from and is responsible to the Chamber of Deputies. The President of the Republic is elected by the legislature for a fixed term of office, and his functions are mainly of an honorary nature.

The draft proposes a unitary state system with the principal organs of government vested in a central legislature, a centralized executive, a centralized judiciary, rather than a federal system emphasizing local units and local authorities. Finally, the draft constitution provides a speedy method of amendment.

The following analysis will show that Israel's constitution makes for government by consent and discussion—in other words, for strictly democratic government.

General Provisions

According to the draft constitution the official name of the State of Israel is Israel. It is the National Home of the whole Jewish people. All citizens of Israel, whether Jewish or non-Jewish, enjoy equal civic and political rights. "No citizen shall be at a disadvantage as a candidate for public office or employment or in the matter of promotion, on account of his race, religion, language or sex." (Article 4) While Hebrew is the official language, adequate facilities must be given to Arabic-speaking citizens for the use of their language in the legislature, before the courts, and before the executive authorities. Citizenship is conferred on all residents of Israel over the age of eighteen who were Palestinian citizens on May 15, 1948, as well as on Jews who were not citizens of Palestine on that date but are resident in the area of Israel "at the time of the enactment of this constitution" or resident of the non-Israeli portions of Palestine opting for citizenship of Israel within one year. (Article 6)

The Bill of Rights

Like most democratic constitutions the draft constitution of Israel contains a comprehensive list of fundamental rights designed to protect the individual and his association with other individuals against legislative and executive abuses. Bills of rights, as such, are no automatic guarantee of human freedom. Compare the "Fundamental Rights and Duties of Citizens" in the Soviet Constitution of 1936 with the arbitrary executive practices in the Soviet Union.* It can only be hoped that the Israeli Bill of Rights, based upon the experiences and aspirations of a people that has cherished freedom throughout the centuries, will be more than paper rights.

It ensures the sanctity of human life and decrees that there shall be no death penalty. It goes further than the United Nations resolution which required Israel to adopt constitutional safeguards protecting "freedom of religion, language, speech and publication, education, assembly and association," by spelling out in detail the protections of the writ of habeas corpus. It prohibits ex post facto legislation and "extraordinary courts." It guarantees the inviolability of the home and bans the interception of mail, telephonic, or telegraphic communications. It assures the tried person "due process of law." (Article 13) Emphasizing the social character of the Israeli economy are those provisions which, as in the Constitution of France, guarantee the rights of workers to form trade unions, to bargain collectively, and to strike in defense of their economic rights and interests. (Article 23)

"Everyone has a right to work"; every citizen is entitled to "a decent standard of living" as well as state insurance against the risks of accident, sickness, disablement, unemployment, old age, and other causes of undeserved want. (Article 23) Working mothers and children,

* Joseph Dunner, *Major Aspects of International Politics,* Soviet Imperialism and the United States, Grinnell College Press, 1948.

widows and orphans are promised special care. Although the right of each religious community to maintain its own schools, to educate its members in its own language and way of life is explicitly confirmed, the state assumes the responsibility for adequate educational facilities for primary and secondary education of both Jews and Arabs in their own language and cultural tradition. (Article 25)

Article 15 provides the answer for those who may ask, "How Jewish will the State of Israel be?" It decrees that the Sabbath and the Jewish Holy Days shall be days of rest and spiritual elevation. But in conformity with the guarantees of freedom of conscience and the free exercise of all forms of worship it adds: "The Holy Days of other religious denominations shall equally be recognized as legal days of rest for the members of such denominations."

The experience of Continental European countries, like the Weimar Republic, which allowed totalitarian forces to destroy democracy in the name of freedom of speech and assembly, is reflected in Article 16. The constitutional guarantee of these freedoms "shall not extend to utterances or publications which are libelous, slanderous or obscene, or which are designed to stir up racial or religious hatred, or to incite to violence or crime, or which advocate the suppression of human rights, or of the democratic system of government. . . ." An analogous position can be found in Article 17, the constitutional guarantee for assemblies and associations except those "aiming at the suppression of human rights or of the democratic form of government." In these instances the legislature is free to act as it deems advisable.

The Legislative Power

The legislative power of Israel is vested in a unicameral legislature, the Chamber of Deputies. The bicameral system, such as the British, is a heritage from the days when a popular assembly like the House of Commons was feared and suspected by the ruling nobility and when the upper house served as a brake against the decisions of the representatives of the "people." In America prior to the Philadelphia Convention of 1787 the legislature had but a single house, and the New Jersey plan contemplated the continuance of that arrangement. With the smaller states insisting upon equality for all and the larger states demanding representation in proportion to population, the most feasible way of reconciling the conflicting interests and keeping all states in line was to create a legislature consisting of two branches. One house was based on representation according to number, the other on equal representation of all member states irrespective of their population. This plan had the additional advantage of balancing major economic interests, since the more populous states were mainly industrial and commercial and the less populous ones mainly agricultural.

Bicameralism in both Britain and the United States has also its distinct disadvantages. It makes for deadlocks and delays, duplication of effort, and buck passing, which clog the wheels of government. In the United States the state of Nebraska, therefore, broke new ground in 1934 by adopting a constitutional amendment of its state constitution under which, since 1937, the legislature of that state has consisted of but a single house.

Hasty and ill-considered legislation which an upper house is supposed to veto can be prevented by other devices than a second chamber, be they an advisory council of the Republic, as in the new French constitution, or committee hearings on major bills, or a special legislative drafting authority. The most important safeguard is the parliamentary system itself, under which most legislation is proposed by the Cabinet. The Cabinet then has the task to guide its passage through the legislature.

Such considerations, I suppose, caused the draftsmen of the Israeli constitution to adopt the unicameral system. In accordance with Article 29 of the Israeli constitution the Chamber of Deputies is to be elected by equal, direct, universal suffrage and by secret ballot on the basis of proportional representation. Ten thousand persons are entitled to send one representative into the Chamber. He is elected for four years. All citizens over twenty-five years of age are eligible for a seat. Ordinarily the Chamber meets twice a year. It may, however, be called into special session by the President of the Republic acting on the advice of the Executive Council or at the request of one-third of the deputies.

The Executive Power

Article 48 vests the executive power in the State of Israel in the President of the Republic and in the Executive Council.

The President represents the unity of the state. Unlike the President of the United States, who in spite of the filtering medium of an electoral college represents popular verdict, the President in a parliamentary democracy possesses relatively little power. Chosen by the Chamber of Deputies, and therefore not subjected to the turmoil that goes with popular elections, he is supposed to stand serenely above the parties. According to the Israeli constitution he is elected by secret ballot for a five-year term, and he may be reelected for one additional term. If no candidate receives a clear majority of the house in the first two ballots, the person receiving the highest number on the third ballot shall be deemed to have been elected. (Article 50)

The President, after consultation with the leaders of the political parties, appoints the Prime Minister. Upon the advice of the Prime Minister, he also appoints the other members of the Executive Council. The new French constitution rigidly limits the exercise of the President's power to dissolve the National Assembly. By contrast, the Israeli President may dissolve the Chamber of Deputies prior to the expiration of its term if the Executive Council has resigned or if there is no stable majority in the legislature. (Article 34) He appoints the Commander in Chief of the armed forces. He commissions the officers of these forces. He promulgates the laws enacted by the Chamber of Deputies. Diplomatic representatives are accredited and received by the President. He also concludes international treaties after having obtained the authorization of both the Executive Council and the Chamber of Deputies. He has the power of pardon and commutation of sentences.

The crucial question of the executive-legislative relationship in modern democratic government is solved in the Israeli draft constitution by making the Executive Council (like the British Cabinet) the executive committee of the Chamber. The President of the Republic appoints the Prime Minister and, upon the latter's proposal, the heads of the Departments of State and the Ministers without Portfolio. All of them must be members of the Chamber, and their total number is not to exceed fifteen. (Article 62)

The Israeli constitution recognizes the primacy of the Prime Minister over his Cabinet colleagues by making him responsible for the coordination of all executive and administrative functions (Article 63) and by stipulating that "the resignation of the Prime Minister shall entail that of the Executive Council as a whole." (Article 64)

Under the proposed draft, the Executive Council has the main initiative in introducing legislation. Legislative measures proposed by members of the House if recommended by a Select Committee of the Chamber "shall be introduced by the Executive Council . . . in the form recommended by that committee." (Article 42) The Executive Council also has the power to make orders and regulations within the framework of the existing laws. (Article 68) To prevent abuses of authority, the Chamber of Deputies may render them inoperative, however. The Executive Council must maintain the confidence of the Chamber of Deputies. (Article 64)

In view of the multiplicity of political parties in the State of Israel, the parliamentary system could easily lead to instability of government. This instability, however, is not inherent in the system of parliamentary democracy itself. It is related rather to the method by which the legislature can be dissolved. Under the Third Republic of France, the Chamber of Deputies could not be dissolved during the period for which it was elected. The deputies, therefore, could provoke one cabinet crisis after another without having to risk a new election in which their own careers were at stake. In Britain the Crown, that is, the King acting on the advice of the Cabinet, can order new elections to the House of Commons whenever a Cabinet chooses to dissolve the House. In general this causes the members of the majority party or a party coalition in power to abstain from voting against the Cabinet, as defeat of the Cabinet in major legislative measures would involve them in a general election.

The Israeli constitution tries to steer the middle course between the French and British extremes. As stated before, the power to dissolve the Chamber is vested in the President under two conditions: (1) when the Executive Council has resigned; (2) when no alternative Executive Council can be formed on the basis of a stable majority in the Chamber. It is hoped that this power in the President will prove adequate to prevent irresponsible cabinet crises and to ensure parliamentary stability.

The Judiciary

The administration of justice, one of the most important aspects of any ordered society, is vested by the Israeli constitution in a hierarchy of courts comprising magistrates' courts, district courts, a High Court "with exclusive original jurisdiction in all questions relating to the validity of any law having regard to the terms of the constitution," (Article 70) and a Supreme Court as final court of appeal. In addition the constitution sanctions a special system of ecclesiastical courts of the Jewish, Moslem, and Christian communities, exercising jurisdiction "in matters of personal status and of religious foundations and endowments." (Article 70)

The judges of the nonecclesiastical courts are appointed by the President of the Republic, who acts on the advice of the Minister of Justice. The Minister of Justice, in turn, relies on the recommendations of a special Selection Board composed of members of the court hierarchy, his own Department of Justice, representatives of the Bar Association and of the Chamber of Deputies. The judges of the ecclesiastical courts are appointed by the President of the Republic on the advice of the Minister for Religious Affairs who in turn shall be guided by the recommendations "of the Supreme Religious Council of the community concerned." (Article 72)

Civil judges, once appointed, may be removed from office, by a two-thirds vote of the Chamber of Deputies, only for stated misbehavior or incapacity. The removal of religious judges requires in addition a motion of the Supreme Religious Council of the community concerned. (Article 73) The proposal for the creation of special ecclesiastical courts and their functions was inspired by a United Nations resolution which stipulated that "the family law and personal status of the various minorities and their religious interests, including endowments, shall be respected." The term "personal status" generally implies such matters as marriage, divorce, alimony, adoption.

Amendment of the Constitution

Most constitutions provide for a rather complex amending process. The Israeli draft requires only the assent of two-thirds of the total membership of the Chamber of Deputies at two successive sessions with a period of at least six months between the two enactments. (Article 75) This relative ease of amendment will facilitate the adoption of experimental solutions to constitutional problems. It will also act as a counterweight to the power of the Supreme Court to declare laws unconstitutional since the legislature, by amendment, can overcome such strictures of the judiciary.

There is, however, a danger that a legislature which can amend the constitution without requiring popular ratification (as provided in the constitutional practices of Australia, Switzerland, and the State of New York) may be inclined to increase its own power and privileges unduly. The question may also be asked whether this simple process of amendment might not lead to the circumvention of certain basic constitutional guarantees such as the protection of ethnic and political minorities.

Constitution and Legislation

To prevent violations of the constitution, the Israeli draft confers on the High Court and the Supreme Court the power of judicial review. If the courts find a proposed amendment to the constitution or any other law "repugnant to any of the provisions of this Constitution," they have the power of voiding such a legislative measure. (Article 76)

The laws which Israel inherited on May 14, 1948, were a colorful mixture of Turkish statutes, mandatory regulations, and English common law. These laws continue in force so long as they are consistent with the terms of the constitution until the Chamber of Deputies explicitly repeals or amends them. All future legislation in Israel shall be guided, as Article 77 demands, by the basic teachings and ideals of the Mosaic tradition.

A Critical Evaluation

The student of government will have little difficulty in detecting a number of shortcomings in this constitutional draft. There are a number of errors in form. Of greater importance and highly questionable is the automatic conferment of citizenship on Jewish residents of Israel who may be citizens of foreign countries. Assuming that these Jews retain their original citizenship, a large category of people with dual citizenship is created, which, as experience teaches, is no unmixed blessing. Dr. Benjamin Akzin, for many years adviser of the American Zionist Emergency Council, in a very able critical analysis of the draft constitution points to the fact that the right of property is not listed in the catalogue of fundamental rights.

> Undoubtedly [he writes] the formula of property rights in the constitution of Israel ought to be circumscribed and limited in the interests of the general welfare, but to ignore the matter altogether would be both unjustifiable per se and lend itself to serious misrepresentation.

I agree with Dr. Akzin's suggestion that the expression "due process of law" be replaced by the words "before duly established tribunals," since the due-process concept which developed in Anglo-American tradition lends itself to a great deal of abuse and confusion.

The wording of Article 25 could be interpreted as meaning that only Jews and Arabs are entitled to adequate facilities for primary and secondary education. It is questionable whether Article 42 does not too greatly restrict the legislative initiative of the Chamber of Deputies. In British practice most legislation emanates from the Cabinet and is implemented by the administrative process, while the House of Commons emphasizes today the function of policy "control" more than that of "lawmaking" in the strict sense. I am inclined to consider such "delegated legislation" unwholesome, if not dangerous to the democratic process, as it gives the permanent officials in the various executive departments too much power.

In spite of the United Nations resolution I see no valid reason for religious courts. If their jurisdiction is to be compulsory, what about those citizens of Israel who do not accept any religious discipline? The guarantee of "freedom of conscience" is seriously jeopardized if religious law is imposed on individuals who may not wish to be guided by it in questions of personal status. Moreover, as Dr. Akzin points out, the expression "personal status" is by no means unequivocal. The draft authorizes the President of the Supreme Court to decide which religious court is to have jurisdiction when persons of different faith are involved. This provision, too, conflicts, in my opinion, with the article which guarantees "freedom of conscience." The British, who liked to encourage divisions along communal and religious lines in their colonies, gave to the religious courts in Palestine a great deal of exclusive jurisdiction. There should be no reason for the State of Israel to perpetuate a fundamentally imperialistic scheme.

As already indicated, there is a real danger in the system of proportional representation. It makes for excessive fragmentation, for indifference in the relation between voter and deputy, and it creates an omnipotent party machine. The Israeli draft makes no provisions for trial by jury in either civil or criminal cases. It does not mention double jeopardy, the right to counsel in criminal cases, and bills of attainder. It authorizes "preventive detention" and "preventive censorship" in time of war or national emergency. The "preventive detention" of some 100,000 Americans of Japanese ancestry during World War II in the United States is not an act to be emulated.

Article 8 declares that natural resources "belong to the state subject to any rights therein vested in any person or body." Provisions of this sort could be more specific. Others, like the provisions of Article 12, are perhaps too specific and could be embodied in ordinary legislation.

But as a whole the draft is an admirable basis for a final text. It is permeated with a profound devotion to political democracy. It is equally concerned with the economic well-being of all citizens. In structure and philosophy it demonstrates that its draftsmen have learned from the constitutional experiences of the great Western democracies. At the same time they have not forgotten the precious heritage from the honored Prophets of Israel, who were the first in the human race to proclaim the brotherhood of man under the fatherhood of God.

Chapter Nine: POLITICAL PARTIES IN THE CONSTITUENT ASSEMBLY

MAPAI · MAPAM · UNITED RELIGIOUS BLOC · HERUT · GENERAL ZIONISM · ARAB REPRESENTATION · ORIENTAL JEWS · COMMUNISTS · CHAIM WEIZMANN, FIRST PRESIDENT OF ISRAEL

One of the characteristics of political democracy is that major divisions of public opinion find their expression in organized political parties. The constitutional structure of legislative, executive, and judicial powers is maintained and developed by these "extralegal" associations. Their leading representatives, the politicians, handle the business of nominating candidates to elective office, of staffing the executive agencies; they influence the nominations of the court hierarchy. By articulating the interests and wishes of their supporters, the party politicians participate in formulating the policies of government. In spite of the factionalism which political parties introduce in the life of every nation, they render an indispensable service to the operation of modern democratic government.

The new State of Israel took a major step toward establishing itself on a permanent basis when, on January 25, 1949, its political parties competed for membership in the *Knesseth*, or Legislative Assembly. Prior to that date, the infant republic had been governed by a Provisional Government, a Provisional Council of State and Cabinet, whose members had been appointed by agreement among the major parties in the Zionist movement. By and large the Provisional Government had been representative of the major currents of political opinion in Jewish Palestine, as demonstrated in elections to the various Jewish bodies under the mandatory regime. But the population of the territory assigned to the State of Israel had grown substantially since the last elections;

and new political issues had arisen as a result of the establishment of the state. The Assembly elected in January was, therefore, the first governing authority of Israel to be chosen in accordance with standard democratic procedure.

All persons, without distinction of race, creed, color, or sex, who were within the boundaries occupied by the Israeli armed forces were allowed to vote if they signified their intention of becoming citizens of Israel. In accordance with the draft constitution, the list system of proportional representation was used. But, whereas in Continental Europe it is customary to divide a country into electoral districts and allot seats on the basis of votes obtained within each district, Israel for reasons of military security was treated as one large constituency. The electorate was presented with 21 lists, comprising a total of 1,288 candidates, from which 120 members of the Assembly were to be elected. The total number of votes cast, 440,095, divided by 120, gave a unit number of about 3,600. This meant that a political party was entitled to as many delegates in the Constituent Assembly as the votes polled by that party divided by 3,600.

The parties which competed in the election are in large part identical with those active in the world Zionist movement. But the existence of the new state and the problems engendered by this fact have led to some political realignment expressed in the development of some new political parties and the merger or split of old ones. These parties compose the Constituent Assembly.

The Israeli Labor Party—Mapai

Mapai (Hebrew abbreviation of *Miflegeth Poale Eretz Israel,* Party of Workers of the Land of Israel) won forty-six seats in the Assembly.

It has an interesting history. While most of the Jewish Socialists in Europe and the United States were opposed to Zionism, while the few Jews who turned Communist after the Russian October Revolution denounced Zionism as a "devilish device of the bourgeoisie to deflect the attention of the Jewish working masses from the class struggle," a fringe of Jewish Socialists remained loyal to the interests of their people. It brought about a socialist faction within the Zionist movement, the *Poale Zion* (Workers of Zion). Among their leaders was Ber Borochov, who realized the error of his contemporaries in following blindly the utopian notions of cosmopolitanism and who attempted a synthesis of Marxian ideas and Zionism. Another was Nachman Syrkin, who also under the influence of Karl Marx undertook to justify the historic inevitability of Zionism and the collaboration with "bourgeois Zionists."

Besides the Poale Zion there was another party in the Zionist movement with socialistic tendencies—the *Zeire Zion* (Young Zionists). Unlike the Poale Zion, the Young Zionists rejected Marxism. In Palestine they were known as *Hapoel Hatzair* (Young Workers). Their most eminent representative was Aaron David Gordon. At the age of forty-eight he left his business post in Europe to take up agricultural work in Palestine. He became an almost legendary figure in Galilee, where he spent the last fifteen years of his life as an agricultural worker in Daganyah, sharing a room with three other men, tilling the soil, and participating in the communal life of that settlement. The question which had preoccupied him in most of his essays—"Will not our Jewish people at all times prefer trading, speculation, especially business in which others will labor while they will manage the enterprises?"—he answered in his own change of profession and his advocation of the doctrine of a "religion of labor." In 1929 both groups, Poale Zion and Zeire Zion (Hapoel Hatzair) merged into one party under the name of Mapai. Its program is a combination of Zionism and socialism. It reads in part:

> Devotion to the construction of the Jewish people in Israel as a free working people rooted in . . . agricultural and industrial economy and developing its own Hebrew culture. . . . Membership in the world movement of the working class and cooperation in the struggle to abolish class subjection and social injustice in any form . . . nationalization of natural resources and means of production, and building a commonwealth of labor, equality and freedom. . . .

The growth of Mapai paralleled the development of the Jewish National Home. Its influence is exercised mainly through the *Histadruth*, the General Federation of Labor, which embraces over 75 per cent of all wage earners in Israel. This dominant position of Histadruth is due to the fact that it is not only the representative of organized employed labor but also the largest single employer in Israel, controlling numerous cooperatives and holding companies, operating transportation, industry, and banking. During the period of the British Mandate the Histadruth organized many agencies which are customarily the concern of government, such as a labor educational system and a special health service for workers and their families. It is for this reason that the Histadruth has sometimes been referred to as a state within a state.

While the Histadruth is supposed to be politically impartial, since its members belong to different political parties, Mapai commands the largest following within the Histadruth. In the elections in that organization, held immediately after those for the Constituent Assembly,

Mapai received three-fifths of the vote. In practical politics Mapai, like the social democratic parties of the Scandinavian countries, Switzerland and Belgium, stands for the social welfare state but welcomes private capital under proper safeguards, as this contributes to the development of the economy of the country. In tradition and present outlook Mapai adheres to the principles of Western democracy. Had it not been for Mr. Bevin's anti-Zionist policy, Mapai would probably have chosen a close alliance with the British Labor party.

One of the assets of Mapai lies in the fact that it includes in its ranks many of the outstanding leaders of Zionism. First among these is the present Prime Minister of Israel, David Ben Gurion, who for many years served as general secretary of the Histadruth and chairman of the Executive of the Jewish Agency. As Prime Minister and Minister of Defense in the Provisional Government he could rightly claim credit for the successful establishment of the new state. He has at times been referred to as the Churchill of Israel; and, indeed, what Churchill was and did for England during the Nazi war on Western civilization, Ben Gurion was and did for Israel under even more trying circumstances. Similarly, the diplomatic achievements of Foreign Minister Moshe Shertok (now known as Sharett) also redounded to the advantage of Mapai. Sharett has been chief of the political department of the Jewish Agency for Palestine since 1933; he was in San Francisco at the organization meeting of the United Nations; and, together with Ben Gurion, he presented the Jewish case to the General Assembly of the United Nations prior to November 29, 1947. Among other Israeli leaders affiliated with Mapai are Finance Minister Eliezer Kaplan, Minister of Labor Golda Meyerson, Minister of Communications David Remez, and Zalman Shazar, the brilliant writer and editor of the largest newspaper of Israel, *Davar.*

The United Workers Party—*Mapam*

The second strongest party in Israel is *Mapam* (Hebrew abbreviation of *Miflegeth Hapoalim Hameuchedeth B'Eretz Israel,* United Workers party) with nineteen seats in the Assembly. It was formed in January, 1948, by the merger of three groups, Achduth Avodah, a leftist offshoot of Mapai, the "left" Poale Zion which withdrew from the European Zionist labor movement after the bolshevist revolution and which espoused a closer collaboration with the Soviet Union (following in this respect the example of the Austrian Social Democrats), and Hashomer Hatzair, one of the most zealous of the pioneering groups in Palestine. The members of *Hashomer Hatzair* (Young Guardians) have been responsible for many of the most daring and most dangerous settlement projects in Palestine. With iron discipline they went into the malaria-infested swamps, braving Bedouin assaults, hunger, disease, and death. Unlike Achduth Avodah, which was orthodox in its Zionism, Hashomer Hatzair advocated a union of Jews and Arabs against "British imperialism" and a binational Palestinian state. It was, therefore, in opposition to the Biltmore program of 1943 in which world Zionism called for the establishment of a Jewish state in Palestine.

The distinguishing feature of Mapam since the merger has been its strong pro-Soviet orientation. It holds that Great Britain is the arch-enemy of Israel and that the United States is influenced by the British Foreign Office and its own interests in the Arabian oil fields. Israel, therefore, must rely on the Soviet Union and the "peoples' democracies" of eastern Europe for support. Mapam takes credit for the flow of arms and ammunition to Israel from Czechoslovakia. It can, unfortunately, point to the sad fact that the United States, by enforcing an arms embargo, and Great Britain, by actually supporting the Arab States, practically compelled the military missions of Israel to turn to the eastern European nations for assistance. Nevertheless, Mapam is not a communist party. It has rejected Communist proposals for a united front in Israeli politics. Mapam, whatever its attitude on foreign policy, places Zionism first on the agenda; and it knows that the Communists are not Zionists but agents of the Soviet Union. Mapam's influence in Israel stems partly from the very constructive role which Achduth Avodah and, especially, Hashomer Hatzair, played in training and settling pioneers in Palestine. It was largely young settlers from the communal villages of these two groups who manned Palmach, the elite commando of Haganah. To some extent Mapam has gained support from elements which were simply restive as a result of Mapai's long dominance in Palestinian Jewish affairs and impatient at the absence of striking successes. Its leaders, Meir Yaari, one of the founders of Histadruth, Aaron Zisling, who was Minister of Agriculture in the Provisional Government, Dr. Moshe Sneh, former Defense Member of the Jewish Agency Executive, Israel Galili, former commander of Palmach, Mordecai Ben Tov, who was Minister of Public Works in the Provisional Government, are well-known and devoted Zionists.

The United Religious Bloc

On the heels of Mapam, with sixteen seats in the Constituent Assembly, followed the United Religious Bloc, a cartel of four political parties which emphasize Jewish religious tradition—the Mizrachi, Hapoel Hamizrachi, Agudath Israel, and Poale Agudath Israel.

In its beginnings the modern Zionist movement had to contend with determined opposition on the part of most orthodox Jews. They insisted that the return to Zion was a task to be performed by the miraculous intercession of God and his Messiah and that human endeavor in that direction was not only futile but fraught with danger. Nevertheless, some orthodox Jews, foremost among them Rabbi Samuel Mohilever and Rabbi Zvi Hirsch Kalisher, had been among the outstanding forerunners of Theodor Herzl. To make the spirit of Jewish religion influential in Zionism, Rabbi Isaac Jacob Reines and the Hebrew writer, Zeev Yaavetz, founded in 1902 in Vilna a Zionist-religious faction, the Mizrachi. While the Hebrew word *Mizrachi* means "Eastern," the name in reality stands for a combination of two Hebrew words, *Merkaz Ruhani,* which means "Spiritual Center." A succinct statement of Mizrachi principles can be found in a pamphlet published by the Mizrachi of America in 1940:

> Mizrachi is that party in Zionism which strives for the upbuilding of the Jewish National Home in Palestine on the basis of Israel's religious traditions in the belief that *Eretz Yisrael* was not intended to be merely a dwelling place of the Jewish people but also the abode of the Jewish spirit. The party's synthesis of its philosophy is well indicated in its slogan: *Eretz Yisrael L'am Yisrael al pi Toras Yisrael* (The land of Israel for the people of Israel on the basis of the Torah of Israel).

Hapoel Hamizrachi (Mizrachi Workers) is a labor organization which emerged from the middle-class Mizrachi Movement and adopted as its main slogan: *Torah V'Avodah* (Religious Law and Labor). It maintains a number of collective farms and cooperatives in Israel in which the traditions and practices of religious Judaism are strictly observed.

Agudath Israel (Association of Israel) is the party of extreme Jewish orthodoxy. For many years its members were bitterly opposed to Zionism, even to the religious Zionism of the Mizrachi. Recently the party decided to approve the establishment of the Jewish State and to participate in its government. Like Mizrachi it has a labor branch called *Poale Agudath Israel* (Workers of the Association of Israel).

In November, 1948, these four groups formed the United Religious Bloc. The bloc's foreign policy does not differ materially from that of the leading party of Israel, Mapai. On social and economic issues its policy resembles that of the Christian Democratic party of Italy and the French Popular Republican Movement (MRP). Among its leaders are Rabbi Judah L. Fishman, who was Minister of Religious Affairs in the Provisional Government, now known as Maimon; Rabbi I. M. Levin, and Moshe Shapira.

Freedom Party—Herut

Fourth in the returns to the Constituent Assembly was Herut, the political outgrowth of the former Irgun Zvai Leumi, a terrorist military organization. The ideological forebear of the Irgun was the Revisionist party, organized in Berlin in 1924 by Vladimir Jabotinsky, the founder of the Jewish Legion in World War I and a brilliant writer and orator. His party accepted the name "Revisionist" because its members felt that a revision was needed in the policy of the world Zionist movement toward Great Britain. The Revisionists demanded a Jewish state on both sides of the Jordan River including all western Palestine and all Trans-Jordan. During the period of the mandate they were violently opposed to the Histadruth. They favored private enterprise. They demanded that strikes be outlawed and that conflicts between capital and labor should be settled through compulsory arbitration. In many respects Jabotinsky's foreign policy was considered a revival of the political Zionism of Theodor Herzl, in contrast to Weizmann's emphasis on practical achievements. But its antilabor platform drew the fire of the majority parties in Palestine, who viewed it as a menace to the rights of the Jewish pioneers. At one time, in 1934, the youth group of the Revisionist party, the Betar, became involved in a series of clashes with the Histadruth. During that period the Labor Zionist leader Chaim Arlosoroff was assassinated.* In 1935 the Revisionist party broke away from the World Zionist Organization and established itself as the New Zionist Organization.

Whatever chances the Revisionists may have had to grow into a movement powerful enough to compete with the World Zionist Organization were ended by the outbreak of World War II and the destruction of eastern European Jewry. It was from its desperate middle class that the party drew its main strength. In 1940 Jabotinsky died. Zionism lost in him a leader who combined exceptional propagandistic qualities and a profound devotion to the cause with sometimes reckless and undiplomatic political action. In 1947 the Revisionists officially renounced terrorism as a weapon and returned to the World Zionist Organization.

But meanwhile, nourished by Revisionist ideology of former years, there had grown up in Jewish Palestine an underground terrorist organization, the Irgun Zvai Leumi. During the Arab riots in 1936–39 the Irgun

* The Betar, or B'rith Trumpeldor (named after Joseph Trumpeldor, the prominent defender of Tel Hai) denied responsibility for Arlosoroff's assassination.

met Arab terror by reprisals—in contrast to the policy of the Yishuv. During World War II it was unconditionally pro-Allied, which caused some of its members under the leadership of Abraham Stern to split off and to found a new group, the Fighters for Freedom, better known as the Sternists. This group toyed with the idea of supporting Mussolini. With the collapse of the Axis both the Irgun and the Sternists expanded in scale. They conducted their own fund-raising activities in the United States, the Irgun through the American Committee for Free Palestine; the Sternists through the Political Action Committee for Palestine. When the Arab-Jewish war broke out, the terrorist groups at first operated independently. While the Irgun never denied the bombing of the King David Hotel in the summer of 1946 and similar terrorist acts during the months preceding the proclamation of the Jewish State, it took issue with the reports that emanated from Palestine in November, 1948, accusing it of "an act of wanton massacre" in the capture of the Arab village of Deir Yassin. The following is a part of a statement made in the *New York Times* of December 15, 1948, by the American Committee for a Free Palestine in the name of Irgun and signed by a number of prominent Americans including Senator Guy M. Gillette, Louis Bromfield, Paul O'Dwyer, and others:

> The capture of Deir Yassin was vital to the defense of Jerusalem. At the risk and cost of a number of Hebrew lives the Irgun gave loudspeaker warnings to the inhabitants to withdraw peacefully. The Arab marauders from Syria and Iraq, who were using the village as a vantage point against the Tel-Aviv-Jerusalem road, prevented the population from leaving and made it necessary for the Irgun to conduct a house-to-house struggle for the village. Loss of life is highly regrettable, but it is one of the unfortunate concomitants of war. The atom bomb which leveled Hiroshima was incapable of distinguishing between soldier and non-combatant, but its use was nevertheless justified. It is in this light that Deir Yassin must be viewed.

Shortly after the Deir Yassin affair the terrorist groups were incorporated into the Jewish Army but permitted to retain their own units and officers. This privilege ended when the Irgun attempted to land an illegal cargo of arms in the port of Tel Aviv—the Altalena incident. From then on the Irgunist and Sternist units in the army were distributed among other contingents, and all political armies were abolished. Finally, following the assassination of Count Bernadotte, the government outlawed both terrorist groups. They accepted the decision and converted themselves into political parties.

Irgun took the name of Herut (Freedom Party). Its program is essentially the old Revisionist program, a Jewish state including all western Palestine and all Trans-Jordan. It is anti-Histadruth in domestic policy. But it denies that it is a fascist party. Its foreign-policy orientation is anti-British and anti-Soviet. While the Revisionist party of Israel polled less than 1 per cent of the vote and secured no seats in the Assembly, Herut, led by Menachem Beigin, received fourteen seats.

More than four-fifths of the votes of Israel went to the parties discussed so far. No other group has shown itself strong enough to play a significant political role. Nevertheless there are several other parties which are potentially capable of influencing the course of political life in Israel, partly because of their strength in world Zionism, partly because of their value as members of a coalition combination.

General Zionists

Among these minor parties special mention must be made of the General Zionist party. While the General Zionists received only seven seats in the Constituent Assembly, they form the strongest Zionist party in other countries, notably the United States of America. The Zionist Organization of America under the guidance of Rabbi Abba Hillel Silver, Emanuel Neumann, Louis Lipsky, Rabbi Israel Goldstein, Judge Morris Rothenberg, Judge Louis E. Levinthal, and its present president, Daniel Frisch, is certainly one of the most influential Zionist parties in the world. In view of Israel's dependence on foreign financial support, the General Zionists of Israel have at times been able to exert a larger influence in the Jewish Commonwealth than their numbers there would by themselves justify.

General Zionism considers itself a party of integration seeking to harmonize the various elements of Jewish nationalism, religion, and social justice. It tries to overcome partisanship and emphasizes the unity of the main streams in Jewish life. For a number of years the Palestine General Zionist party operated with two independent wings: Group A—left of center, oriented toward the Histadruth, drawing its support from artisans, small farmers, and the members of the liberal professions; Group B—right of center, drawing support from industrialists, merchants, citrus growers, and landlords. In 1946 the two groups were united into the General Zionist party. Fritz Bernstein, for years editor of the Hebrew daily *Haboker,* and Isaac Gruenbaum, a member of the Jewish Agency Executive, were the outstanding leaders of the combined party and ministers in the Provisional Government. After the establishment of the State the differences between the two groups became so marked, however, that the leaders of the former Group A broke away and formed the Progressive party.

The Progressive party, composed of former Group A, Haoved

Hazioni, a General Zionist labor group with membership in the Histadruth and Aliyah Hadashah (New Immigration, mainly from Germany and Austria) resembles the present Liberal party of the United Kingdom in social outlook and foreign policy. Its main representative is Dr. Felix Rosenblueth, one of the outstanding leaders of German Zionism, who was Minister of Justice in the Provisional Government. The party secured five seats in the Constituent Assembly.

Arab Parties

Of considerable potential significance, although at present rather weak, are the parties which represent the Arabs, who at the present writing form about 15 per cent of Israel's population. The names of these parties are: the Arab Workers Bloc (affiliated with Mapai), the Arab Peoples Party (affiliated with Mapam), and the Democratic List. Only one of these three parties, the Democratic List, was able to poll sufficient votes to gain two seats. The other two parties obtained no seats. The reason for this may be that the Arabs do not consider them as genuinely independent organizations. But as the Arabs in Israel recover from the effects of the war and as at least some of the refugees begin to trickle back, it seems likely that they will turn to political action to improve their position. In view of the divisions within Jewish political life, a political representation of the Arabs might well have considerable bargaining power.

Oriental Jews

There are ethnic minorities within the Jewish community itself that have not as yet been fully assimilated. These are the Sephardic and Oriental Jews. Economically and culturally they constitute an underprivileged group whose mode of living is closer to that of the Arabs than to that of the other Jews. Since hundreds of thousands of Jews from North Africa and Israel's neighbors seem to be determined to leave their former homes for settlement in the Jewish State, their political representation might some day become highly significant. At present the Union of Sephardic Jews and Oriental Communities has four seats in the Assembly.

Another party, representing this group, in particular those Jews who stem from Yemen in the Arabian peninsula, the Yemenite party, gained one seat in the Assembly. This, however, does not represent the real strength of the Yemenites in Israel. Belonging to a somewhat depressed group which has never known the Western standard of living and particularly susceptible to the appeal of terrorism, some Yemenites probably voted for Herut and the Stern group, while other Oriental Jews filled the ranks especially of the Religious Bloc.

Like the Yemenite party, the Sternists, calling themselves Fighters and Soldiers Party, and the Women's International Zionist Organization (Wizo) secured one seat each in the Assembly. Wizo, like Hadassah in the United States an agency devoted to constructive social service, entered the political race because, among other things, it hopes to prevent the inclusion in Israeli law of those provisions of Jewish religious law which belong to an outmoded past and discriminate against women.

The Communist Party

Jewish life in Palestine has not been conducive to the growth of a communist party. Since Soviet Russia and its Communist agencies in the rest of the world have traditionally condemned Zionism as a particularly flagrant form of "bourgeois nationalism" and a "tool of British imperialism," the Jews who went to Palestine demonstrated by their very going that they had no regard for the Kremlin dictum. Nevertheless, when as a consequence of the Hitlerian persecutions some Jewish Communists from Europe, having been denied entry into the "fatherland of the proletariat," considered the Jewish National Home a good-enough place of refuge, a small communist party came into being. It followed, of course, the Moscow line which called for "Arab-Jewish unity against British imperialism." In furtherance of this aim the Communist party in Palestine was asked to support all Arab riots, which caused the Jews of Palestine to attribute this motto to the Jewish Communists: "Let's kick ourselves out of here!"

After the official dissolution of the Comintern (replaced later by the Cominform), the Communist party of Palestine received special permission from Moscow to revise its stand. By agreement the Arab Communists in Palestine continued to support Hitler's friend, the Mufti of Jerusalem, and demanded the immediate stoppage of all Jewish immigration. The Jewish Communists demanded free Jewish immigration and a binational state. When Soviet Russia switched to support of the partition of Palestine, both the Jewish and the Arab Communists likewise supported the partition scheme.

In the elections to the Constituent Assembly they presented a unified list. They polled 3.5 per cent of the entire vote and won four seats. Tewfik Touby, one of the Communists in the Assembly, is an Arab. More important, half the Communist vote came from Arabs, which means that something like a fifth of the Arabs in Israel cast their ballots for the

Communist party while only a fiftieth of the Jews voted Communist. In addition, the Arab Democratic List, which gained two seats in the Assembly, is reputed to be a Communist-front organization. It seems likely that the Communist agents in Israel will seek to capitalize on the deep-rooted discontent which pervades the Arab masses all over the Near East. On the other hand, the return of the Soviet Union and of the international Communist movement to anti-Zionism, a policy that is already discernible in the Communist press, will prevent Communist inroads into the Jewish vote. Already, a few days after the election, the Communist party of Israel felt obliged to "purge" one of the three Jews elected on its ticket, Eliezer Preminger, on the familiar charge of inclining in the direction of "bourgeois nationalism."

On February 14, 1949, the members of the Constituent Assembly, the first parliament of Israel, met in Jerusalem. The choice of Jerusalem as well as of the date were of symbolic significance. Jerusalem, the ancient capital of the Jewish State, had at the time of meeting the status of "Israeli-occupied territory." It was administered by a military governor, Dr. Bernard Joseph, who was formerly the legal adviser of the Jewish Agency.

The Jewish festival of the Feast of the Trees, celebrating the first signs of spring, fell this time on February 14. During the more peaceful years of the mandatory regime there used to be folk dances in the streets, and the children would hike into the fields to plant new trees and to pick wild flowers.

The Arab-Israeli war was at a standstill, and sunshine bathed the Holy City when the delegates walked through flag-bedecked Herzl Street, the city's main thoroughfare, toward the Jewish Agency Building. Their first task was to elect their own presiding officers. As speaker of the leading party, David Ben Gurion suggested the election of three vice-presidents representing Mapai, Mapam, and the Religious Bloc. This suggestion was accepted against the protests of Herut and the Communists. The high spot of the day was the stirring address by Dr. Chaim Weizmann, who opened the Israeli Constituent Assembly with these words:

> It is with a feeling of deep reverence and consecration that I rise to open the Constituent Assembly of the State of Israel—the first Knesseth Israel (Assembly of Israel) of our time, in this, our eternal city of Jerusalem.
>
> This is a great moment in our history. Let us give thanks and praise to the God of Israel, who, in His mercy, granted us the privilege of witnessing the redemption of our people after centuries of affliction and suffering. . . .

After paying tribute to the Jewish pioneers who carved out the road of return, to Herzl, Ahad Haam, Chaim Nachman Bialik (the great Hebrew poet), Louis Brandeis (the pride of American Jewry), and others, Weizmann added significantly:

It is our people who once gave the whole world the spiritual message fundamental to civilization. The world is watching us now to see the way we choose in ordering our lives, how we fashion our State. The world is listening to hear whether a new message will go forth from Zion, and what that message will be.

A new message is not born without some sore travail of the creative spirit. The creative force of our nation will soon meet a new and serious challenge. The constitution which this Assembly has been called upon to frame will be the supreme test. . . .

Today is a great day in our lives. Let us not be thought too arrogant if we say that it is also a great day in the history of the world. In this hour a message of hope and good cheer issues from this place, from this sacred city to all oppressed people and to all who are struggling for freedom and equality. . . . From this place we send fraternal blessings to our brethren throughout the world. We stretch out our hand in peace to the neighboring countries and extend friendship to all peace-loving peoples of the world. . . .

On February 17 Dr. Weizmann was elected the first President of Israel. When an honor guard of officers of the armed forces led him to the dais of the Assembly, the delegates and the diplomatic corps rose in silent tribute to the scientist-statesman who had devoted a lifetime to the cause of his people. The spell was broken by the shrill notes of the *Shofar* (ram's horn) and the singing of "Hatikvah," the Jewish national anthem. Dr. Weizmann took the oath, "I, son of Ozer and Rachel Weizmann, undertake as President of the state to maintain allegiance to the State of Israel and its laws."

He immediately called on David Ben Gurion to form a cabinet in order to replace the Provisional State Council which had been created on May 14, 1948. The Cabinet was formed on March 3, 1949, consisting of seven representatives of Mapai, three representatives of the Religious Bloc, and one representative each of the Progressive Party and the Union of Sephardic Jews and Oriental Communities. With seventy-four delegates in the Assembly, the Cabinet was assured a safe majority even if Mapam and the General Zionists who were invited to join the government bloc should prefer to stay in opposition. In the present government Mapai sets the tone. Not only does it have the absolute majority of cabinet positions, but it can count on the support of the Progressive representative, Minister of Justice Dr. Felix Rosenblueth, on almost all questions, on that of the Religious Bloc on foreign policy, and on the representatives of Religious Labor within the Religious Bloc on economic problems. It, therefore, appears likely that the new state will bear the impress of Mapai's secular, social democratic, and, as a whole, pro-Western program.

Chapter Ten: SOCIAL AND ECONOMIC OUTLOOK

KVUTZAH AND MOSHAV · SECONDARY AND TERTIARY INDUSTRIES · FOREIGN TRADE AND TOURISM · JORDAN VALLEY AUTHORITY

The late Arthur Ruppin, one of the fathers of modern Jewish colonization in Palestine, foresaw the most pressing problem of the Jewish State when in his address at the Thirteenth Zionist Congress in Carlsbad, in 1923, he said: "If we have great financial means at our disposal, the obstacles to immigration will be brushed away like cobwebs; without such means they will prove insuperable barriers." He warned his fellow Zionists not to pursue the line of least resistance by adopting a policy of short-term relief for immigrants instead of the more difficult long-term planning aimed at the permanent integration of the newcomers.

In the new state, immigration and its attendant financial, social, and psychological problems have assumed proportions unknown in the three decades following the Balfour Declaration. The government of Israel must think today in terms of settling 1,500,000 new Jewish immigrants from Europe and the Middle East within five years. By comparison this is as if the United States government had to plan to settle in the United States some 80,000,000 newcomers within that same brief period. Obviously such mass immigration necessitates careful planning. Dr. Ruppin, like others in the Zionist movement, knew that the rebuilding of the ancient homeland could be achieved only by the creation of a new type of Jew who would be willing to forego the amenities of city life and devote himself to agricultural occupations. So far as could be observed, the majority of the former DP's are not drawn toward the life of agricultural pioneering. They are town dwellers without the spirit of sacrifice that animated former Jewish immigrants to leave their urban professions and to accept willingly and almost joyfully the hardships of a farmer's life.

As a democratic government the government of Israel will not be able to coerce the newcomers into leaving the cities. But in the interest of a well-balanced economy and an equitable social order it will have to find ways and means of inducing at least a substantial number among the recent immigrants to settle on the land.

Dr. Ruppin, who was by no means a champion of collectivism, saw very soon that the collective settlement alone could safeguard the principle of self-labor in the pioneering Jewish society of Palestine.* Economic realism as well as ethical considerations led him to advocate those types of agricultural settlement which are known today as Kvutzah and Moshav. They were a creation chiefly of the second and third immigration waves.

The first group of immigrants who sailed from Europe in 1882 had planned to establish themselves on a communal basis. But their initial effort in *Rishon le Zion* (First of Zion) proved unsuccessful. Coming from the Jewish middle class of eastern Europe, with some meager financial means at their disposal and apparently unable to change their lives too radically, they preferred in the end private ownership of the land, buildings, animals, and machinery. Rishon le Zion and similar settlements, therefore, developed as the prototype of the individualistic, capitalistic village in the Jewish Commonwealth. It is called *Moshavah* (colony). Many of the farmers in these villages devoted themselves almost exclusively to the production of citrus fruit. They employed cheap Arab labor. Although they started with the best intentions, their insistence on unrestricted private property in agriculture militated against the idea of "self-labor" and further Jewish mass immigration to Palestine.

Those immigrants who came in the early twenties realized that communal living and mutual help were necessary at least in the primary stages of colonization since they lacked agricultural experience and the means, however small, which were at the disposal of the settlers of Rishon le Zion. Moreover, under the impact of Western socialist ideas they were acutely disturbed by the question which they asked themselves over and over: "Are we not escapists leaving the liberal and radical struggle of the Western world to go off to an island far away from the centers in which this struggle takes place?" The answer, finally, was that they had not abandoned the battle for democracy and freedom. They were carrying it on in their own way, not through pamphlets, pro-

* The first plan of cooperative settlement in Palestine was evolved by the German-Jewish economist, Professor Franz Oppenheimer of the University of Frankfurt am Main.

tests, strikes, but by the attempt to create a social and democratic commonwealth in Palestine. Zionism was for them the instrument set aside by history for a particular Jewish interpretation of the modern struggle for human progress.

Palestine was suffering from centuries of neglect. Means of communication were primitive. The early settlers were exposed to frequent attacks by marauding Bedouins. Under such conditions a closely knit cooperative development offered greater chances of success than the individual effort. Economic necessity, national and social idealism met. As a result the *Kvutzah,* or communal settlement, and the *Moshav Ovdim,* or smallholders' settlement, developed in the years after World War I. Since the Kvutzah forms a unique achievement of Jewish colonization, indeed an original contribution of the Jewish homeland to agrarian reform, I shall describe it in some detail. Its roots go back to the period immediately before World War I.

The Kvutzah is engaged mainly in agriculture. It originated in Sedjera, a colony in lower Galilee. A few workers of that colony pooled the wages which they had earned for their work in the fields and orchards of the colony and established a commune of their own with common living quarters and a common kitchen. On the strength of their experiment in living together, they later leased from the Jewish National Fund a tract of land in the valley of the Jordan near the city of Tiberias. There, in 1909, they founded the first agricultural commune of Palestine, Daganyah.

Daganyah, like the many communal settlements that followed its example, resembles a large working family of several hundred members, with an equal standard of living for all. No money whatsoever is used in the internal relations of the settlement. Each works according to his ability and within the framework of a general plan devised by all the members in a sort of town-hall meeting. There is an equal allotment of living quarters. A common kitchen and a common commissary cater to the various needs of the community. Not only the means of production are owned in common, but all the personal things of life are also possessed by the group as a whole. Everyone draws his clothing from the common stock. His wants are satisfied in accordance with his needs. Everyone gets his tobacco or cigarettes from the common supply. He who requires more, gets more. Those who need less do not envy the others. The communal library provides everybody with literature. He who joins a Kvutzah gives up his money, his private home, furniture, books, clothing, all his earthly possessions. No individual accounts are kept.

The woman is accorded absolute equality. She has an equal voice in all decisions of the settlement, and she participates in all branches of agricultural work. The most striking feature of the Kvutzah, however, is its *Bet Jeladim* (the children's house). It is always the largest and most comfortable building in the collective settlement. From the moment of their birth the children of the members spend all their time, day and night, in the children's house and the adjacent gardens. They see their parents twice a day, during the luncheon recess and after working hours before dinner time. Separated into age groups, they pass the rest of the time under the supervision of carefully trained nurses and teachers who in general are also members of the Kvutzah.

Only the external financial relations of the settlement are governed by customary capitalistic standards. The Kvutzah sells its surplus production for money which in turn pays for improvements of the collective, the repayment of loans from the Jewish national institutions and those means of life which must be acquired from the outside. He who leaves the settlement for a vacation, a necessary journey, or some specialized education is given his expenses from the common treasury. Concerts, plays, motion pictures offered by the cities are paid for from the cooperative earnings of the community. The community as a whole also takes care of aged and impecunious parents whether they reside in Israel or abroad.

During the early years of their existence these communal settlements were frequently criticized as hopelessly utopian efforts. They were branded as wasteful undertakings that would never pay. But today the overwhelming majority of the Kvutzoth (plural of Kvutzah) are on a self-sustaining basis. Many of them have accumulated considerable wealth, and a younger generation has grown up in them who cannot think of any better way of life.

In addition to the Kvutzah, the fully established communal settlement, there exists a modified form of communal enterprise, the Kibutz. It could perhaps be described as a Kvutzah in the making. Its members, though not yet permanently settled on their common land, live as a commune, sharing all property and income collectively. Many members of the Kibutz are still doing work outside the settlement, on private farms, or in private industries. No distinction is made between an unqualified laborer who earns relatively little and a qualified worker who earns twice, or even three times, as much. All their earnings are invested in the cooperative with the objective of widening its agricultural basis and enabling all its members to live from its production. The mode of life in the Kibutz resembles that of the Kvutzah. Each worker works according to his ability, while his needs are taken care of collectively from the common resources. Some of the Kibutzim (plural of Kibutz) operate bakeries, trucks for transportation, carpentry and other shops serving neighboring communities. Thus they combine agriculture, urban trades, and outside work to establish some economic security for the collective.

The second type, the Moshav Ovdim, or smallholders' settlement, resembles the ordinary European peasant community. But its guiding principle is self-labor, and its members are imbued with a social spirit rarely found among peasants and farmers of other countries. The land of the Moshav does not belong to its members as private property. It remains the permanent possession of the Jewish National Fund, that is, the Jewish people as a whole. It is understood, however, that the settlers, their children, and children's children will be permitted to stay on that land as long as they are willing to cultivate it. The statutes of the smallholders' settlements provide that in case one of their members is too ill to work his farm, his fellow members must take turns to attend to it with the same care that they give their own farms. All farm products are sold cooperatively. Manufactured articles, in particular farm machinery, are purchased in the same way. In a number of these villages there is collective cultivation of the fields, restricting the individual effort to dairying, poultry raising, fruit growing, and vegetable gardening.

The first settlements of this type—Nahalal and Kfar Yehezkiel—were founded in the summer of 1921 at the beginning of the colonizing activities in the valley of Jezreel. In contrast to the capitalistic Moshavah, the Moshav is characterized by its emphasis on mixed farming. The unit of land per family is about 120 dunams (30 acres) in regions without artificial irrigation. In settlements which enjoy ample water supply the unit of land is smaller. In the plantation zone of Israel 20 or 25 dunams is considered a large enough holding to support a farmer and his family.

Our age is characterized by its quest for new methods of intensifying production. In 1947, at the Pan-Asiatic Conference in New Delhi, the Jewish delegates from what is now Israel were assailed with questions about the Kvutzah and the Kibutz. Visitors to Israel are amazed to see in the midst of a capitalist economy these islands of collectivism based on solely voluntary efforts and maintaining the creative spirit of man. It is this elasticity and absence of coercion which distinguishes the collective farms of Israel from the kolkhozes of the Soviet Union. Moreover, the kolkhozes never applied communistic principles in the relations of their members to the extent of Israel's Kvutzoth and Kibutzim. The earnings of the "kolkhoznik" are calculated according to working hours, efficiency, and skill. Besides, he owns some private property, usually even a small garden.*

Whether the Kvutzah type of settlement could be profitably emulated by other nations depends, of course, on the number of men and women who can free themselves completely of the idea of all private property and who at the same time are willing to work to the best of their ability irrespective of the quality and amount of work done by others. It is even questionable whether the former Jewish DP's—with few exceptions—will be able to undergo the spiritual transformation which entry into a Kvutzah necessitates.

The Department of Agriculture of the Israel government has plans for a large-scale colonization program in three strategic sections of the country—in Galilee, the Jerusalem area, and in the Negev. Hundreds of new settlements are to be established on land acquired by the Jewish National Fund. Success of this effort will depend in part on the generosity of world Jewry, especially American Jewry, which will be called upon to help provide the initial means of resettlement. But in part it will depend on the readiness of the newcomers themselves to display the same quiet heroism which characterized former groups of settlers.

An ever more important potential source of absorption of the new immigrants is, of course, the local industries. At the end of World War II the industries of the Jewish National Home employed about 55,000 workers producing goods valued at over $160,000,000. Despite the uncooperative attitude of the British mandatory government, Jewish industry underwent a careful renovation of exhausted plant and equipment. With the reopening of the Mediterranean and larger facilities for shipping, Jewish manufacturers began to market their commodities abroad. Belgium and Switzerland buy furs, knitwear, leather clothing, and fancy leather goods from Israel. Holland and Norway buy textiles. Greece is a market for chemicals, ironware, and stationery. The Union of South Africa imports from Israel women's and children's apparel. Australia imports stationery. Many European countries and the United States import wines from Rishon le Zion and the old Rothschild colonies.

Israel has little chance to develop primary industries. It has no iron or coal mines. It lacks well-developed forests. It must, therefore, concentrate on secondary and tertiary industries—textiles, from the imported raw materials to the finished products; furs, from foreign and domestic skins to the finished products; leather, from the imported raw-

* There is a trend in the communal settlements of Israel pointing to increased private ownership of personal effects.

hide to the finished product; foodstuffs, canned vegetables, fruit juices, citrus by-products and wines; pharmaceutical products, cosmetics, plastics, furniture, diamonds, books and films, shellac, pencils, metals from semifinished materials to the final products like silver plate and stainless steelware.

The new state will require substantial foreign investments from both large and small investors to implement these industrial developments and their expansion. As Albert Schiff, president of the Israel Corporation of America, emphasized in an address in March, 1949, Israel's "national economy must be developed to support the growing population by a well planned and amply financed process of industrialization which will enable Israel to gain substantial weight in the domestic and foreign markets."

Growing industrialization demands a large volume of imports, especially of machinery and raw materials. In 1939 Palestine's total foreign trade was already four times as great per capita as that of Syria and Iraq and three times as great as that of Egypt. The per capita rate is today similar to that of the United Kingdom and Sweden.

As long as Palestine was mandated territory it had to grant an "open-door" trade clause, providing equal treatment to all foreign countries regardless of the customs policy which they applied toward Palestine. The effect of Article 18 of the British Mandate, containing the "open-door" clause, was so harmful to Palestine's trade that the Royal Commission of 1936 stated:

> The provisions of Article 18 are out of date . . . the application of the principle of the open door to mandated territories was certainly never intended to have an injurious effect on their well being and development.

Palestine's foreign-trade system was largely designed not so much to meet the needs of its own population as to assist Great Britain's economic requirements. Palestine's foreign exchange was manipulated by the Bank of England. Palestine was not allowed to retain the foreign currencies which it earned but had to turn them over to the London pool against sterling credit. In this way Britain compelled the Jews to buy only in the sterling area although they could have done much better elsewhere. While after World War II British manufacturers obtained licenses to import American heavy machinery, radios, and refrigerators, His Majesty's Government made it largely impossible for Jewish firms in Palestine to obtain similar licenses, in spite of the fact that the "gift dollars," that is, money sent from America by the Zionist funds, covered the desired imports from America several times over.

Now at last Israel is free to pursue its own trade policy. In possession of excellent modern harbors and the oil refineries in Haifa, it can use its economic position to become an outstanding oil center in the Middle East, although Israel itself is not yet an oil-producing country.

A very important item in its foreign trade will be the so-called invisible exports, foremost the tourist business. For it can be safely assumed that with improved tourist accommodations, Israel will attract more tourists eventually—Jews and non-Jews—than any other country in the Middle East. Israel will soon become the hub of Middle Eastern air traffic. Air France, KLM, TWA, the Czech Air Lines have already begun service to Israel, using the airport facilities of Lydda. In addition Lydda is the home port of the youngest air line in the world, El Al, the Israel National Air Line.

During the period from June to October, 1948, Israel's imports from the United States amounted to $11,131,000, against exports to the United States in the amount of $1,743,000. It can be expected that for many years to come the new state will be a good customer of the United States. While the American standard of living is unsurpassed in all the world, Israeli wages and salaries in terms of purchasing power compare favorably with those of Great Britain and other Western nations. The government of Israel has appointed a special subcommittee to draft proposals for a social welfare plan which, like the Beveridge plan, is to include these main features: (1) free medical aid, including hospitalization, for all citizens of Israel; (2) compulsory social insurance for all wage earners, including members of the professions and artisans. This insurance is to comprise workmen's compensation, special allowances for expectant mothers and maternity aid, unemployment insurance, old-age pensions, sickness benefits, and special assistance to widows and orphans. It will be financed through contributions from employers, employees, and the State. A number of social-insurance schemes are already in existence in Israel. The object of the Cabinet subcommittee is to introduce uniformity and thereby to reduce overhead expenses.

The social impulses permeating the Jewish colonization work are not confined to the agricultural sectors. Nowhere in the world have workers succeeded to the same extent in creating and operating cooperative enterprises in the cities.

Much of Israel's motor transport—passengers and freight—is in the hands of a powerful cooperative, Egged. Over a hundred cooperatives are engaged in production and public services. The urge to permanency which characterizes the Jew of Israel expresses itself in his desire, not to own real estate but to have a home of his own. In many instances the home-building cooperatives, instead of erecting separate small houses for every individual member, have resorted to building large blocks of modernistic apartment houses in which each member is allotted an apartment with a share in courts and gardens.

Israel knows the co-op store of the more usual consumer type. But it plays a much smaller role than the cooperative in the field of production. The workers of Israel never lost track of their chief national goal. They were, therefore, not too interested in cooperatives which compete with private stores without providing working opportunities for new immigrants. The only trading cooperative which has achieved significance in Israel's economic life is Tnuva. This cooperative sells the products of the communal farms and the smallholders' settlements in the inner markets of the country. The sale of citrus fruits in foreign markets is likewise conducted by cooperatives. The most prominent among them is Pardess, which is controlled by the planters of the capitalistic village type, the Moshavah.

Whenever an opportunity for a new cooperative effort is offered, Histadruth, the main organizing spirit behind Israel's cooperative movement, can be counted upon to try the venture. Thus when the Israelis penetrated into all kinds of maritime trades, Histadruth established a special corporation, Nakshon, to build the port of Tel Aviv and enlarge the Haifa harbor facilities.

Much of Israel's economic future will depend on the Jordan Valley Authority plan of Dr. Walter Clay Lowdermilk, formerly of the United States Soil Conservation Service. Dr. Lowdermilk, who studied the Middle East on an official American government mission in 1938 and 1939, has written an excellent book on his observations and the plan itself, *Palestine, Land of Promise.* He had seen how the Dutch had made fertile farm land of 550,000 acres on the floor of the Zuider Zee, how the French had changed sand dunes into productive forests; and he had studied the Tennessee Valley Authority, the Boulder Dam, the Grand Coulee power and irrigation projects in the United States. These projects demonstrated how modern engineering can harness wild waters to produce electric power and how scientific agriculture can transform wastelands into orchards and vegetable gardens. Going back to an idea of Theodor Herzl, Lowdermilk realized that the valley of the Jordan offers the possibilities of a reclamation project along the lines of the TVA.

Israel needs water and power. Water is available in the flow of the Jordan. Potential power is locked in the swift descent of the river to the depth of the Dead Sea, 1,300 feet below sea level. The Jordan Valley Authority, therefore, envisages the diversion of the sweet waters of the Jordan and its tributaries for the purpose of irrigating the adjacent lands. A surplus of water is to be channeled to the valley of Jezreel and to Galilee. The power program calls for the introduction of sea water from the Mediterranean into the Jordan River Valley in concrete-lined canals for the double purpose of compensating the Dead Sea for the loss of Jordan waters and of utilizing the sea water for the creation of hydroelectric power estimated at a yield of over one billion kilowatt hours per year, enough to serve the needs of well over a million of additional population.

The Jordan Valley Authority would promote the conservation of farm and grazing lands and the reforestation of lands unsuited to farming and grazing. This in turn would provide Israel with much-needed fuel and timber. An important part of the authority would be the extraction of valuable minerals from the Dead Sea on a scale far larger than the present one. The Jordan Valley Authority would also include the reclamation of the Negev by using floodwaters for its irrigation.

Equipment, labor, and materials are at hand. The financing could be done through a governmental loan and the United Nations with the active participation of private capital. If properly organized, the Jordan Valley Authority will benefit not only Israel but all its neighboring countries. In fact it could produce the economic union of Israel and Trans-Jordan which neither the British Mandate nor the Bernadotte proposals were able to create. It would solve the problem of Jewish immigration, and it would improve the standard of living of many Arabs.

Due to the creative talents of her citizens, which count for more than ready accessibility of raw materials, Israel might well become another Switzerland.

Chapter Eleven: *EDUCATION AND INFORMATION*

PRIMARY AND SECONDARY SCHOOLS · THE HEBREW UNIVERSITY · THE HEBREW PRESS · THE HEBREW THEATER

Modern scientific and agricultural growth and industrialization are intimately related to the educational system of a country. The problems which confronted the Jewish educators under the British Mandate were not only technical and financial but ideological and traditional as well. Their task was to synthesize Jewish cultural heritage, in particular the study of the Bible and Talmud, with modern Western experience. While the primary purpose of all schooling is to prepare the student for useful membership in society, the Jewish educational effort in Palestine had to produce an additional result. It had to prepare youth with a sense of responsibility not only toward the country and its residents but also toward those Jews still to come. The continuous stream of Jewish immigrants from different cultural backgrounds, speaking a plethora of languages, far outweighed the native Jewish population. It was chiefly through the Jewish schools in Palestine, therefore, that the revived Hebrew language and the new Hebraic culture had to emerge.

The first modern Jewish school in Palestine was founded in 1867 in Jerusalem by Baron von Laemel. It was followed by an agricultural school, Mikveh Israel, established in 1870 by a French-Jewish aid society, the Alliance Israelite Universelle. In 1901 a German-Jewish organization, the Ezra Relief Fund, founded a number of kindergartens and elementary schools in Jerusalem and Jaffa. In 1906 the first secondary school, the Herzlia Gymnasium, was opened in Tel Aviv.

As early as 1915, when Zionists in England began to intensify their agitation for the recognition of Palestine as the Jewish homeland, provisions to guarantee the Jews autonomy in the conduct of their educational system were written into all proposals. Their main principles were incorporated in Article 15 of the British Mandate providing: "the right of each community to maintain its own schools for the education of its own members, in its own language. . . ."

In 1932 the Vaad Leumi (National Council of Palestine Jewry) set up a Department of Education which attempted to coordinate the educational activities of a variety of Jewish organizations. Immediately a rather heated debate took place about the desirability of a centralized educational system as against a decentralized one.

The primary school course comprises eight years of study. Its general curriculum is about the same as that of primary schools in western and central Europe. The Bible is a major subject in all schools, as it forms the cultural and literary background of the Jewish renaissance. While modern Hebrew is the main language, Arabic is also taught in the last two years. The majority of primary schools are so-called "general" institutions, leaning to no particular party or creed.

While the majority of the schools resembled the public schools in any democratic country, there were two separate school systems sponsored by political parties. The Histadruth (Jewish Federation of Labor) maintained a far-reaching net of kindergartens and elementary schools in the agricultural settlements and the cities. Its own educational department supervised educational activities in some ninety different localities. In addition it had created a number of district schools corresponding in their curriculum to American high schools. It insisted on educating the children of its members in the spirit of the Jewish Labor Movement in the National Home, of instilling in them a readiness for agricultural and industrial pioneering, of awakening in them the idea of mutual help and love for social justice. There is no Histadruth school without gardens cultivated by the pupils themselves, without special workshops in which the rudiments of carpentry and other trades are taught. In the Kvutzoth (communal settlements) the children raise in their own school gardens most of the vegetables which come to their tables. They help the cooks; they take turns in washing dishes; they clean their dining room after each meal. Here education through work, the ideal of progressive educators, is daily and self-evident practice.

Another Zionist organization, the religious Mizrachi, maintained its own schools, laying special stress on religious instruction and the observance of religious precepts. No matter what their philosophy, all the schools were eventually included in the network of the educational department of the Vaad Leumi. It limited its supervision, however, to creating some general educational standards and to financial matters.

The secondary schools, too, provide for an eight-year course. A student may enter a secondary school in his sixth year, go through four preparatory classes and eight regular classes, or he may attend a primary school for four years and then enter the first grade of a secondary school. The purpose of the secondary schools is to provide a complete education for those students who after graduation wish to earn a living and the necessary preparation for those who want to continue their studies in the Hebrew University or other institutions of higher learning.

In secondary schools the main subjects are Hebrew literature, history and geography, mathematics, physics, biology, Arabic, French, and English. In the last two years the studies are of a more specialized nature. Final written and oral examinations in Hebrew composition, Bible, mathematics, and foreign languages are taken by all students before graduation. Candidates majoring in science take additional examinations in higher mathematics, chemistry, physics, and biology. Candidates in the arts undergo special tests in Talmud, literature, and history. The holders of graduate certificates from the secondary schools are admitted without special entrance examinations to the Hebrew University in Jerusalem, the Technion at Haifa, and similar institutions of higher learning in Israel and abroad.

The Hebrew University on Mount Scopus near Jerusalem goes back to a plan developed by Hermann Schapira, professor of mathematics at the University of Heidelberg, during the First Zionist Congress in Basel in 1897. However, not until July 24, 1918, when Dr. Chaim Weizmann laid the foundation stone of the university, did the project begin to take shape. Seven years were to pass before the university became more than a plan with a cornerstone. In the meantime a Hebrew University Committee had been founded, which counted among its members Menachem Ussischkin, for many years president of the Jewish National Fund, Ahad Haam, Dr. Judah Magnes, Dr. Joseph Klausner, now professor of modern Hebrew literature at the Hebrew University, and Norman Bentwich. On December 24, 1924, Dr. Magnes, a former American Reform rabbi who devoted himself entirely to the university project, opened the Institute of Jewish Studies. Four months later, on April 1, 1925, Hebrew University was formally opened by Lord Balfour in the presence of Chaim Weizmann, Sir Herbert Samuel, the first High Commissioner for Palestine, Field Marshal Viscount Allenby, the conqueror of Jerusalem, diplomatic representatives of various European and American governments, and delegates of the great universities of the world. It was the first time in two thousand years that nations had gathered to pay homage to the spiritual heritage of the people of Israel.

The intention of the founders of the university was to create a purely research institution. At the beginning only institutes or departments of research were established, in which specially selected students and scholars carried on research programs without expectance of academic degrees. So great, however, was the demand for undergraduate teaching, especially from students of European countries, that it became necessary to add new departments and extend the teaching facilities. A combination of undergraduate and graduate instruction is now based on a four-year course leading to degrees of M.A. (Master of Arts) and M.S. (Master of Science). Intensive graduate studies can also lead to a doctorate.

In addition to the Institute of Jewish Studies, the Institute of Chemistry was founded in 1924. The School of Oriental Studies, the Institute of Palestine Natural History, and the Department of Hygiene and Bacteriology followed in 1926, the Institute of Mathematics in 1927. In 1928 the Division of the Humanities, comprising the Jewish, Oriental, and Arts Institutes, was established. In 1935 the Division of Sciences came into existence. In 1936 Hebrew University awarded for the first time the degree of Doctor of Philosophy.

In the same year a Department of Medicine for postgraduate study was established by the university, together with Hadassah (the Women's Zionist Organization of America). In 1939 instruction in a number of clinical subjects for practicing physicians was instituted, and some departments of the Rothschild–Hadassah Hospital in Jerusalem were given university status. Ten years later, in April, 1949, Hebrew University—at last—was able to open its medical school to undergraduates, especially veterans of the Israeli army. It came into existence as the result of the combined financial efforts of Hadassah and the "American Friends of the Hebrew University." In addition to regular medical instruction the school plans special courses for the retraining of refugee physicians whose practice was cut short by the Nazis.

In 1940 a School of Agriculture was started by the university in cooperation with the Agricultural Research Station at Rehovoth. The course, which leads to the degree of Master of Agriculture, includes two years of natural-science studies in Jerusalem, one year of practical work on the land, and two years of specialized studies at Rehovoth.

Today, under the presidency of Professor Selig Brodetsky, the well-known mathematician, Hebrew University has a faculty of some 180 full professors, lecturers, and instructors, and a student body of close to 1,200 men and women. Faculty and students have at their disposal the Jewish National and University Library, with its collection of over 400,000 volumes in every known language—the largest library in the Near East. It is an integral part of the university, with whose aid it publishes the biographical quarterly, *Kiryat Sefer*. Another important part of the university's activities is the Hebrew University Press, which publishes the scientific quarterly, *Tarbitz,* as well as a complete series of scientific books, edited with a view to the immediate needs of the students of the university. Among them are the Hebrew translations of Plato, Aristotle, Descartes, Locke, Hume, Leibnitz, Kant, John Stuart Mill, and others. The university serves Israel and the whole Jewish people. Teaching the Talmud and natural sciences, Hebrew literature, alongside Greek and Latin, Jewish and general philosophy, it is bound to bring about a fusion of many civilizations. This work of synthesis is underlined by the fact that both professors and students come from countries all over the world, bringing with them something of every kind of culture. It is significant that close to one-third of the student body are women, who do not restrict themselves to general studies but take a part in the studies of traditional Jewish knowledge. This alone might produce decisive changes in Jewish religious affairs, which to this day have been the monopoly of the men.

Students are accepted at Hebrew University without discrimination as to creed, nationality, or race. On Mount Scopus Moslem and Christian students can study fields which few other universities can offer and under teachers who would rank with the best of the Western world.

Among other institutions of higher learning in Israel mention must be made of the Technion, the Hebrew Institute of Technology in Haifa. Founded in 1909, the institute did not open its doors until 1924. At the beginning its major departments were architecture and civil and industrial engineering. Due to the rapid industrial development of the National Home, additional departments—mechanical and chemical engineering, in particular—had to be added. The faculty of the Technion consists of forty full professors and sixteen instructors. The school's enrollment is over seven hundred with about 5 per cent of the student body doing intensive graduate work. In addition to full-time academic instruction the Technion conducts special evening courses for workers and an extension service for agricultural settlements.

In 1938 the Technion established a Nautical School to train officers and personnel for a Jewish merchant marine. It was a far cry from that year 1419, when Prince Henry the Navigator invited Juda Crescas, a Jew, to become the first director of the newly established nautical observatory at Sagres, Portugal, under the name of Maestro Jacomo de Majorca. For hundreds of years most Jews had completely lost contact with the sea and seafaring. Now the Jewish National Home was reawakening the desire in Jewish boys to make the sea an important part of their lives.

A number of institutions are devoted exclusively to research. The Agricultural Research Station in Rehovoth has already been mentioned.

The Daniel Sieff Institute, also in Rehovoth, with Dr. Weizmann as its honorary director, dedicates itself to research projects for the development of Israel's industry, particularly in the fields of chemistry, physical chemistry, physics, and bacteriology. The late Nobel Prize winner, Fritz Haber, like Dr. Weizmann one of the world's outstanding chemists, helped plan the institute and willed it his famous library. On November 2, 1949, in observance of the Balfour Declaration and the seventy-fifth birthday of Dr. Weizmann the Daniel Sieff Institute celebrated the inauguration of its new physics and physical chemistry building, which bears Weizmann's name, in the presence of eminent scientists and educators from all over the world. Dewey Stone, chairman of the American Committee for the Institute, described the dedication as "the completion of the first unit of a great project on which we embarked five years ago" and, symbolically, Harry Levine, the treasurer of the organization, placed a scroll in the cornerstone of the proposed Institute for Biology and Biochemistry, which will be the next scientific structure to arise in Rehovoth.

Like Israel's school system, the Hebrew press—the most important medium of informing and educating the general public—can stand comparison with any in the world. Although the Jewish population of Israel is at present only about 1,000,000, it nevertheless supports ten Hebrew morning papers, five evening papers and about one hundred periodicals —weeklies, monthlies, and technical journals in all fields. There are two special weeklies for women and a monthly devoted to military problems. There are illustrated magazines and digests of the world press as well as of the world Jewish press.

There were Hebrew periodicals in Palestine long before the Balfour Declaration was issued. As early as 1863, a monthly in the Hebrew language, *Halevanon* (*The Lebanon*), and a weekly, *Havatzelet* (*The Lily*) appeared in Jerusalem. Both publications were promptly suppressed by the Turkish administration. Between 1883 and 1915 Eliezer Ben Yehuda, author of the most comprehensive Hebrew dictionary and an outstanding pioneer in the movement for the revival of Hebrew as a spoken, modern language, published a number of weeklies and monthlies. In 1908 the weekly *Hapoel Hatzair* (*Young Worker*) made its appearance as the official mouthpiece of Israel's Labor party. In 1918 *Haaretz* (*The Land*), the first Hebrew daily in the world, was founded in Egypt. Though considered the party organ of the progressive, liberal wing in general Zionism, it has gained a reputation for political independence and high literary standards. Its authentic news coverage and special sections have brought *Haaretz* great esteem and world-wide circulation.

The largest Hebrew daily is *Davar* (*The Word*) which was founded in 1925 as the organ of Histadruth, the Jewish Federation of Labor. From a four-page paper it grew to sixteen pages with a circulation of about fifty thousand. *Davar* is far from being a house organ of a labor organization. It devotes considerable space to world politics and to Israel's internal situation. It has an excellent literature and arts department; and among its contributors are outstanding figures of contemporary political and literary life in Israel and abroad.

In 1935 *Haboker* (*The Morning*) was founded under the sponsorship of Tel Aviv's present energetic Mayor Rokach. It has the support of the farmers' and the manufacturers' associations and is considered a right-wing Zionist newspaper. *Haboker* has an interesting economics section which was introduced as a special service by its former editor, the Dutch Zionist Fritz Bernstein. The views of religious Judaism are voiced by *Hatzofe* (*The Lookout*), established in 1937 by the Mizrachi. Mapam, the left-wing Labor party, publishes *Al Hamishmar* (*On Guard*). *Herut* (*Freedom*) is the party organ of the former Irgun Zvai Leumi. Together with the Communist *Kol Haam* (*Voice of the People*) it leads the opposition against the present government of Israel.

Most dailies have weekly and monthly supplements. *Davar* publishes a monthly supplement on the cooperative movement, another for women, and a weekly for children. A weekly edition for readers of Hebrew abroad, *D'var Hashevuah* (*Weekly Word*), summarizes events and describes life in the Jewish State. All Hebrew papers devote considerable space to the Arab world. Each maintains at least one desk man who reads the Arabic press and follows events in the Arab countries. As the Israeli reader wants to be informed about Jewish life outside Israel, especially in the United States, every larger Hebrew paper maintains its own correspondents in New York and other Jewish centers. Every newspaper is national in scope. A provincial or local press does not exist, although all papers devote part of their news section to strictly local events.

The party affiliation of a newspaper naturally affects its presentation of the news and creates a specific "angle." While this fact has its negative aspects, it does militate against the exploitation of information for private ends. Party affiliation guarantees a fairly stable circulation. This is perhaps the reason why the Hebrew press refrains from all sensationalism. Absent are the screaming headlines and exciting pictures which form the daily menu of most newspapers in other parts of the world. With the exception of the papers of the extreme parties the Hebrew press is characterized by outstanding self-discipline and by a remarkable awareness of its responsibility toward the community as a whole.

The Jews are known as the people of the book. In addition to the increasing publication of scientific books, printed in the Hebrew language, Israeli publishers produce annually an average of 500 titles in the field of poetry, novels, and stories. Translations (which once formed the most important part of book publishing in Israel) include English, German, Russian, French, Yiddish, Arabic, Persian, and Polish works. Even during the war period from 1939 to 1945, close to 3,200 new titles were introduced by publishing firms in Tel Aviv, Jerusalem, and Haifa. The authors ranged from Galsworthy, Oscar Wilde, Priestley, Mark Twain, and Hemingway to modern Hebrew and Arab writers.

To this day schools, newspapers, and books clearly reflect the distinctive features brought to Israel by the different groups of immigrants. The same influence is apparent in the fine arts field. The excellent Israel Philharmonic Orchestra, which was founded in 1935 by Bronislaw Hubermann and conducted in its first season by Arturo Toscanini, is just beginning to draw on compositions created out of the national landscape.

The Jews in modern times have everywhere evinced an enlightened interest for the theater. Tel Aviv with its rapidly increasing population has three permanent companies, Habimah, Ohel, and the Chambers Theater, operating three separate houses, and a recently constituted Opera Company giving performances in the Habimah building.

Habimah's classics, the *Dibbuk* and the *Golem,* reflecting Jewish mysticism, have their origin in Eastern Europe where Habimah started its career. But to an audience which "has fought seven Arab nations," as the younger Israelis are fond of reminding visitors of their country, *Dibbuk* and *Golem* are museum pieces. They want plays like Mossenson's *In the Wastes of the Negev,* Habimah's first production since its return from America. They want a reflection of their young vitality and patriotism.

Typical of the younger generation's taste is Bar Josef's *Guardians of the Wall,* performed by Ohel, the workers' theater, and Salacrou's *Nights of Wrath,* about the struggle between French collaborationists and the Maquis, a play directed by the young American Peter Frye in the Chambers Theater. This Chambers Theater, of which almost all the actors are beginners, also recently produced a native work, *He Went to the Fields,* following the progress of a boy from life in a Kibutz to death in the Arab-Jewish war.

The youthful spirit is all-pervasive, even in opera performances, which belong to the most popular forms of mass entertainment in the new state. In 1949 the Hebrew National Opera Company, supported, like the theaters and the Philharmonic Orchestra, by the American

Fund for Israel Institutions, presented Rossini's "Barber of Seville," Offenbach's "Tales of Hoffmann," and Massenet's "Manon."

Harold Clurman, the American stage director and critic who directed *Montserrat*, by Robles, in Israel, upon his return to the United States made this comment on Israel's theaters: "Considering the inadequacies of the theater everywhere in the upset world today, what is being done in this new frontier country is amazingly good."

Learning, teaching, and writing have been the most striking fundamentals of Jewish life throughout the ages. Wherever the Jews wandered, the first institution they established was a house of learning, the synagogue (or school). Scores of moving accounts could be told of Jews who even in the concentration camps of Hitler's Europe provided their youngsters with education, both Jewish and general, in the hope that they might survive and remember their parents by their teachings.

When Rome had destroyed the Second Jewish Commonwealth, it contemptuously granted the Jews a little school in Palestine, Yabneh. From the Yabneh Academy, where brave students gathered about their teacher, Ben Zakkai, the voice of the Torah was heard in the dispersion. It found an echo in the Jewish Bible and Talmud schools of eastern Europe, in the classics of Ahad Haam and Bialik, in the Hebrew University on Mount Scopus, the modern Hebrew press, and the modern Hebrew arts. It was never subdued.

Chapter Twelve: ARABS IN ISRAEL

ARAB REFUGEE PROBLEM · ARAB ECONOMY · ARAB POLITICAL LIFE · ARAB FIFTH COLUMN · OTHER MINORITIES

A by-product of the war which the Arab States forced on the Jews when they invaded Palestine in the spring of 1948 is the Arab refugee problem.

It is difficult to determine the exact number of these refugees. In raising the question before the Security Council of the United Nations on August 2, 1948, Sir Alexander Cadogan maintained that there are "certainly not less than 250,000 Arab refugees from Palestine." A few days later Israeli Foreign Minister Moshe Sharett made an estimate of 300,000. At the end of August the Secretary General of the League of Arab States put the number at 582,248. He gave the following breakdown of this figure:

Syria	80,000
Iraq	23,000
Trans-Jordan	72,551
Eastern Palestine	100,000
Egyptian-occupied territory	236,697
Lebanon	70,000
	582,248

On October 18, 1948, Dr. Ralph J. Bunche, the Acting Mediator, in his Progress Report to the United Nations Security Council mentioned that the number of Arab refugees had reached 472,000. At the same time Monsignor George Hakim, the Catholic Archbishop of Galilee, asserted that there were 600,000 Arab refugees seeking aid in the various neighboring Arab states and in the Arab parts of Palestine.

The problem of refugees, regardless of nationality, creed, color, is without doubt first of all a humanitarian concern. But the question of the Arab refugees is also an important political issue. It was made such an issue by the League of Arab States, which demanded the return of the refugees as "an indispensable condition for eventual acceptance of a truce and further negotiations." The political character of the Arab refugee problem was underscored by the British representatives in the United Nations and in unofficial dispatches of the United States State Department to the government of Israel.

In December, 1948, at the annual convention of the American Political Science Association in Chicago, some of my colleagues who had just returned from the UNESCO meetings in Beirut, Lebanon declared that the Jews were solving their own refugee problem by the simple expedient of creating an Arab refugee problem. When I asked them whether they had attempted to secure the Israeli point of view on this matter and whether they had been to Israel at all, their answer was no. Their view was not so extreme as that of the British Government, which wished to stop IRO funds from being used to transport Jews from Europe to Israel. But at least one of the professors expressed the idea that the Jewish community in the United States should be asked to raise substantial funds for aid to Arab refugees. He had completely accepted the Arab accusation that the Jews had thrown the Palestine Arabs out of their villages and towns in order to fill them with Jewish refugees.

This version is shamefully untrue.

When the Arab war against the Jewish community of Palestine began before the end of the British Mandate, the ex-Mufti of Jerusalem from his headquarters in Cairo and his cousin Jamal Husseini in Jerusalem gave express orders to the Arabs in the Jewish territory of Palestine to abandon their villages and towns and carry out a mass exodus. Apparently the Palestine Arab Higher Committee reckoned that their diplomatic game would be up if the Arabs were allowed to settle down quietly in the Jewish-controlled parts of the country. Apparently the ex-Mufti and his henchmen hoped that the flood of Arab refugees would excite public fervor in the Arab countries and force their undecided governments to invade Palestine openly after May 14, 1948. Moreover, world public opinion would be turned against the Jews; and in a short time the Arab refugees would be allowed to come back at the heels of the victorious Arab armies.

An illustration of this Arab strategy is offered by the consistently outspoken anti-Zionist London *Economist*. Speaking of the Arab flight from

Haifa after the conquest of this port city by the Jewish forces, the *Economist* wrote on October 2, 1948:

> During the subsequent days, the Jewish authorities urged all Arabs to remain in Haifa and guaranteed their protection and security. Various factors influenced the Arabs' decision to seek safety in flight. Far the most potent of these factors was the announcement made over the air by the Arab Higher Committee urging all Arabs in Haifa to quit. The reason given was that upon the final withdrawal of the British the combined armies of the Arab states would invade Palestine and drive the Jews into the sea. It was clearly intimated that those who remained in Haifa and accepted Jewish protection would be regarded as renegades.

In those days it apparently did not occur to the Arab leaders that the Jews could defeat the combined regular forces of the Arab League. War is a cruel and uncertain game. The trials of Nuremberg and Tokyo have established as international law that those who start aggressive war must bear the guilt for the suffering which it causes. In the Palestine war Arab responsibility is beyond doubt. If the Arab States had not taken up arms to defeat the decision of the United Nations General Assembly of November 29, 1947, in an effort to "drive the Jews into the sea," if the Arab leaders had not demanded the evacuation of the Palestine Arabs in the pursuit of their own aggressive aims, there would have been no Arab refugee problem. These facts must be known in order to understand the Arab refugee problem.

On August 1, 1948, the Israeli government declared that the Arab mass flight "is a direct effect of Arab aggression from outside. . . . But for the intervention of the Arab states there would have been an overwhelming measure of local Arab acquiescence in the establishment of the State of Israel, and by now peace and reasonable prosperity would have reigned throughout its territory, to the enjoyment of Jews and Arabs alike. . . . The Arab governments and the Great Power which espoused their cause cannot have it both ways: do everything they can to undermine and destroy the State of Israel, and then, having failed, require the State of Israel to take over the liability for the results of their own reckless action."

It further declared that the Arab refugee question could be solved only when the Arab States were ready to conclude a peace treaty with Israel. In the final settlement Israel's counterclaim with respect to the destruction of Jewish life and property would also have to be taken into account.

In a letter to Secretary-General Trygve Lie dated August 17, the representative of the United States in the Security Council expressed the concern of the United States government over the problem of the Arab refugees "not only from a humanitarian point of view . . . but also because of the effect of this problem on the prospects of a peaceful adjustment of the future situation in Palestine."

The government of Israel did not dispute the right of some of the refugees to return. But it warned that their return would create an acute security problem and affect the balance of military advantage which the truce was supposed to maintain. This idea was contained in a statement made by Israel's representative in the United Nations, Major Aubrey S. Eban, before the Security Council on August 18. Pointing out that the League of Arab States had publicly declared its intention to renew the war, he added: "It is obvious, therefore, that we are not yet in a state of armistice . . . in those circumstances . . . any far-reaching measure of repatriation must be weighed in terms of military advantage."

In the United States a number of welfare, educational, and oil business agencies formed the Central Committee for Arab Relief. The Red Cross gave considerable aid. The United Nations set up a Central Relief Office in the Lebanon and IRO advanced funds to the United Nations' relief program.

In this connection I should like to raise an issue which to my knowledge was never raised during all the discussions of the plight of the Arab refugees. Why is it that the League of Arab States has never been asked by the United Nations to make effective arrangements for the housing and provisioning of the Arab refugees in the various Arab countries? The Arab kings are reputedly very wealthy individuals. Their luxury is proverbial. Americans who, like this writer, have been able to observe the splendor of the Egyptian court and the display of munificence on the part of Arab diplomatic missions abroad ought to be acutely puzzled by the fact that the Arab States seek foreign relief for the refugees of their own making. Moreover, as an American taxpayer, interested in the administration of the Marshall Plan, it is my opinion that the British Foreign Office which has allotted millions of dollars to Trans-Jordan and other Arab countries should be asked to predicate such loans on the willingness of the Arab States to help their own refugees with food and medical care before further converting these loans into instruments of warfare.

The question of Arab refugees, spotlighted by the Arab diplomatic missions and their friends in the Western world, has dimmed by contrast the efforts of the Israeli government to create an atmosphere in Israel which will allow Arabs and Jews to live together in harmony.

From the beginning of the building of the Jewish homeland, the Jews felt and said that if the two peoples were to live together there had to be complete equality between them. But for a long time ancient traditions and customs, stagnation in the social, economic, and political spheres of Arab life militated against a genuine equality of Arabs and Jews.

When I first came to Palestine in 1934, an Arab friend with whom I had spent several years of study at European universities invited me to stay at his home in the Wadi Nisnas, the Arab quarter of Haifa. Thanks to him and his relatives in other parts of Palestine I had a good opportunity to observe Arab life.

The Arab village is largely patriarchal. The father or, as was the case in my friend's family, the eldest son rules the family. The family is part of the *hamulah,* the clan. Its members are related through a common paternal ancestor. The average clan is composed of eighteen families with about one hundred and twenty persons. Each village has from three to five clans. As the clans often feud among themselves, they seek alliances with clans in neighboring villages and towns for their protection. This leads to the formation of regional clan associations which in turn form the basis of the political organization of the Arabs. The position of the individual depends on his standing in the clan and the clan's standing within the clan association. If the prestige of the clan is high, his chances for economic well-being are high. If he incurs the disfavor of the clan chief, however, he is degraded both socially and economically. The shepherds in the Arab communities, lowest in the scale of Arab workers, are often men who have incurred the displeasure of their clan chief. If the clan chief expels a family, its members lose all village protection, and their property can be rightfully seized by other families in the village.

The vast majority of the Palestine Arabs are fellahin (small peasants, farm tenants, and agricultural laborers). Harking back to the Ottoman land code, a mixture of older tenures and elements of Moslem religious law, ownership of land ranges from freehold to common property by the entire village. The commonly owned land is divided for cultivation every two or three years. The privately owned land is cultivated by the owner or, in the case of absentee landowners, by a tenant. Because of the family and clan relationships holdings are usually parceled into small strips of land located in different parts of the village. This fragmentation is detrimental to all efficiency and actually restricts the owner's freedom in the use of his soil. The result of this system has been low productivity. In 1934 the production of a male Arab agricultural worker in Palestine was estimated to be 148 international units, compared to 661 in the United States and 579 in Holland. It was higher, however, than that of his Arab neighbors in Syria, Lebanon, and Egypt, which ranged from 90 to 98 international units.*

The houses of the typical Arab village consist of small huts without windows or ventilation. Clay and straw resting on a matrix of twigs form the roof. One end of the house serves as a barn. The other end is the home of the fellah and his family. The whole family sleeps on straw mats in the same room. Cattle dung smoking on a primitive oven warms the house. Food consists of bread, olives, and cheese.

Villagers marry young. They show a tendency to select their wives from the same village, if not from the same clan. Many women marry at the age of fifteen and earlier. The period of fertility is therefore long, and the birth rate is high. But so is the death rate.

One of the greatest obstacles to the progress of the Arab masses is their illiteracy. Most Moslem Arabs do not consider it necessary to send girls to school. Few Arab boys get beyond the fifth grade. In 1931 over 80 per cent of the Palestine Arabs were unable to read and write. In this respect a pronounced difference could be noted between Moslem and Christian Arabs. While over 90 per cent of the children of Christian Arabs attended school, the figure for the Moslem Arabs was only 25 per cent. Also in contrast to the Moslems, Christian Arabs educated their boys and girls on an equal basis. Secondary education among the Palestine Arabs has been the exclusive monopoly of the upper classes. Teachers in the secondary schools were usually graduates of the American University in Beirut. The mandatory government, which made a very noteworthy effort to improve the educational standards of the Palestine Arabs, used to send a number of students on scholarships to Egypt and the United Kingdom.

At the end of World War I approximately a half-million Arabs lived in Palestine. Like most of the Middle Eastern peoples they eked out a meager existence within the framework of a primitive agriculture, supplemented by small handicrafts and a limited trade. The most advanced branch of the Arab economy at that time was citriculture. The Palestine Arabs began to plant citrus trees during the second half of the nineteenth century, and by 1918 citriculture had developed into a substantial industry. Some Arabs, particularly Christian Arabs, tried to improve their lot by emigrating to France and the United States. In 1913 Arab emigrants from the Jerusalem district alone numbered over 2,000.

After Jewish immigration began to improve the standard of living among the Arabs, Arab emigration from Palestine stopped completely.

* The international unit equals the average amount of goods which one dollar could purchase in the United States over the period 1925–1934.

Fellahin sold part of their land to the Jewish National Fund or private Jewish settlers to obtain the necessary capital to develop the land which they retained. Jewish immigration provided the Arab peasant with large urban markets where he received high prices for his produce. It also provided the mandatory government with the means to remit the fellah's taxes and to offer him loans and seeds free of charge. As the income of 1 dunam of irrigated land equals the income of 5 dunam of unirrigated land, the Arab who sold one-third or even half of his land holdings to Jews could improve his living standard considerably. Even during the riots of 1936 to 1939 and after the issuance of the 1939 White Paper Arabs were anxious to effect some land sales.

Beyond the natural interaction of Jewish and Arab economic life there was a great deal of ordinary human cooperation. During my stays in Palestine in 1934, 1936, 1938, and again after World War II, I saw Arab villagers frequently exchange friendly visits with their Jewish neighbors. The fascist gangs of the Arab Higher Committee had to resort to murder of hundreds of Arab villagers before they could—temporarily—impose their will on the Arab countryside.

The existing good will assumed concrete shape when the Histadruth, the Jewish Federation of Labor, took the initiative in sponsoring the formation of Arab trade unions. This move was dictated largely by reasons of self-preservation. The Jewish labor leaders had come to realize that many Jewish entrepreneurs, particularly in the field of agriculture, preferred to employ cheap Arab labor. The years 1929 to 1936 had already brought a considerable influx of Arab laborers from Syria and from Trans-Jordan, where real wages were much lower than in Palestine.

All hopes for a Jewish state would have been frustrated if Palestine had been built by Jewish capital and predominantly Arab labor. For not only would the Jews have remained a hopeless minority in their National Home, but the future of the Yishuv would have been no more secure than that of any Jewish community outside of Palestine.

National and economic needs, therefore, caused the efforts of the Histadruth to organize Arab labor. This was no easy task. To this day the number of Arab urban workers in Palestine is rather small. Many are only seasonal workers who cultivate their fields most of the year and are, therefore, difficult to organize. Moreover, the general backwardness of the Arab masses, their subservience to the will of the effendi, the wealthy clan chiefs, militates against the very idea of a trade-union organization. Only in one case was a consistent effort made to organize Arabs and Jews in the same union. This was the Union of Railway, Postal, and Telegraph Workers. It was strong enough to survive the riots of

1936 to 1939 and World War II. Arab unions were formed in a few places and mainly maintained by the Histadruth. The British administration frowned upon mixed Arab-Jewish unions. In one way or another it let the Arabs know that they would fare better if they dropped all association with their Jewish fellow workers. But the main obstacle to cooperation was the intransigence of the political leaders of the Arabs and their unwillingness to work with the Jews, even in nonpolitical matters.

Comparatively slow as Arab economic progress has been, the Arabs in Palestine have made some strides forward during the last few years. When I returned to Palestine in 1946 I observed that Arab agriculture had become less primitive and more diversified. While many Arab workers were still village-bound, a large number had found permanent employment in urban industries. There were new Arab building companies, cement, soap, and textile factories, and several transportation concerns. Under the influence of the Jewish cooperative movement, Arab citrus and tobacco growers had formed cooperative societies.

The changes were particularly noticeable in regions close to Jewish agricultural settlements and cities. Entirely new methods of cultivation had been developed. In many instances the tractor had replaced the wooden plow. Better breeds of cattle and poultry were being raised. In the wake of Jewish building activity, the Arabs had developed industries which supplied necessary building materials. Arab social and economic progress is well described in *Haaravim B'Eretz Israel* (The Arabs in the Land of Israel) by J. Waschitz. The following quotation from this book characterizes the process of Arab urbanization:

> The unskilled workers originate mainly in the village. They come to the town to escape hunger. They are ready to work at any wage. At first they do not make any demands. But uniting with skilled workers, seeing the progress in the cities, they are compelled to adjust themselves to the new forms of living. The woman does not want to run around barefoot and work outside the home. She brings her sick child to the doctor, and he prescribes new methods of care, the use of soap, feeding the child bananas, eggs, milk and sugar. On the other hand, the husband goes to the coffee house, smokes cigarettes and dresses in European clothes. . . . The character of the dwelling changes, mainly in the large cities. The rent has risen, one must pay for utilities; one starts to use a bathroom. . . .

There is a growing demand among the Arab fellahin and industrial workers for shorter working hours and better wages. In 1934 the workday of the fellah and Arab industrial worker was sixteen to eighteen hours. In 1946 close to half of Palestine's Arab workers had an eight-hour workday, and their wages were not far below the wages of the Jewish workers.

The social and occupational structure of the Palestine Arabs is expressed in Arab political life. The Arabs have not yet developed truly democratic political institutions in the accepted sense of the word. In 1946 the Mandatory administration in "A Survey of Palestine" described the political activity of the Arabs as follows:

> The Palestine Arab political parties which were formed after the British occupation are not similar to the generally accepted conception of such parties in the Western democracies. The differences among their leaders tend to be personal rather than on matters of principle, and party funds are obtained by *ad hoc* collections rather than by the regular dues and subscriptions paid by party supporters. Party organization is loose and a permanent secretariat is usually absent. In general, too, the influence of each party is local and confined to the localities where the family influence of the party leaders is strongest. But, although the history of Arab political parties in Palestine is so largely a history of personal relationships and rivalries, in the absence of any other form of political expression they do represent the feeling of the Arab masses on the broader issues, and particularly on the Jewish question.

In 1920 the spokesmen of the Arab upper classes under the leadership of Muza Kazim Pasha, a member of the influential Husseini clan, organized an Arab Congress in Palestine. It concerned itself mainly with protests against the British Mandate and the Jewish National Home. The Arab fellahin were completely indifferent to the affairs of this Congress. With the death of its founder, Muza Kazim Pasha, in 1934, the whole structure collapsed. After 1934 four political parties made their appearance in the Arab sector of Palestine: the Palestine Arab party, which was largely identical with the Husseini clan; the more moderate National Defense party under the leadership of another clan chief, Ragheb Nashashibi; the Arab Reform party, led by the former mayor of Jerusalem, Dr. Hussein Fakhri Khalidi; and the Istiqlal, founded by Arab intellectuals who had studied in Western universities and who were dissatisfied with the personal rivalries among the leaders of the three other parties.

In 1936 all these Arab parties formed the Arab Higher Committee under the chairmanship of Haj Amin el Husseini, then Grand Mufti of Jerusalem. After the assassination of a number of Englishmen and hundreds of Arabs who were opposed to the Arab Higher Committee, the Palestine administration, in September, 1937, removed the Mufti from his office as head of the Supreme Moslem Council and proscribed the Arab Higher Committee. The Mufti went to the Lebanon, and his cousin, Jamal Husseini, spokesman of the Palestine Arabs during the United Nations deliberations, went to Syria. Even before the official dissolution of the Arab Higher Committee the internal struggle between the Husseini and the Nashashibi had led to the withdrawal of the Nashashibi clan.

After World War II Arab political life was shaped by Jamal Husseini's return to power. The ex-Mufti did not dare to return to Palestine. He probably feared that he would be killed by the Jews or by the relatives of Ragheb Nashashibi, who had been assassinated in Iraq by members of the Husseini clique. To secure representation of the Palestine Arabs in the newly formed League of Arab States, it was first agreed that Musa al Alami, a "nonparty man" who was connected by marriage with the Husseini clan, should serve as the representative of the former Arab Higher Committee. Since his activities aroused the jealousy of the Nashashibi and the other Arab groups, the League of Arab States virtually imposed a new Arab Higher Committee on the Palestine Arabs with Jamal Husseini as Deputy Chairman. The chairman's place was kept open for the ex-Mufti of Jerusalem.

The war which the Arab States had imposed on Israel in 1948, combined with the flight of the large majority of the Moslem Arabs, made it both impossible and unnecessary to put any large-scale Arab program into operation. At present there are about 160,000 Arabs in Israel. Close to half of this Arab population are Christians, the majority of whom live in and near Nazareth. From the beginning of the Arab-Jewish war the Christian Arabs had mixed feelings as to their own stand. As Arabs they probably shared in the swelling nationalism of the Moslem Arabs. As Christians who had suffered frequent persecution at the hands of the Moslem Arabs, they probably were not too unhappy over the Jewish victories. It is significant that a great part of their number refused to leave the State of Israel when the Arab Higher Command ordered the Arabs out.

A special Ministry of Minorities had been set up by the government of Israel to deal with the Arabs and other minorities. It organized an Arab police force. Among its duties was the guarding of abandoned Arab property in Israeli territory. The ministry reopened a number of Arab-owned factories. The former Arab printing concern, Falastin, publishes an Arab edition of the *Official Gazette,* the government organ of Israel. In September, 1948, a new Arab daily, *al-Yom* (The Day), began publication. Arab labor exchanges and workers' clubs place Arab fellahin and industrial workers in private industries and public enterprises. Arabs are on a par with Jewish workers as to job rights and wages. They receive the same medical care as Jews. Their food rations are of the same quantity and quality. The Department for Education and Culture has recently completed a survey of Arab educational needs. Most Arab schools have been reopened, and new ones have been set up where none existed previously. Arab school children receive free lunches.

Arabs participated freely in the elections to the Knesseth, Israel's Parliament. For the first time in the history of the Arab world the Arab women went to the polls. Three Arabs sit in the Assembly; and an Arab interpreter translates all Hebrew speeches into Arabic and all Arab speeches into Hebrew, with headphones available for the deputies just as at Lake Success. Arabs have their representation in the local councils and the public services. They have the fullest freedom of religious worship.

These facts are not lost upon the Arabs of neighboring countries and especially the Arab refugees from Palestine. But under present circumstances no Israeli government, mindful of the country's security, can consent to the mass immigration of persons who are bound to constitute an explosive fifth column.

Some of the Moslem leaders themselves do not at all conceal their plan to this effect. Thus the Lebanese weekly, *as-Seyad,* on February 17, 1949, frankly stated in a leading article:

> Our first urgent request must be the return of the refugees. We are unable to return them honorably. Let us therefore try to make them our fifth column in the struggle yet before us. Once and for all let us put the facts before Israel and say: "We request the return of the refugees. What do you want for it? . . ." Up to now they argued that there was a state of war between us and one could not ask them to accept soldiers, enemies, into their midst. But at present, if we shall appear in the disguise of peace-seekers, they will have no argument. After we shall have solved this problem and decided on the boundaries of Israel—at the same time doing our best to make them as narrow as possible—we shall turn to England, America, and other countries and shall resolve what kind of agreements we should conclude with them and what loans we should accept from them so as to gain strength, rise and take the safe and only path that leads to the destruction of Israel.

On May 19, 1949, Azmi Nashashibi, the manager of the Ramallah radio station, in his English broadcast said:

> Thousands of boys are receiving military training and the girls are learning first aid. [He asked for the return of all the refugees to their homes, and added] We have been attacked, murdered, robbed, ruined—but we shall carry our burdens and when the time comes, we shall show what material we are made of. We, the Arabs of Palestine, shall neither forget nor forgive.

In June, 1949, the Amman paper *an-Nahda* stated that a military training center for Palestine Arabs had been established at Beit Iba, a village near Nablus, and on July 21, 1949, Albion Ross cabled from Beirut to *The New York Times* that, according to a report from Amman, the previously announced course of military training for all able-bodied men between eighteen and forty years old had been initiated in the Jordan-occupied part of Palestine. In the light of these facts and trends, the return of the great mass of Palestine Arabs before the conclusion of binding peace treaties is obviously inconceivable.

There are other minorities in Israel. There are the Druze who practice a variant of Islam, dating from the end of the tenth century. Though they speak Arabic, they do not intermarry with the Arabs and maintain their existence as a separate community. Up to the establishment of the State of Israel it was impossible for the 15,000 Druze of Palestine to break away from Arab domination. But they made their crucial decision to ally themselves with the Jews when Israel's chances of survival were still uncertain. None of them fled from the country, and many of their younger men joined the Israeli army. Other minorities followed their example. The Circassians of Palestine, living in Galilee, like the Druze, contributed military units of their own to Haganah. They are descendants of a Caucasian Moslem tribe which immigrated to Palestine at the end of the nineteenth century. Traditionally warlike, they served in large numbers in the Palestine police under the British Mandate. When the Arab States began their invasion, the Arab Higher Committee hoped that the Circassians would turn their arms against the Jews. But the Elders of the Circassian communities approached the Jewish authorities in Tel Aviv and said: "Our people have decided to assist David against Goliath."

III

ISRAEL IN WORLD AFFAIRS

Chapter Thirteen: THE NEW STATE AND THE MIDDLE EAST *

ARAB NATIONALISM, ISLAM, AND THE JEWS · ARMISTICE PACTS WITH EGYPT, LEBANON, TRANS-JORDAN, AND SYRIA · HOPE FOR THE NON-MOSLEM MINORITIES

That Arab-Jewish harmony is a Jewish interest may be considered a self-evident truth. For the most wholehearted support of Israel in Europe and America can never fully compensate for the absence of friendly relations with the predominantly Arab world in which Israel must live. This fact was recognized by all responsible elements in the modern Zionist movement since the days of the Balfour Declaration. As long as Arab nationalism, however, refused to compromise with its Jewish counterpart, it was, at least temporarily, a "lost cause."

Historically, the nationalism of the Arabs springs from two major sources, both of which developed in the outgoing nineteenth century. One source was the British-inspired revolt in the Arabian peninsula which found an echo in the dynastic ambitions of the Hashimite family ruling the Holy City of Mecca. The other source of Arab nationalism, with centers in Syria and in the Lebanon, bore the stamp of the French Revolution and was cultivated by France. One emphasized a revival of Islam and of the glorious era of the caliphate; the other was secular and liberal.

After World War I the two movements coalesced for a fleeting moment when Faisal left his native Hejaz, led his horsemen to Damascus, and established himself as King of Greater Syria under the guidance

* At the beginning of World War II, the British forces based on Egypt were called the "Middle East" Command. Since then it has become the practice to use the term "Middle East" to cover the Arabian peninsula and the countries of the former Ottoman Empire.

of Britain's empire builder, T. E. Lawrence. But by 1920 Faisal was forced to surrender the Levant States to the French. Through the British he subsequently was offered the throne of Iraq, while Abdullah, his brother, was made regent of Trans-Jordan, also under British auspices.

A few years later, in 1925, their father, Husein ibn-Ali, Sherif of Mecca and King of Hejaz, was deposed by Abdul-Aziz ibn-Saud, who started his career as the chieftain of a humble and obscure tribe in the Nejd and who, also with British political and financial help, has become the leading potentate in the Arabian peninsula. Since 1925 there has been bitter hatred between the ruler of Saudi Arabia and the Hashimite rulers of Iraq and Trans-Jordan. The partition of the Arab world, initiated by the rival imperialisms of France and Britain, was thus widened by an inter-Arab conflict.

After World War I the more liberal Arab nationalists in the Fertile Crescent and in Egypt hoped that the attainment of "self-determination" would release sufficient progressive forces in the Arab countries to sweep away their social and economic disabilities. But now, having achieved official independence, Arab nationalism became more and more a tool in the hands of the propertied effendi, who, to divert popular attention from an oppressive semifeudal social order, encourage xenophobia, in particular anti-Zionism.

For years the existence of the unsolved Palestine problem has aided this class in perpetuating reaction throughout the Arab world. It ensured the dominance of men like Haj Amin el Husseini, the ex-Mufti of Jerusalem. It enabled Arab politicians to cover the cracks in the façade of Arab unity, and it served to incite Moslem fanaticism to oppose any constructive economic measures.

It would be a mistake to assume that there are no Arabs who advocate improved health services, free and better education, adequate water supplies, and other badly needed reforms. But it must be remembered that some 75 per cent of the male and 90 per cent of the female population of the Arab countries are illiterate. The utter lack of an enlightened public opinion permits a coterie of political careerists and feudal landowners to push the progressive elements against the wall, thus preserving the antisocial *status quo*.

In this respect the Western powers, Britain first and foremost, have their share of guilt. For years the British civilian and military services in the Middle East have catered to the Bourbons in Arab society and increased their anti-Zionist intransigence. As a result, the younger generation, rebelling against the feudal magnates and the inefficient administrations in the Arab States, began to look to Moscow rather than to the West for guidance. The social democracy of the Western world which might have appealed to those who desire a "New Deal" for the Middle East is obscured for them by the conscious identification of the Western diplomatic services with the most reactionary cliques in Arab life. Inspired by Moscow's agents who quite naturally hoped to take advantage of a potentially explosive atmosphere, not a few of the younger Arabs came to decry Zionism as the Trojan horse of Anglo-American "imperialism," while the remainder of the Arabs saw in Zionist Jews foreign and dangerous iconoclasts.

It was against this background that Jewish Palestine had to find a *modus vivendi* with the Arab world. Animated by a great deal of unjustified optimism but also genuine sincerity, one school of thought, the *Ihud* (Unity) hoped that the formula of binationalism would suffice to draw Arabs and Jews into a common political orbit and into a mood of acquiescence to each other's central national objectives. Its spokesmen, particularly the late Chancellor of Hebrew University, Dr. Judah Magnes, claimed that from time immemorial Jews and Moslems had lived side by side in amity. They reminded their fellow Jews of the famous "Golden Age," those two hundred years of peace and creative development for the Jewish community of Spain following the Arab conquest of that country in the Middle Ages. They were convinced that a Jewish-Arab agreement was largely a matter of subjective attitude; and, consequently, they took their main concern to be the persuasion of both Arabs and Jews into an acceptance of a moderate cultural Zionism with cautiously limited political objectives.

During the Middle Ages the Moslem world compared favorably indeed with the Christian society of Europe in its treatment of the Jews. Especially the Jews in the Spanish outposts of the Moslem Empire enjoyed the rare opportunity of participating freely in all civic affairs and of living their own cultural life to the full. Under Abd-er-Rahman III, who ascended to the throne of Spain in 929, a Jew, Hasdai ibn-Shaprut, was the foreign minister of the Spanish realm. It was during the "Golden Age" that Solomon ibn-Gabirol wrote his famous *Fons Vitae*, that Judah ha-Levi, the great troubadour of the Jewish people, and Maimonides, the synthesizer of Jewish with Greek thought, enriched the spiritual treasures of humanity. But it would be a misinterpretation of history to suppose that Moslem-Jewish relations were always amicable.

It must be realized that orthodox Islam was and still is fundamentally intolerant toward all nonbelievers, Jews and Christians alike. At the earliest stage of his ministry, Mohammed probably did not regard himself as the originator of a new religion but rather as one who came to warn his fellow Arabs to give up their polytheistic idolatry and to turn either to Judaism or to Christianity. When after the Hegira, his flight from Mecca to Medina, Mohammed began to realize that the Jews would not honor him as *rasul Allah,* an apostle of God, he resorted to active persecution of the Jewish tribes in the Arabian peninsula. Later on, when the initial impetus of fanaticism, in particular the duty of jihad, the holy war against nonbelievers, had run its due course, the followers of the Koran imposed on their non-Islamic subjects, both Jews and Christians, a code of observance which bore close resemblance to the repugnant treatment of the Jews by the medieval Christian world. The humiliating Badge of Shame was a Moslem and not a Christian innovation; and the thought cannot be suppressed that the "Golden Age" of Spanish Jewry under the pallid light of the Crescent was due to the precarious position of Moslem rule on a predominantly Christian European continent rather than to any genuine sense of justice and tolerance.

Although the Moslem world has known relatively little of the infamous blood libel, the charge of ritual murder, directed against the Jews of Christian Europe, it has known massacres of Jews for other "religious" reasons. To this day the Jews of Morocco in their synagogue services mourn the slaughter of the most prominent members of their community who during the accession of Muley Yazid to the throne in 1789 were faced with the alternative of conversion to Islam or the martyr's death for Judaism. To this day the Jews of Yemen are officially degraded as a penalty for the refusal of their ancestors of thirteen hundred years ago to accept the Prophet of Islam as Israel's Messiah. Fundamentally, Arab-Jewish relations throughout the centuries were based on the same principle as the relations between Christians and Jews. Wherever the Jews formed a small and defenseless minority, they were likely to become the scapegoat of the majority in times of political, economic, and psychological upheaval.

The vast majority of Zionists, therefore, argued that a solid agreement between Arabs and Jews could only follow the creation of a Jewish state in which the Jews would form the majority of the population. They admitted that in a truly just world Dr. Magnes's attempt to secure Arab consent to Jewish aspirations might have been the proper approach. In the world of reality, however, prudence compelled them to consolidate the Jewish position in Palestine to such a degree that the surrounding Arab world would perforce abandon its intransigent attitude toward Zionism.

In this connection the historians of our time will be interested in a conversation between Aubrey S. Eban, the representative of the Israeli government in the United Nations, and Azzam Pasha, the secretary of the League of Arab States, as reported by Eban in the September, 1948 issue of *Commentary:*

In September 1947 [Eban writes] when I was attempting (with complete failure) to persuade Azzam Pasha of the virtues of prior consent, he swept all argument aside with his doctrine of historic fatalism. "The Jews will have no state unless they obtain and hold it. By the logic of our history we shall fight it. Unless you can first resist the entire Arab world you cannot even be entitled to discuss agreement. We once had Spain and Persia. If anyone had come beforehand and asked us to surrender Spain or Persia he would have received the same negative response as I now give you."

If the League of Arab States has failed to wipe the Jewish National Home off the map, if today an Arab-Jewish accord is on the horizon, the credit belongs not to the leaders of the Arab world but to those Jews who, rather than wait for Arab consent, established their commonwealth in a status of political, economic, and military equality with the surrounding Arab countries.

The first move to end the Arab-Jewish struggle in Palestine was made by the Egyptian government. On January 6, 1949, it notified the Acting Mediator, Dr. Ralph J. Bunche, that it was ready to discuss an armistice with Israel. Egypt had suffered defeat in the Negev. The only Arab army that could have come to the assistance of its forces was the Trans-Jordan Legion. But Abdullah preferred to keep at a safe distance and to let Egypt lose the battle. Knowing that emissaries of the Hashimite King had already put out feelers for possible peace negotiations with Israel, Egypt jumped ahead and declared herself willing to come to terms with the Jewish State.

On February 24, after protracted negotiations, Dr. Walter Eytan for Israel and Colonel Seif ed Din for Egypt signed the armistice agreement. Under the settlement Israel received more than 700 square miles of the Negev area which had been seized by the Egyptian forces in May, 1948. Egypt retained a coastal strip of about 135 square miles from its border to Gaza. Israel retained its military possession of Beersheba. The final disposition of that city, as well as the disposition of the Israeli-held eastern Negev southward to the Red Sea and of Arab-occupied east-central Palestine, was not considered to be within the scope of the armistice.

Although the pact was largely concerned with military matters, it became an important milestone toward a political solution of the conflict. For it marked the first definite Arab acceptance of the fact that Israel is an established state. The Acting Mediator did not exaggerate the significance of the armistice when he declared at the signing ceremony that it was "an epochal event in the history of Palestine and in the relations between Israel and the Arab States."

It was also a demonstration of the skill, the wisdom, and the impartiality of Dr. Bunche, who had the task of carrying out the resolution of the Security Council of the United Nations of November 16, 1948. That resolution summoned the parties to enter into armistice negotiations which would end the war without prejudice to a final political solution. It was a difficult task, indeed, to induce the Arab States to consent to such an arrangement, since negotiations with Israel naturally implied a tacit recognition of the existence of a Jewish state—the very thing against which most of the Arab leaders had been fighting. Dr. Bunche had to send his roving ambassadors repeatedly into the Arab capitals before he could hope to secure an official reply. He had to discuss procedures and proposals with each delegation separately before any agreement could be reached in common. At the same time he had not only to maintain close contact with a vast network of United Nations observers and traveling delegates entrusted with the enforcement of the truce but also to preserve his liaison with United Nations headquarters at Lake Success. Nominally, he was only the "Acting" Mediator. Nevertheless, the Rhodes negotiations will forever be linked with the name of the American Negro professor who, imbued with a deep sense of humanity, was ideally suited for the job of peacemaker.

Soon after the Israeli-Egyptian armistice negotiations had begun, Dr. Bunche asked the Lebanese government whether it would accept an invitation to enter likewise into armistice discussions.

The Republic of Lebanon is the most westernized of the Arab States. Its population, close to 1,200,000, represents a mosaic of numerous religious sects and faiths precariously balanced between Moslems and Christians. Most of the Christians, particularly the more than 300,000 Maronites, were opposed to the war with Israel. Unlike their fellow Arabs of the Moslem persuasion, they had no interest in acquiring territory in Palestine. For they realized that an increase in the number of Moslems might eliminate the Christian character of Lebanon.

Characteristic of their attitude is the letter which the Archbishop of Beirut, Ignatius Mourabak, sent on August 5, 1947, to Judge Sandstrom, Chairman of UNSCOP:

> It is an incontestable historical fact [the Archbishop writes] that Palestine was the home of the Jews and of the first Christians. None of them was of Arab origin. By the brutal force of conquest they were forced to become converts to the Moslem religion. That is the origin of the Arabs in that country. Can one deduce from that that Palestine is Arab or that it ever was Arab? . . .
>
> Major reasons of a social, humanitarian and religious nature require the creation of two homelands for minorities: a Christian home in the Lebanon, as there has always been, a Jewish home in Palestine. These two centers

connected with each other geographically, and supporting and assisting each other economically, will form the necessary bridge between West and East, from the viewpoint of culture and civilization. The neighborly relations between these two nations will contribute to the maintenance of peace in the Near East which is so divided by rivalries and will lessen the persecution of minorities, who will always find refuge in these two countries.

That is the opinion of the Lebanese whom I represent; it is the opinion of these people whom your Committee of Enquiry was unable to hear.

Behind the closed doors of the Sofar Hotel you were able to listen only to the words dictated to our so-called legal representatives by the lords and masters of the neighboring Arab countries. The real voice of the Lebanese was smothered by the group who falsified the elections of May 25.*

The Lebanon demands freedom for the Jews in Palestine—as it desires its own freedom and independence.

The Arab-Jewish conflict had accentuated the economic difficulties of the small republic. The end of the French Mandate in 1944 and the departure of the last French troops in the summer of 1946 were profound psychological experiences for the politically mature elements in Lebanese society. They brought a new sense of pride and prestige. But they also brought an acute postwar depression, with steadily rising unemployment. Before and during World War II the country's two main industries, fruit raising and the tourist trade, had found an expanding market in Jewish Palestine. But when in 1946 the League of Arab States forced the Lebanon to participate in its boycott of the Jews, the Jews in turn stopped importing Lebanese fruits and vacationing in the resort places of the Lebanese mountains.

The administration of Lebanon, as of all Arab states, is notoriously wasteful. In spite of the fact that the military contribution of the Lebanese government to the invasion of Palestine did not consist of more than a token force, the campaign expenditures cut sharply into the country's meager financial resources. As a final burden, depleting the national treasury, there came in the summer of 1948 the influx of the Palestine Arab refugees, who did not wish to endanger themselves by fighting against the Jewish State and rather depended on the promise of the Arab League to "liberate" them.

While the Lebanese units held a strip of Israeli territory on the border between Palestine and Lebanon near Ras en Naqura, Israeli forces had occupied some fifteen Lebanese villages and towns and could have marched on Beirut had they so desired. When the whole Arab

* May 25, 1947, was the date of the last national elections for the Lebanese Parliament. In order to keep the Christian majority from electing its candidates, the government resorted to fraud and violence, with the result that Lebanese public opinion has become bitterly antigovernment.

invasion appeared ready to collapse by the end of the year, Lebanon was most anxious to conclude an armistice. Unofficial talks between representatives of Israel and Lebanon were held throughout the month of December. But the government of Lebanon, conscious of its unique position in a league of Moslem states, denied officially that it was conferring with the Israeli. So delicate was the situation for a while that Dr. Bunche had to deny reports of even having extended an invitation to Lebanon to join the armistice negotiations.

It was not before March 1, 1949, that the informal talks gave way to an officially acknowledged armistice conference under the chairmanship of Dr. Bunche's associate, Henri Vigier. On March 23 the final agreement was signed by Lieutenant Colonel Mordecai Makleff for the government of Israel and Lieutenant Colonel Tewfiq Salim for the government of Lebanon. The armistice demarcation line followed the international boundary between Lebanon and Palestine as established by the League of Nations after World War I. In spite of the fact that Israel had militarily the upper hand, neither side lost nor gained territory. As in the Israeli-Egyptian agreement, provision was made for the full exchange of prisoners of war and a mixed armistice commission composed of representatives of the former warring parties as well as United Nations officials to supervise the execution of the agreement. Like the Israeli-Egyptian armistice, the Israeli-Lebanese treaty entered into force upon signing and was not subject to ratification.

The third Arab state to conclude an armistice with Israel was Trans-Jordan.

From the beginning of the Arab-Jewish war in Palestine it was evident that Abdullah had the most to gain. The immediate collapse of the Palestine Arab resistance movement had utterly discredited the ex-Mufti and those Arab leaders who might have frustrated his plan to declare himself king of at least the Arab part of Palestine. The Trans-Jordan Legion under the command of British officers, by far the most efficient of all Arab armies, was stationed in the very heart of Palestine already under the British mandatory regime. Abdullah knew that in any final political solution of the Palestine problem he had the support of the British Government.

But the other Arab countries could not possibly leave the invasion of Palestine to Abdullah, as a successful occupation of that country would have completely changed the balance of power within the League of Arab States. Moreover, they feared that Abdullah might make a deal with the Jews at their expense. Mutual distrust rather than a sentiment of patriotism produced the display of Arab "unity" when Trans-Jordan,

Egypt, Syria, Lebanon, and Iraq sent their troops simultaneously into the Holy Land.

Since already the first few weeks of fighting disposed of any possibility of an Arab victory, Mr. Bevin, who had hoped to put the Jews in their place, probably advised Abdullah not to risk defeat but rather to come to terms with the Israeli government. There was another reason which may have induced Abdullah to accept the existence of a Jewish state as a *fait accompli.* The great oil fields of Arabia gush their black gold within the very territory which Abdullah's family contend is rightfully theirs. To overpower the Saudi-Arabian potentate, who is backed by a population of millions and very considerable annual royalties from the American oil companies, Abdullah needs a greater reservoir of manpower than he can muster from among his 350,000 Trans-Jordanian subjects. This manpower lies in the area of Greater Syria, including Trans-Jordan, Syria, Lebanon, and Iraq. Abdullah probably calculated that an alliance with the new State of Israel, would provide him with armaments and means of transportation in return for certain economic concessions such as the exploitation of the Jordan River in Trans-Jordanian territory.

On January 30, 1949, after having received an official invitation from the Acting Mediator, Abdullah announced that he was ready to enter into formal armistice negotiations. The Israeli delegates at Rhodes, being in the midst of conferences with the Egyptians, were not too eager to assume any new responsibilities. Abdullah, on the other hand, anxious to keep a watchful eye on the other members of the Arab League, called on them to join him in the negotiations. Not one replied. But on February 27 the Cairo newspaper *Al Assas,* the organ of the predominant faction in the Egyptian government, abandoned all reticence and declared frankly:

> Syria rightly believes that Trans-Jordan's expansions are a prelude to a Greater Syria plan that threatens her very existence. Hence her justifiable desire to annex Galilee to protect herself against danger.
>
> Further, Saudi Arabia cannot be happy about this Trans-Jordanian expansion for two reasons. First, expansion of Trans-Jordan would constitute a threat to her, if not today, certainly in the future. Second, the Regent of Trans-Jordan is only human and cannot forget that the crown of Hejaz would have been his after the death of his father, King Husein ibn-Ali, had Saudi Arabia not conquered Hejaz and thrown out the Hashimites.

Significantly the paper added:

> We have to face certain facts. Partition is effected. The Arab countries that are opposed to it could not have prevented it without waging war, not only

against the Zionists but against Trans-Jordan, Iraq,* Britain, America and Russia.

For the first time the anti-Hashimite bloc within the League of Arab States openly admitted that it considered Trans-Jordan and Iraq to be arrayed on the side of the "enemy."

On March 4 the representatives of Trans-Jordan and Israel met in Rhodes in an atmosphere chilled by reports from Amman that Abdullah would ask for access to the Mediterranean through the port of Jaffa and the return of the Arab refugees to Ramle, Lydda, and Beersheba, which the United Nations partition plan had awarded to Arab Palestine. The Israeli, who had conquered the port city opposite Tel Aviv and the inland area, realized that turning them over to Trans-Jordan would cut Israel in two and bar her road to Jerusalem.

Before the discussions began, the Trans-Jordan delegation indicated that it would also speak for Iraq. Although the Iraqi government failed to verify this statement, it recalled its troops from the Jenin-Tulkarm-Nablus triangle and allowed Trans-Jordanian units to move into the area. Apart from being Britain's protégé, Trans-Jordan had a military position different from that of Egypt and Lebanon. Israel had defeated the Egyptian and Lebanese armies in the field. Trans-Jordan's Arab Legion and the Israeli had fought each other to a standstill. From a purely military point of view neither side felt that an armistice was imperative. Nevertheless the negotiations would probably have proceeded with less complication had it not been for the interference of the British Middle East Command and the Foreign Office.

Britain "pays the piper" to the tune of some $11,000,000 yearly for the Trans-Jordanian military administration. Why should she not call the tune?

After World War I Britain had been successful in using Egypt and the Fertile Crescent as a shock absorber between her European rivals and her Indian Empire. But the growing nationalism of both Arabs and Jews had brought her military and economic penetration of the area into sharp conflict with the principle of national self-determination. After World War II, realizing that the melody of the white man's burden was no longer considered good music, Britain conceded self-government to the countries within her sphere of influence. She consoled herself with a number of strategic bases to maintain control over her oil fields around the Persian Gulf and to safeguard her communications with Australia, New Zealand, and the other Far Eastern portions of the Com-

* After Faisal's death in 1933, his son Ghazi came to the throne of Iraq. He was killed in a motor accident in 1939. Ghazi was succeeded by his infant son, Faisal II, under the regency of Emir Abdul Illah, a representative of the Hashimite family.

monwealth. While British troops would no longer interfere in the functioning of the Egyptian government nor encroach upon its sovereignty, yet no British government could divest itself completely of all interest in the defense of the Suez Canal. The primary objective of the Egyptians, on the other hand, was to bring about the withdrawal of British troops from the canal area and to achieve a permanent unity with the Sudan in order to gain complete freedom along the fertile upper valley of the Nile.

In 1945 the British chiefs of staff began to consider Soviet Russia as a potential aggressor in the Middle East. It was the consensus of military opinion that in the event of war the Nile Delta and Suez would once again become a major zone of British operations. The problem, therefore, was to find an alternative military and naval base near enough to Egypt to permit a speedy reentry into that country in the event of an emergency. Syria and Lebanon had just secured the withdrawal of all foreign troops. Iraq was too distant and unsafe. In 1939 the British consul was murdered in Mosul. Since that year popular sentiment against Britain had led to a number of revolts and to one political assassination after the other. The British Middle East Command chose Palestine as the main British base. Its advantages were the port of Haifa, second only to Alexandria as a naval station, and the Negev, which could be used to replace the vast cantonments of the Suez zone. Britain left the frying pan only to fall right into the fire. She had antagonized the Egyptians and those Arabs who habitually follow Egypt's lead. Now her empire policy came into conflict with the Jews.

There is little doubt that if some of the British generals and the Jewish terrorists had been permitted to wage the war which they both quite obviously desired, the Jewish National Home might have been destroyed. But all politically mature elements in the Labor party as well as the opposition parties balked at a war of extermination. The result was that Bevin fell between two stools, angering both Arabs and Jews by his half-hearted measures to ensure the British position in the Holy Land. When he finally decided on his policy of "bag and baggage" and ordered the evacuation of British troops, there remained only one secure bastion, Trans-Jordan. Low as British prestige may have sunk in other parts of the Arab world, it was, and is, still high in Amman. When Abdullah's emissaries presented their credentials at the Hotel des Roses in Rhodes, it was, therefore, quite clear that Britain too had entered into negotiations with Israel.

Suddenly, on March 9, 1949, five days after the beginning of the Israel–Trans-Jordan armistice talks, the British Foreign Office reported Jewish troop movements in the eastern Negev in the direction of the port of Aqaba on the Red Sea and emphasized that Britain would come to Abdullah's assistance in the event of an Israeli invasion of Trans-Jordanian territory. On March 12 London issued the terse statement, "The War Office announces that the British detachment at Aqaba is being reinforced." * Aqaba, a strategic port in the Middle East, offers the only access to the sea routes for Abdullah's otherwise landlocked kingdom. It was in the area of Aqaba that King Solomon once built a harbor for his ships sailing the Indian Ocean to the Orient. Although the Israeli government denied military operations in the southern Negev, which, incidentally, had been allotted to the Jewish State by the partition resolution of the United Nations, the British battleship "Magpie" arrived at the port. The next day, March 14, Amman claimed that 3,000 Israeli troops were concentrated in Elath on the gulf, while United Nations observers testified that there were only 150 Israeli in the area. On March 20 the whole scheme of "crying wolf" exploded. Trans-Jordan, in the midst of negotiations with Israel, formally asked the British Government for military assistance against Israel. In practical terms this meant that British troops previously sent to Aqaba would occupy the southern Negev and release sufficient Arab forces to take over other critical areas on the Palestine front. At this point the Israeli government warned that if British forces took over the Trans-Jordanian position near Aqaba, Israel would have to reconsider its cease-fire agreement with Trans-Jordan. There now was every chance that Israel might walk out of the Rhodes conference when, probably acting on the advice of Washington, the British Government decided not to comply with the Trans-Jordanian request.

After the British retreat, the Acting Mediator was able to submit a final draft to both delegations. On April 3 the armistice was signed by Reuven Shiloah and Lieutenant Colonel Moshe Dagan for Israel, Colonel Ahmed el Jundi and Lieutenant Colonel Muhammad Muayatah for Trans-Jordan.

Article Five of the Israel–Trans-Jordan Treaty, dealing with the

* Two months before, on January 7, 1949, the Foreign Office had announced the landing of the first detachment of British troops at Aqaba. On this same January 7, the British Government stated that five Royal Air Force planes were shot down by Israeli fighters near the Egyptian-Israeli frontier and that Sir Terence A. Shone, British delegate to the Security Council, was ordered to present to the Israeli representative the British Government's rights, "both as regards a claim for compensation and as regards possible further action." Britain's military position in the Arab world can easily be deduced from the concluding words of the official British communique: "In view of these unprovoked attacks, our aircraft have now been instructed to regard as hostile any Jewish aircraft encountered over *Egyptian territory.*"

demarcation lines, provided for a minor adjustment in favor of Trans-Jordan in the Hebron–Dead Sea region. South from the Dead Sea to Aqaba the line followed the international boundary between Palestine and Trans-Jordan. Article Six recognized the substitution of Trans-Jordanian for Iraqi forces in the Jenin-Tulkarm-Nablus sector and freed the Haifa–Tel Aviv railway in favor of Israel against a promise of the Israeli government to reimburse Trans-Jordan for the cost of constructing 20 kilometers of first-class road. Provisions were made for setting up a special committee composed of representatives of Israel and Trans-Jordan for "the purpose of formulating agreed plans and arrangements designed to enlarge the scope of this agreement and to effect improvements in its application." Among the issues upon which agreement was reached in principle but which the armistice did not specifically mention were the free movement of traffic on the Bethlehem-Jerusalem and Latrun-Jerusalem roads, resumption of the normal functioning of the educational and hospital institutions on Mount Scopus, and free access to all holy places in Jerusalem.

Since the Israel–Trans-Jordan pact was also binding upon Iraq and since ibn-Saud had been very careful not to join the military invasion, only Syria was left as an active combatant with whom the Jewish State had yet to negotiate.

In Syria the Republican Nationalists, who had groomed Fawzi el Kaukje as their field marshal in the war against the Jews, were compelled to embark on a costly face-saving adventure. On March 30 the Syrian army seized control of the government in a successful *coup d'état* led by General Husni Zayim, a graduate of the French military academy at St. Cyr. A week later armistice talks began between Israel and Syria. At the same time Zayim made it clear that his government would not support Abdullah's claim to the Greater Syria which his brother Faisal ruled from 1918 to 1920. In an open challenge to Abdullah and the British the General called additional troops to the colors, closed the Syrian–Trans-Jordan frontier, and declared in a public address that Syria would refuse to be annexed by Trans-Jordan but would rather itself annex the Hashimite Kingdom. Political observers seeking the source of the General's confidence noted that whereas Britain had withheld recognition from his government, the United States and France were the first governments to extend him recognition. In May Damascus ratified an agreement permitting the Trans-Arabian pipe line of America's oil interests to pass through Syria. These events linked together lent credence to the rumor that Zayim had joined Saudi-Arabia in the "American Axis."

On July 20, 1949, in the presence of Henri Vigier, personal deputy of the United Nations Acting Mediator and Brigadier General William Riley, United Nations Chief of Staff of the Truce Supervision Organization, Lieutenant Colonel Mordecai Makleff on behalf of the Israeli government and Colonel Fozi Selo on behalf of the Syrian government signed the armistice agreement. As "Armistice Demarcation Line" the two signatories determined a frontier midway between the existing truce lines which in turn coincided largely with the international boundary between Syria and Palestine.

Israel signed individual armistice pacts with Egypt, Lebanon, Jordan, and Syria. Because of the internal rifts within the Arab League it could not reach an agreement with them all simultaneously. If there could be armistice agreements, there could also be peace pacts. But the Conciliation Commission of the United Nations (which had been charged by the General Assembly decision of December 11, 1948, with the task of assisting the governments "to achieve final settlement of all questions outstanding between them") soon experienced how significant a bar to peace the disunity within the Arab League could be.

The main problems that demanded settlement were the final boundaries of the State of Israel, the status of Jerusalem, and the resettlement of the Arab refugees from the Palestine war. When the three members of the United Nations Palestine Conciliation Commission, Mark F. Ethridge (U.S.A.), Hussein C. Yalcin (Turkey), and Claude L. Boisanger (France), began their tour of the Arab countries and arrived in Cairo in February, 1949, Azzam Pasha declared that the Arab States had decided to negotiate with the commission only en bloc. Soon afterward the Egyptian government, to the surprise of all other Arab countries, proposed the "Gaza Plan," offering the Gaza strip of land on the Mediterranean to Israel in return for taking a quarter of a million Arab refugees in that area off Egypt's hands. About the same time a new development took place within the Arab sector of Palestine. In the triangle under Trans-Jordanian control the newspapers reported the rise of a new political party which openly demanded the evacuation of the Trans-Jordan Legion and the annexation of the Jenin-Tulkarm-Nablus area to Israel. In July the American delegation in Damascus was about to arrange a meeting between the foreign ministers of Israel and Syria, and it seemed certain that the Syrian dictatorship would be the first Arab government to go beyond an armistice and sign a permanent peace with Israel, when Husni Zayim was suddenly assassinated.

Zayim had attempted to copy Mustafa Kemal in modernizing the Syrian Republic. Like the first President of the Turkish Republic he proclaimed the separation of state and church, the right of women to vote and to unveil their faces. But his plans for a gradual democratization of

Syria remained a midsummer night's dream. On August 14th his own military colleagues, headed by Colonel Sami Hennavi, overthrew his paternal government in a second military coup, which, in turn, led to a third coup within one year, the seizure of power by Colonel Adiv Chichickli and other army officers.

Into this internal Syrian struggle enter many elements. There is the Greater Syria movement, the pet scheme of Abdullah and his British backers. There is the question of the proposed federation of Syria and Iraq. There is the wide gap between the armies and the masses of the Arab peoples as the result of Arab defeat. Syria is probably the shakiest spot in the League of Arab States. But the whole structure is shaken.

Far from being the unified "Arab world" of British Foreign Office propaganda, the Middle East abounds in subterranean conflicts for place and power. In spite of their unity in United Nations circles, one Arab state fights the other. Moreover, ethnic and religious minorities which have for centuries held on to cultures of their own, Maronites, Kurds, Assyrians, Druze, have just begun their struggle for autonomy. For them the emergence of the State of Israel, the fact that one non-Islamic, non-Arab nationality in the Middle East has been able to establish itself as sovereign in its own territory, symbolizes a first encouraging change in a long succession of defeats. Just as the Christian leaders of the Lebanon have more than once asserted that the Lebanon will be able to preserve its Christian tradition only in alliance with the Jewish State, most of the other Middle East minorities have come to see Israel's resurrection as the test case for themselves. There is now a chance, they feel, for all of them to make the Middle East more hospitable and tolerant.

Chapter Fourteen: THE FIFTY-NINTH MEMBER OF THE UNITED NATIONS

BRITAIN ABSTAINS FROM VOTING · PAKISTAN BELIEVES IN DIVIDED JUSTICE · HERZL COMES HOME

Throughout the first year of her national independence, Israel demonstrated her aim of securing an enduring peace with her Arab neighbors provided that the peace was based on equity and was achieved through the orderly accommodation of all differences.

In pursuit of this aim, Foreign Minister Moshe Sharett (Shertok), on November 29, 1948, the first anniversary of the United Nations partition resolution, presented to Secretary-General Trygve Lie the application of Israel for membership in the United Nations.

On May 14, 1948 [Sharett wrote] the independence of the State of Israel was proclaimed by the National Council of the Jewish people in Palestine by virtue of the natural and historic right of the Jewish people to independence in its own sovereign State and in pursuance of the General Assembly Resolution of November 29, 1947. Since that date Israel has been consolidated administratively and defended itself successfully against the aggression of neighboring States. It has so far achieved recognition by nineteen Powers.

On behalf of the Provisional Government of Israel, I have now the honor to request the admission of Israel as a member of the United Nations in accordance with Article 4 of the Charter. . . .

An attached declaration read:

On behalf of the State of Israel, I, Moshe Shertok (Sharett), Minister for Foreign Affairs, being duly authorized by the State Council of Israel, declare that the State of Israel hereby unreservedly accepts the obligations of the United Nations Charter and undertakes to honor them from the day when it becomes a member of the United Nations.

(Article 4 of the Charter stipulates that membership in the United Nations is open to all peace-loving states which accept the obligations contained in the Charter and, "in the judgment of the Organization, are able and willing to carry out these obligations." Article 4 further directs that the admission of a new state to membership in the family of nations "will be effected by a decision of the General Assembly upon the recommendation of the Security Council.")

Within three days the Security Council took up Israel's application for admission. Dr. Philip Jessup, the well-known political scientist of Columbia University who represented the United States in the Council, urged acceptance. With regard to the question of whether or not Israel formed a state, Dr. Jessup reminded his colleagues in the Council that Israel possessed the four qualifications which international law has come to recognize as the main criteria of a state—population, territory, government, and sovereignty. He pointed out that Israel exercised independence of judgment and will in its foreign policy and added, "I think the world has been particularly impressed with the way in which the people of Israel have organized their government and have established a firm system of administration and of law making under the most difficult conditions."

Turning to the other requirements of Article 4, Dr. Jessup expressed the view of the United States government that Israel was a peace-loving nation and that she could be trusted to carry out the obligations imposed on members by the Charter. He substantiated this statement by recalling the major events following the November 29, 1947 Resolution of the General Assembly and the consistently cooperative attitude which the government of Israel had demonstrated. In summarizing the position of the United States toward Israel's application he said:

> As a result of any inspection of the requirements for membership in the United Nations, as set out in Article 4 of the Charter, and of their application to the specific situation of Israel, my delegation reaches the definite conclusion that the State of Israel is qualified for membership and that its application should be endorsed by the Security Council.

Soviet Russia's delegate likewise supported the immediate approval of the application. But Sir Alexander Cadogan, speaking for the United Kingdom, declared that His Majesty's Government considered Israel's application "both premature and rather doubtful." He felt that there was no urgency in the matter and that the question of final boundaries and other issues should be solved before consideration was given to the admission of the Jewish State. Alexander Parodi of France suggested that the Security Council defer consideration of the application until the General Assembly, which was about to conclude its session in Paris, had acted on the Palestine issue. The President of the Council, in accordance with the rules of procedure, turned the application over to the membership committee. This committee came to the conclusion that it was not "in possession of the requisite information to enable it to come to any decision." On September 17 the eleven members of the Security Council voted on the application. Argentina, Colombia, Russia, the Ukraine, and the United States voted in favor. Belgium, Canada, China, France, Great Britain abstained. Syria voted against approval. The vote was a rejection of the application.

On February 24, 1949, the same day the armistice between Israel and Egypt was signed, Aubrey S. Eban requested the Security Council to reconsider Israel's application for membership in the United Nations. Since the General Assembly was to reconvene at Flushing Meadow on April 5, he expressed the hope of his government that the Security Council would reach a decision in time for the General Assembly to take action.

Meanwhile, the number of countries which had extended recognition to the new state had risen to forty-four. Elections had been held in Israel, and a permanent government had replaced the Provisional State Council. France announced that she considered Israel as worthy of membership and that this time she would vote in favor of her application. China's delegate, too, indicated that he would vote for Israel's membership in the United Nations.

On March 4 the debate started anew. In the absence of Sir Alexander Cadogan, Sir Terence Shone declared that utterances of responsible Israeli representatives had demonstrated the unwillingness of the young state to abide by a number of United Nations resolutions, particularly the resolutions concerning the internationalization of Jerusalem and the resettlement of the Arab refugees. He conveniently forgot to add that there was a time—not so long ago—when Britain herself appeared to be willing to forego Jerusalem's internationalization and to recognize the Holy City as the capital of King Abdullah. In fact, none of the Arab governments had ever agreed to an international administration of Jerusalem. Yet Britain had never questioned their right to membership in the United Nations. Since British delegates on several occasions had emphasized that the United Kingdom, one of the Big Five, would not use its privileged veto right to block the admission of any state which obtained the requisite majority, Britain could not well vote against Israel's admission either. Sir Terence, therefore, concluded his remarks by stating that he would abstain from voting.

The only opponent was Mahmoud Bey Fawzi, Egypt's representative, who had replaced the Syrian delegate on the Security Council. He pointed out that the armistice signed between Egypt and Israel was a

Citriculture and industrial development represent two chief aspects of Israel's economic program. *Courtesy of United Palestine Appeal.*

Aforestation—not reforestation—planting trees where none had been before. *Courtesy of United Palestine Appeal.*

Artificial fishponds in the settlements of the Jordan Valley, where carp breeding has been developed to enlarge the country's food output. *Courtesy of United Palestine Appeal.*

purely military matter and did not imply any Egyptian willingness to vote for the admission of Israel to the United Nations. Like the British delegate he emphasized that Israel had done nothing to solve the Arab refugee problem. The Soviet delegate, Jacob A. Malik, answered both the British and Egyptian delegates that in the opinion of his government Israel was not responsible for the plight of the Arab refugees and that in any case this issue could best be solved by a peaceful settlement of the whole Palestine problem.

At the end of the debate Warren R. Austin, the representative of the United States, introduced the following resolution:

> THE SECURITY COUNCIL,
>
> HAVING RECEIVED and considered the application of Israel for membership in the United Nations;
>
> DECIDES in its judgment that Israel is a peace-loving State and is able and willing to carry out the obligations contained in the Charter; and
>
> ACCORDINGLY RECOMMENDS to the General Assembly that it admit Israel to membership in the United Nations.

Britain abstained from voting. Egypt opposed the resolution. Argentina, Canada, China, Cuba, France, Norway, the Ukraine, the U.S.S.R. and the United States voted in favor. The President of the Council, Alberto y Alvarez of Cuba, ruled:

> According to the established practice of the Security Council, whenever the rule of unanimity of the permanent members is concerned, the abstention of one of those permanent members does not invalidate the favorable vote of the Security Council.

Austin's resolution was adopted despite the fact that Great Britain, one of the permanent members of the Council, had abstained from voting.

On March 7, Alberto y Alvarez notified Dr. Herbert V. Evatt of Australia, President of the General Assembly, that the Security Council recommended Israel's admission to the United Nations. Over a month later, on April 13, the Assembly decided to refer the application to its Political Committee before including it on the agenda of the plenary session. From the Political Committee, which was overloaded with work, the application was transferred to the ad hoc Political Committee. The ad hoc committee convened on May 3.

Pakistan's representative, Sir Mohammed Zafrullah Khan, attempted immediately to push Israel's application to the end of the list of items which were before the committee, hoping that in this way the Israeli application would never reach the plenary. Like the Jewish minority in the Arab-Moslem world, the Moslem minority in the Hindu world gained its national independence by stressing that religious distinctiveness is in itself sufficient reason to justify the establishment of a separate statehood. But this did not prevent the Pakistan delegate from exerting every effort to deny Israel's admission into the world community of independent nations. When the chairman, General Carlos P. Romulo of the Philippines, ruled that Israel's application would be the first on the agenda, Sir Mohammed insisted that the Assembly had no right to even consider Israel's application, since Great Britain had abstained from voting on it in the Security Council.

The chairman then declared that it was "beyond the competence of the committee to question the regularity of the vote in the Security Council and the validity of the decision taken." This ruling was at once challenged by the Iraqi delegate, who suggested that the International Court of Justice be asked for an advisory opinion on the validity of the recommendation.

The main issues in the committee debate were again the establishment of an international regime for Jerusalem and the resettlement of the Arab refugees. The Arab representatives in the committee reversed their original position according to which the United Nations resolution of November 29, 1947, was invalid and demanded that Israel comply with all the provisions of this resolution before she could be admitted to United Nations membership.

On May 3 El Salvador introduced a resolution inviting a representative of the Israeli government to the meeting of the ad hoc Political Committee in order to clarify Israel's position. Meanwhile, encyclicals of Pope Pius XII, asking for free access to the Holy Places and for guarantees of security for Catholic institutions, had sufficiently disturbed the delegate from Argentina to introduce a resolution inviting the Holy See to present a report "on the guarantees which, in its exalted opinion, would be necessary for the protection of the Sacred Places in Palestine and for free access thereto." Greece immediately offered an amendment to include the Greek Patriarchate in the Jerusalem area. Saudi Arabia demanded the inclusion of the Moslem religious authorities. To the delight of the Arab-Moslem bloc, the list threatened to become inexhaustive. Nevertheless, El Salvador's resolution, amended by Australia and Denmark, to invite the government of Israel to send a representative to the ad hoc Political Committee was passed by a vote of 35 to 6, with 11 abstentions.

On May 5 Israel's representative, Major Eban, addressed the committee. He stressed that Israel was ready to cooperate with the United

Nations, that, indeed, Israel had been the only country which had displayed any initiative in solving the problems involved in the Palestine issue. He pointed out that the November 29, 1947 Resolution of the General Assembly was based on the assumption that the Arab member states in the United Nations would comply with a United Nations decision; that they and not Israel had fought with violence against it; that the Security Council had been unable to implement the partition of Palestine, and that the Trusteeship Council had refused to implement the Jerusalem provisions of internationalization. He stated that his government favored an international regime for the rule of Jerusalem but one that would be restricted functionally so as to concern itself solely with the protection of the religious shrines and not with the purely secular aspects of life and government.

As for the refugee question, he insisted that primary responsibility rested on the Arab States which created the whole problem when they invaded Palestine and incited the Palestine Arabs to leave their homes. "The government of Israel," Eban said, "has already announced its acceptance of obligations to make compensation for lands abandoned. The entire question of compensation may well be settled by negotiations at Lausanne."

In answer to Denmark's questions, the Israeli representative declared that the assassinations of Count Folke Bernadotte and his military aide, Colonel André Serot (who had tried to protect Bernadotte), were "a source of deep distress and acute mortification to the government and the people of Israel" and added frankly that his government felt "a deep sense of failure" in not having been able yet to arrest and punish the assassins. He assured the committee that the Israeli authorities did not consider the case closed and would continue their endeavors to apprehend the perpetrators of the crime.

The next day, May 6, Australia introduced a resolution calling for approval of the Israeli application. The resolution read in part:

The General Assembly,

Acting in discharge of its functions under Article 4 of the Charter and rule 125 of its rules of procedure,

1. Decides that Israel is a peace-loving State which accepts the obligations contained in the Charter and is able and willing to carry out those obligations;
2. Decides to admit Israel to membership in the United Nations.

The Arab Delegations resorted to filibustering. Late on May 7 a motion was carried to limit the discussion. Two days later the Australian draft came to a vote. It was passed by roll-call vote, 33 to 11, with 13 abstentions.

On May 11, the plenary of the General Assembly experienced a repetition of the debate which had taken place in the ad hoc Political Committee. Finally at 7:23 P.M. the vote was taken. The General Assembly adopted the Australian resolution, 37 to 12, with 9 abstentions. Dr. Evatt declared Israel a member of the United Nations. Outside in front of the Assembly Hall, on the fifty-ninth flagpole, the blue and white flag was raised. While Israeli's foreign minister, Moshe Sharett, was escorted to his country's seat, the hundreds of spectators in the public gallery rose to pay their tribute to a people that for so long had been outcast and that now had been welcomed back into the community of nations, proudly vindicated and justified in its faith.

Israel's admission to the United Nations involved more than legal issues. It symbolized a drama of profound majesty. The nation that was so often consigned to death, the nation that had first kindled for mankind the vision of universal brotherhood, had risen at last from its immemorial crucifixion and had returned to sovereign national life.

It was also the crowning achievement of the indefatigable efforts of Theodor Herzl. The founder of modern Zionism had asked in his testament that his fellow Jews should bring his remains to Israel as soon as the nations of the world had recognized Jewish statehood in its ancient land. Once before in the history of the Jewish people, one of its great sons, Joseph, viceroy of Egypt, had left as his last will the request that, if the Jews would leave Egypt and return to the land of Israel, they should take his body with them. As Moses in ancient days fulfilled Joseph's will, the government of the new State of Israel now fulfilled the will of Herzl.

On August 14, 1949, Herzl's coffin was exhumed in the cemetery of Vienna, covered with the Israeli flag, and flown aboard an Israeli C-54 to Lydda airport. As the silvered contours of the plane circled out of the blue sky and the motor came to a stop, Prime Minister Ben Gurion and the members of the Israeli Cabinet received the casket on the soil of the Holy Land. In Tel Aviv the bier rested on the esplanade in front of Israel's Parliament. From there the mortal remains of the prophetic pioneer traversed exactly the same route that Herzl had traversed decades ago to meet the German Kaiser at the Jaffa gate of Jerusalem in order to make his first bid for the charter of the great powers.

The landscape had changed its complexion. Barren desert in the days of Herzl, it was dotted now with villages and orange groves, and everywhere laborers, artisans, farmers poured out to join the ascent of the dead leader to Israel's ancient capital.

There, in Jerusalem, the entire population formed a living avenue for the cortege. On the highest hill, visible for miles around, a grave had been hewn out of solid rock. As the casket was lowered into the massive walls, delegates from all towns, villages, and hamlets deposited small bags of soil from their communities in the grave, that the soil of the whole of Israel might mingle with Herzl's body. While the guards presented arms, the multitude recited Kaddish, the prayer said by Jews the world over at the grave of their closest and dearest relatives.

The nations of the world had at last recognized the burning desire of the Jewish people to acquire the status of national equality. And Herzl had come home.

Chapter Fifteen: IF I FORGET THEE, OH JERUSALEM

JERUSALEM'S PLACE IN JEWISH HISTORY · THE HOLY SHRINES OF JUDAISM, CHRISTIANITY, AND ISLAM · THE DRAFT OF THE CONCILIATION COMMISSION AND THE NEW HOLY ALLIANCE

To the Biblical chronicler of the reigns of the kings of Judah and Israel, Jerusalem was the city which God "had chosen out of all the tribes of Israel." For the exiles of Judah weeping by the rivers of Babylon, the name and memory of Jerusalem summed up all their agony and all their faith: "If I forget thee, oh Jerusalem, let my right hand forget her cunning. Let my tongue cleave to the roof of my mouth, if I prefer not Jerusalem above my chief joy." It was concern for the welfare of Jerusalem that caused Nehemiah, one of the founding fathers of the Second Jewish Commonwealth, to leave the comforts of his post in the Persian government of the fifth century before the Christian Era. "Why should not my countenance be sad," he said to the king of Persia, "when the city, the place of my fathers' Sepulchres, lieth waste, and the gates thereof are consumed with fire"?

For the builders of the Second Commonwealth and the Jews of the Diaspora of those days, Jerusalem was not only the cherished spiritual and temporal capital of the Jewish people but the very center of the earth. When in 165 B.C. the Syrian Antiochus occupied the land of Israel, prohibited the traditional services in the Temple, and ordered sacrifices of swine's flesh to the idols of Greece and Macedonia, the Maccabees kindled the flame of revolt for the sake of Israel's holy city. To this day Jews the world over commemorate the rededication of the Temple in Jerusalem by the victorious Jewish forces under Judas Maccabaeus in the festival of Chanukah.

The preservation of Jerusalem's spiritual character was the test of all Jewish independence movements against Rome, starting with Pompey's conquest of Judea in 63 B.C. When sixty-two years after the destruction of the Temple Emperor Hadrian proclaimed plans for rebuilding Jerusalem as a Roman city with a new temple dedicated to Jupiter Capitolinus, Jews from their dispersion in Europe and the Near East hastened to Palestine to fight under Bar Kochba against the Roman legions.

After three years of warfare the dream of physical reconquest of Jerusalem ended with Bar Kochba's defeat. But the spiritual attachment to Israel's religious shrine and national center never died in Jewish hearts. During the eighteen hundred years of the second dispersion, the liturgy, the customs, the literature, the thoughts of Jews throughout the world reverted again and again to Jerusalem. Daily the pious Jew repeated in prayer the plea, "Build Thou Thy Holy City, Jerusalem." Every year when Jews gather around the Seder table to celebrate Passover, the festival of liberation, they climax the reading of the Hagadah, which relates the story of Jewish deliverance from Egypt, with the passionate words, "Next year in Jerusalem!"

When in 640 Jerusalem fell to the Moslems, Jews from Babylonia, Egypt, and Syria bought the slopes of the Mount of Olives facing the remnants of the Temple; and there, together with Jewish pilgrims from other parts of the world, they celebrated the Feast of Tabernacles and other solemn days of the Jewish calendar. The conquest of Jerusalem by the Crusaders in 1099 brought virtual annihilation to the Moslems and Jews of Jerusalem. But in the twelfth century Jewish pilgrims, among them Judah ha-Levi, the great poet and philosopher of Spanish Jewry, returned to the city and the land of Israel. Ha-Levi—as legend has it—died at the foot of the Wailing Wall. In 1267, following the Mongol devastations, the Jewish philosopher Nahmanides reorganized the Jewish community of Jerusalem. In 1700 the Jews within the walled Old City built the synagogue Hurvat Rabbi Jehuda Hahasid, which was demolished in 1948 by the Trans-Jordan Arab Legion. In the middle of the nineteenth century the British Jew Moses Montefiore and the American Jew Judah Touro became the founders of the New Jerusalem built outside the walled Old City; and by 1895, 15,000 of the then 28,000 Jews of Jerusalem lived outside the walls. During the mandatory regime Jerusalem was the seat of the British administration and of the Jewish Agency. The Jewish Agency building, the Hebrew University, the Hadassah Hospital, the offices of the Chief Rabbinate—all the central religious, educational, and administrative institutions of Jewish Palestine were concentrated in the New City. When, on May 14, 1948, the mandatory government completed the withdrawal of its security forces from Jerusalem, close to 100,000 Jews and some 30,000 non-Jews lived in the New City.

On November 29, 1947, the whole of the Jerusalem area had been assigned international status by the partition resolution of the United Nations General Assembly. Although bitterly disappointed that Jerusalem was not included in the Jewish State, the Jews were at first willing to accept internationalization as the price of peace with the Arab countries. They assumed that implementation of the partition plan would be brought about by the instrumentality of the United Nations. But the United Nations were neither willing nor able to implement their own resolution. The statute for Jerusalem's internationalization lay in the files of the Trusteeship Council discarded and unratified. On the critical morning of May 15, 1948, when the armies of the neighboring Arab countries invaded Palestine, it was apparent to the Jews of Jerusalem that they could expect from the United Nations neither defense nor administration, neither a focus of allegiance nor the means of subsistence. Their choice was to sit back, paralyzed and inert until the Arab conquerors would destroy their homes and lives or to fight and organize their individual and collective future. They chose the second alternative.

For the historical record it must be emphasized that at the beginning of the Arab-Jewish war, the representatives of Egypt, Syria, Lebanon, and Iraq opposed the establishment of an international regime in Jerusalem. They argued that the protection of the Jewish, Christian, and Moslem Holy Places required no special political status. In the Trusteeship Council the representative of Iraq said: "It is my duty to show that the plan for the city of Jerusalem is illegal. . . . Neither the Iraqi Government nor other Arab states are prepared to enter the details or to participate in the discussion of the plan." For the historical record it must also be emphasized that the Jewish representatives of Jerusalem, especially the Jewish mayor, time and again appealed to the Security Council of the United Nations to isolate Jerusalem from the general conflict by some assertion of United Nations authority. But their appeals fell on deaf ears as the Arab States and their friends in the United Nations hoped for a victory of the invaders and the inclusion of Jerusalem in an Arab-dominated Palestine. In fact—and this should not be forgotten either—Count Bernadotte, the United Nations Mediator, himself frankly advocated the complete abandonment of the international principle and suggested that Jerusalem should become part of an Arab state—a proposal evidently based on what appeared to be the military logic at that time.

Meanwhile, most Jewish religious buildings and living quarters within the Old City of Jerusalem were destroyed by the Trans-Jordanian Arab Legion. Egyptian and Trans-Jordanian forces surrounding Jerusalem from all four roads cut off its food and water supply and brought the New City to the verge of capitulation. Nearly all normal foodstuffs were absent, and a quart of water per day had to suffice for all needs. Thirst and pestilence threatened the population. The economy had been struck a nearly fatal blow. Civilians, women, and children were killed by Trans-Jordanian artillery and Egyptian-piloted British Spitfires. When the Haganah units finally forced their way through the Arab lines in the west to bring relief to their besieged compatriots, the illusion that an international status for Jerusalem could assure its security lay buried amidst thousands of Jewish graves in the war-shattered cities and along the coastal roads.

The life line thrown from the State of Israel to the New City reached Jerusalem when it had little breath remaining. The Provisional Government of Israel reorganized the economy of the city, repaired its buildings, cleared the damaged areas. Jews from all over the world sent funds to assist the hard-pressed Israel treasury in the restoration of Jerusalem. To stabilize the situation, the government of Israel, on July 26, 1948, proclaimed the city Israeli-occupied territory and appointed a military governor. Finally, in the spring of 1949, after the Israel–Trans-Jordan armistice, a Jewish civil authority replaced the military regime.

In a similar way the 30,000 Arabs in the Old City under the control of the Trans-Jordanian Arab Legion began to adapt themselves to a regime of peace under Trans-Jordanian authorities. The Old City is the site of the Holy Places of Judaism, Christianity, and Islam. The chief Jewish Holy Place is the Western Wall, or, as it is often called, the Wailing Wall which was part of the wall around the Temple. Ever since the destruction of the Temple by Titus, Jews have come to this wall to mourn the loss of their glory and to pray for the restoration of Zion.

The main Christian Holy Places are the Holy Sepulchre, the Church of the Nativity, the Garden of Gethsemane, the Mount of Olives, the Grotto, the Shepherds' Fields. All these places of religious interest are under the control of the Trans-Jordanian Arabs who also police the Dome of the Rock, built by Caliph Abdel-Malik at the end of the seventh century and erroneously called the Mosque of Omar.

These realities confronted the United Nations Palestine Conciliation Commission which, on December 11, 1948, was charged by the General Assembly with the task of preparing plans for a "special and separate treatment" of the Jerusalem area because "of its association with three world religions."

On September 1, 1949, without previous announcement and without consulting the inhabitants of the city, the Conciliation Commission produced its plan for Jerusalem. It contained the following provisions:

The boundaries of the area are to be the same as those outlined in the partition resolution, but the area is to be divided into two zones, Jewish and Arab.

A local authority is to be created by the residents of each zone.

The responsible authorities in their respective zones are not to establish administrative organs or agencies or appoint officials beyond those required for strictly municipal affairs.

They are not to permit immigration beyond the present respective demographic equilibrium.

The General Assembly of the UN is to appoint, for a period of five years, a Commissioner who will be responsible to the Assembly.

The functions of the Commissioner are to ensure the protection of and free access to the Holy Places, supervise the permanent demilitarization and neutralization of the area, ensure protection of human rights and the rights of the distinctive groups.

A General Council for the entire area is to be established, composed of fourteen members appointed for a period of three years and presided over by the Commissioner or his deputy. Five members are to be appointed by the Jewish authorities, five members by the Arab authorities, and two each by the Commissioner from the residents of the Jewish area and from the residents of the Arab area respectively.

The functions and powers of the Council are to prescribe rules for the coordination and operation of the main public services of common interest to the area; plan and supervise the execution, on an area-wide basis, of matters of municipal concern; prescribe rules in matters relating to the protection of sites and antiquities and town planning; guarantee machinery for the maintenance of public order; allocate the contributions of each zone toward expenditures in the common interest; recommend to the authorities of the zones economic and commercial agreements to permit the economic development of the area; facilitate trade both between the two zones and between the area and the world outside.

The proposed draft clearly violates the principle of self-determination by vesting all decisive powers in external agencies outside the control of the peoples concerned. The "General Council" is no representative authority of the people. Yet this council determines levies to be paid. Here is taxation without representation—made worse by the likelihood that one part of the city will be asked to subsidize the other at the expense of its own development. According to the draft the responsible authorities shall take no steps in matters of immigration which might alter the present demographic equilibrium of the Jerusalem area. In view of the fact that the Arab birth rate is the highest in the world, this clause virtually asserts in the name of the United Nations, "No Jews allowed!"

Jerusalem is to be divided into two zones. But neither the Arab nor the Jewish zone would be integrated with the contiguous Jewish and Arab states. The people of each zone are euphemistically referred to as "residents." Apparently, they are to bear allegiance to no national authority. Internationalization is not a concept readily acceptable to any people. Many sentiments, pride, common history, and devotion to a common destiny, give meaningful content to the idea of national allegiance. The establishment of the State of Israel and the stout and successful defense of Jerusalem have made it possible for former homeless and stateless refugees to assert their own nationality. The United Nations Organization should be the last agency in the world to deny them this newly won right.

Moreover, statelessness implies physical, economic, and juridical disabilities. The residents of the Jerusalem zones, citizens of no country, will have to ask themselves: "Provided we shall receive international passports, who will protect us from personal indignities abroad? In view of the non-existence of an international police force, who will defend us from external aggression? Who will stand up as our spokesman in international councils, defend our interests, express our views, make our proper contributions to international affairs"? It is a curious paradox that the internationalization of Jerusalem, as proposed by the Conciliation Commission, would remove its population from the international arena.

On September 26, 1949, Aubrey S. Eban, Israeli Representative in the United Nations, declared before the General Assembly:

> We regard the Jerusalem problem as composed of two elements. First: there is the responsibility of the United Nations for ensuring that Holy Places and sites are reverently preserved and that religious institutions are assured full liberty in the exercise of their functions. The other purpose, no less valid, and for the Government of Israel not one whit less compelling, is the need to assure the Jewish population of the city the full enjoyment of its democratic political rights in association with the only government to which it is now prepared to offer its allegiance.
>
> We see no incompatibility between these two purposes. Conflict can arise only if there is an unjustified encroachment by one upon the other. Thus, if the political aspirations of Israel and of Jerusalem's population were carried to the point of repudiating the concern of the United Nations for the safeguarding of Holy Places and sites there might be an encroachment upon a universal religious interest. No such eventuality will take place. On the other hand, if the United Nations were to impose upon the population of

Jerusalem any burden or deprivation not strictly related to the satisfaction of universal religious interests, an encroachment would take place upon cherished political freedom. . . .

Ruhi Abdulhadi, Foreign Minister of Trans-Jordan, cabled that Jordan considered the internationalization of Jerusalem as "harmful to its vital interests" and that it would "oppose the execution of whatever is decided contrary to its rightful wishes."

Article I of the United Nations Charter affirms the principle of self-determination. Nowhere is the United Nations Organization or any of its organs empowered to coerce peoples into non-self-government. Since the Jews, who constituted the overwhelming majority of the population of the entire Jerusalem area, and even the Arabs of the Old City, preferred the partition of the area as effected by the Armistice Pact between Israel and Trans-Jordan to "internationalization," a United Nations Organization true to its charter would have seen no reason for unmaking what had become a basis of a permanent peace.

But the political game rarely lacks an element of cynicism and can become doubly cynical when it is pursued in the name of religion. The Arab States which in 1948 had fought against the internationalization of Jerusalem, driven by jealousy of Abdullah and hatred for the Jews, now invoked the sacredness of Jerusalem and agitated in favor of the internationalization of the whole Jerusalem area. The Holy See, anxious to strengthen itself in the Middle East and to make Jerusalem a Roman Catholic center, stated on October 23, 1948: "It would be expedient [notice the word 'expedient'], as a better guarantee for the safety of the sanctuaries under the present circumstances, to give an international character to Jerusalem and its vicinity. . . ." On April 15, 1949, Pope Pius XII added: "We are impelled also to urge our children wherever they may live to work for this just cause to the end that their governments which are competent to act in a matter of such consequence may be persuaded that Jerusalem and its surroundings should be given a juridical status, the security of which under existing conditions should be insured with the support and cooperation of all peace-loving nations respectful of one another's laws." Inspired by these messages of the Vatican, Dr. Rudolf Manoz of Argentina told the General Assembly: "The tradition of my country which is widely Catholic could not but react favorably to the idea of internationalization." Other Latin American countries followed suit.

There have been few opportunities for the creation of confusion and turmoil which Soviet Russia has missed. Here was another chance. Since the Soviet Union, a permanent member of the Trusteeship Council, hoped to use the internationalization of Jerusalem as a means of extending its influence in the Middle East, and since, moreover, the State of Israel had incurred the wrath of the Communists by orienting itself toward the United States, the Politburo ordered its satellites to join the new Holy Alliance of those who demanded the internationalization of the Jerusalem area.

On December 9, 1949, the General Assembly adopted the proposals of the Conciliation Commission. The vote was 30 to 14 with 7 abstentions. While the United States and the United Kingdom as well as most of the nations with large Protestant populations voted against the commission's plan,* the Arab-Soviet-Vatican blocs carried the day.

Legally the new Holy Alliance could, of course, point to the original partition resolution of November 29, 1947, providing for the internationalization of Jerusalem. But the original resolution was meant to establish peace in Palestine. Instead of peace there was the Arab war on the Jews. Max Lerner in the *New York Post* of December 12, 1949, rightly asks the question: "If that war had ended with the Jews being pushed into the sea, would any great power or great church today be moving heaven and earth to fish the Jews out of the sea and restore them to their land?" As it turned out the Jews won the war and held out in the New City of Jerusalem which was theirs also by right of history and population. Trans-Jordan and Israel had been willing to come to terms as neighbors in the Jerusalem area. Skimpy as its legal garments are, an implementation of the new General Assembly decision could but unsettle the peace in Palestine.

There is the religious issue. The professed idea was to give the adherents of the three great religions free access to the Holy Places in Jerusalem. A glance at the map of Jerusalem shows that the Holy Places, churches, synagogues, patriarchates, and monasteries, the historic streets, such as the Via Dolorosa and the sites of the Stations of the Cross, are all in the Old City. A special United Nations commission could easily be entrusted with the responsibility of guarding all shrines and the Holy Places and guarantee worshipers free access to them. The government of Israel had expressed its willingness to cooperate with such a commission and to accept the fullest international safeguards and controls for the protection and immunity of the Holy Places. Abdullah of Trans-Jordan had made similar statements. The United States delegation in the United Nations went further and proposed a limited United Nations police force to administer the Holy Places. All these offers met the issue squarely. But they were rejected in favor of a

* Australia's delegation voted for internationalization. Australia's Labor government was about to fight an election and was wooing the Catholic vote. It lost the election anyway.

resolution which lacks justice, common sense, and historical perspective.

Jerusalem, high up on the plateau of the mountains of Judea, between the Mediterranean and the Dead Sea, has been the center of Jewish life since the day when King Solomon dedicated the Temple. Throughout three thousand years Jews fought and prayed for their Holy City. They show little insight into the meaning of history who believe that a three-thousand-year-old bond can be broken by political expediency.

Chapter Sixteen: ISRAEL—EAST OR WEST

BRIDGE BETWEEN ORIENTAL AND WESTERN CIVILIZATION · NATIONALISM AND INTERNATIONALISM

The mendacious propaganda asserting that the State of Israel has made concessions to Soviet Russia in return for a favorable Soviet vote in the United Nations was blown to bits on that December 9, 1949, when Soviet Russia and her satellites together with the Vatican bloc joined the Arab States in a united front and attacked the very heartbeat of Jewish group existence.

What is Israel's position in the over-all East-West conflict of these fateful years? What is Israel's position in the postwar game of the big powers which began with the ousting of France from the Levant states, the reappearance of Russia on the Mediterranean scene, and the general political and social unrest within the Middle Eastern lands? What will be Israel's prospects of integration into its immediate environment? Is one justified at all in speaking of the significance of a tiny strip of land populated by slightly more than one million people for a region which is so many times larger than the new state in area and in population?

The answer given by history to the last question is that the huge empires of antiquity, developed as they were on the military and administrative side, left less of a cultural legacy to coming generations than did the city states of Phoenicia and Greece and the little Hebrew tribe that fled from the fleshpots of Egypt to form a people whose greatness lay only in its spiritual freedom. Ancient and also modern history provides many examples which should teach us not to overrate population statistics and square miles of area.

The emergence of the new Jewish Commonwealth as an independent political unit in a region characterized by feudal bonds and backward economic conditions is actually a revolutionary event. So far as most countries of the Middle East are concerned, the French Declaration of the Rights of Man might never have occurred. The partial conversion of Egypt, Lebanon, and Syria from a precapitalist to a capitalist economy during the last thirty years has tended to increase rather than to reduce the disparity between the landowning and mercantile upper class and the fellahin. The growth of parliamentary institutions in their outward façade should not be allowed to obscure the fact that in the larger part of the Arab world only a few wealthy families enjoy a modicum of political and personal freedom; that even political parties, which, like the Egyptian Wafd, claim to represent the masses, are upper-middle-class organizations. The doctrine of individual equality, of personal safety and welfare, the idea of the emancipation of the woman has not yet taken root in Arab lands.

To the student of politics it is obvious that the basic conditions for a functioning democracy are not the external forms of parliamentarianism but a literate electorate with supreme controlling power over all public functions. None of the great powers has the human resources and the necessary patience to bridge the gap between Oriental and Western civilization. They must content themselves with sending out some missionaries of their material and ideological strength; and their struggle for supremacy retards rather than accelerates the forward march of the Middle Eastern peoples.

Unlike Americans, British, and Russians, the Jews are settling in the Mediterranean area as a nation, not singly or in small groups but en masse. They are eager to integrate themselves into the local setting which was their traditional home and which is destined to be their actual home. To be sure, they must not try to impose their institutions upon their Arab neighbors. But the living example of a new progressive statehood in the center of the Middle East cannot fail to attract attention.

Political maturity is a sociological phenomenon which does not lend itself to statistical analysis. Economic progress, however, is measurable. The social disabilities of the Middle East spring from no lack of resources. The Middle East oil fields, which began to be exploited only at the beginning of this century, are estimated to contain over 30 per cent of the total world reserves of crude oil. There are other mineral resources; there are, as history shows, the potentialities of a flourishing agriculture. But antiquated methods of technique, organization, and distribution have made of the Middle East one of the worst slum areas of the world. In Egypt increasing multitudes have to live on static resources of wealth. While close to 40 per cent of the arable land is held in large estates by one-half per cent of the total number of landowners, two-thirds of the landowning peasants must be satisfied with an average

Jewish children arriving in Israel. Many of these children have never had a chance to attend school, but have crowded a lifetime into a few years of fighting for survival. *Courtesy of United Palestine Appeal.*

Israeli children planting seedlings for arbor day. *Courtesy of United Palestine Appeal.*

Allenby Road, Tel Aviv. *Courtesy of Israel Office of Information.*

Haifa. *Courtesy of Herbert S. Sonnenfeld.*

holding of only two-fifths of an acre each. Iraq, the eastern extremity of the Fertile Crescent, was known in antiquity as the seat of the empires of Sumer, Akkad, Babylonia, and Assyria. Iraq formed the center of gravity in the rise of Moslem civilization. During the European Dark Ages Baghdad kept alight the lamps of learning and preserved the Greek culture which was carried thence to Moslem Spain and the Western world. Today in the midst of ruin, with the majority of Iraq's four million inhabitants living in indescribable poverty, the splendor of the past can scarcely be believed.

It is in the economic field more than in the area of politics that Jewish incentive may justly be regarded as an example serving to show what can be done in an Oriental setting. No other country in the Middle East has been able to point to signs of progress in agricultural and industrial productivity, in social forms of enterprise, and in the status of the working man and woman so remarkable as that of Israel. Jewish society based on Western science and skills is shaping itself on the very doorstep of the Arab world to which it must strive to adapt itself. Arab society, on the other hand, starts off with an Oriental environment into which its more progressive elements hope to assimilate some Western ingredients. The needs of both are bound to produce a vitalizing effect upon the entire region.

In this respect the present phase of world politics is of significance for the role which the Jewish Commonwealth has carved out for itself in its international relations. The social order of Israel is a symbiosis of free-enterprise capitalism with the radical socialism of the early Judaeo-Christian sects, doctrines of economic and social organization which are generally considered as irreconcilable. The unique harmonious coexistence of individual initiative and social cooperation within the Jewish community is reflected upon the international scene in the already obvious capacity of the new state to approach both the Eastern and the Western worlds with understanding and impartiality.

Ideologically, Israel is a nation imbued with Western ideals which before the rise of Bolshevism were also the ideals of Russian and Eastern European humanity. Politically, Israel values its newly won status too much by far to permit itself voluntarily to become a satellite of either of the two main power blocs. Its leaders believe, as Washington and Jefferson one hundred and fifty years ago believed, that a small state just starting out on its way should not entangle itself by foreign commitments. Its leaders believe that the Middle Eastern countries by learning to practice a similar detachment from the international struggle would not only achieve their own economic and political rehabilitation but also serve the cause of world peace. In appealing to the peoples of the

Middle East to assume the intermediate position of a "third force," Israel allies itself with similar pronouncements of India's Pandit Nehru. From the Hindu as well as from the Jewish point of view the present political divisions of the world are transient. What alone counts against the background of human history in its totality is the gradual synthesis of Western and Eastern forms of life.

Israel has a very firm belief in its sovereign independence. This belief rests on an acute awareness of the distinctiveness of human groups as to historic origin, language, social and economic standards. For centuries, ever since their dispersion, the Jews hoped to take their destiny again into their own hands and live their lives in the image of their own tradition. As other national units emerged in recent years out of regimes of tutelage into national independence, the Jewish community, no less advanced, likewise demanded its own frontiers of authority. Anyone who approves the American Declaration of Independence will sympathize with Israel's insistence on its national separateness. Anyone who has observed how the Netherlands, Belgium, and Luxembourg, once united under one state, seceded from a superimposed political yoke and developed their political independence in conjunction with regional cooperation will realize that Israel's nationalism does not preclude its cooperation with other national units.

Only confused minds regard nationalism as the antithesis of internationalism. No one will deny that nationalism has had a checkered career and that it has often been synonymous with narrow political ambitions, economic exploitation, and militaristic adventurism. But if we are to regard all nationalism as ungodly because it has been debased by men like Mussolini and Hitler, why not also regard religion as synonymous with human sacrifice, forced conversions, and the horrors of Hell? Actually both nationalism and religion are expressions of group personality springing from motives of spiritual self-preservation. It is to Amos and Isaiah rather than to the totalitarian despots that Jewish nationalism looks for guidance.

There is no conflict between Israel's pride in its own free polity and the universalistic trend of our time. Internationalism, as is too often forgotten, means a relationship between nations and presupposes the existence of national units as essential elements in a wider system of human association. Just as the full expression of individual civil rights is the best guarantee of national loyalty, so the full expression of a people's civilization is a necessary condition to its successful integration into the world community.

Political discussion in Western circles during recent years has been focused on the question of world government versus national sovereignty.

If world government is to mean a single political unit enforcing the allegiance of all humanity, I wonder whether its advocates have ever thought about the possibility that in the end Moscow and not Washington, D.C. would be the commanding center of their supranational world. Those who in good faith wish to harmonize the activities of national units in a general stream of universal peace will do well to allow the human spirit the right to express its differences in a variety of social and political organisms instead of pressing them into a totalitarian strait jacket. I, for one, have no quarrel with modern concepts of federalism provided that their standard-bearers allow for the free interplay of different cultures and the organic development of the federal structure. In every example of successful federation, the individual units cooperate on a voluntary basis simply because they realize the benefits of their cooperation. This is the reason for the strength of the United States. This is the reason why Napoleon and Hitler failed.

The rise of Israel as a Jewish commonwealth, the existence of Christian Lebanon and of non-Arab states like Turkey and Iran in the Middle East point in the direction of a regional organization based on economic cooperation rather than racial and religious ties.

To remove a standing invitation to Soviet interference in this area, to prevent its complete Balkanization, the Western powers, in particular Britain, would be well-advised to cease the arming of the Arab States and to discourage further hostilities. Arming and being armed will not help the Arab nations to achieve economic solvency. Once relieved from the waste of playing power politics, they could concentrate on all that is worth while in human life.

Israel's pioneers reclaimed the desert and the swamps before they were forced to take up arms and defend themselves against the mercenaries of an arrogant, albeit cultured, effendi class. Not in warfare, not in dynastic rivalries, but in the redemption of their lands, in guarantees for individual freedom and social progress, lies the hope of Middle Eastern humanity.

Chapter Seventeen: ZION AND THE JEWS OF THE WORLD

JEWS IN THE SOVIET UNION · EMIGRATION FROM EASTERN EUROPE · THE YEMEN AIR LIFT · THE STATE OF ISRAEL AND THE JEWS OF AMERICA

When the white and blue flag with the blue six-pointed Star of David was hoisted on the grounds of the United Nations, symbol of a new state with its own domestic administration, its own armed forces, its own foreign policy, not a few Jews outside the borders of Israel must have asked themselves: "What is my relationship toward this new democracy in the Middle East?"

Before the Nazi fury raged over the European continent close to nine millions Jews, over half the Jewish population of the world, lived in eastern Europe. By V-E Day the Jews of eastern Europe had been reduced to less than three million. The majority of these Jews were in the Soviet Union, where half the Jewish population survived. In Poland, where 3,250,000 Jews had lived before the war, only 80,000 Jews escaped the gas chambers and slaughterhouses of the Hitlerian beasts. In Rumania 300,000 Jews out of a Jewish population of 900,000 are still alive. In Hungary, where some of the leaders of the Horthy regime sabotaged the Nazi demand for the annihilation of Hungarian Jewry, close to half the 470,000 Jewish citizens were rescued. In Czechoslovakia with its 380,000 Jewish inhabitants in 1939, some 50,000 survived the Nazi policy of extermination by going "underground." Another 50,000 fled from Czechoslovakia immediately after the Munich Pact.

Before the war Eastern European Jewry, except for the Jews of Soviet Russia, was the chief source and repository of Jewish cultural life. The overwhelming majority of Eastern European Jews spoke Yiddish, the German of the late Middle Ages which the Jews had acquired on their enforced wanderings through Bohemia and other Germanic lands. In this language, written in Hebrew characters, a vast and beautiful literature had grown up which mirrored the unique Jewish group existence in a predominantly Slavic–Roman Catholic environment. Hebrew, though chiefly the language of the prayer-book, was not forgotten; and at the end of the nineteenth century, inspired by modern Zionism, a Hebrew renaissance was ushered in by the Jewish intelligentsia of Russia, Lithuania, Poland, and Rumania.

In Czarist Russia as in all Eastern European nations, notwithstanding the fact that they were deeply infected with the virus of anti-Semitism, Jewish communal life was extremely well developed. Family ties and common cultural, economic, and social attitudes had led the Jews to build up a complex network of religious, educational, and philanthropic institutions. They had their own newspapers, their own labor unions, their own political parties. Even their legal relationships revolved around rabbinical law and the synagogue rather than the secular courts.

In Russia proper all this came to an abrupt halt after the bolshevist *coup d'état*. Even in the writings of men who ought to know better, one finds the contention that bolshevism, with all its faults, after all abolished such objectionable characteristics of the czarist regime as the "Pale of Settlement" * pogroms against the Jews, and the general discrimination against all non-Russian nationalities. Actually the so-called October Revolution was not directed against an intolerant clique of power-thirsty despots but against the only truly democratic government Russia ever had. It has almost been forgotten that in March, 1917, following the abdication of Czar Nicholas II a provisional government had come into existence which represented a coalition of the main democratic parties of Russia. One of the first acts of this government was the abolition of the "Pale of Settlement" and all other discriminations against Jews. Under the premiership of Prince Lvov and later Alexander Kerensky Russia made up for her previous backwardness and lethargy by creating in a short time democratic institutions which were in many respects the equal of the Western world's. When the Bolshevists seized the reins of power, they immediately destroyed the political liberties for which the liberals of Russia had struggled for generations. Freedom of cultural development, freedom of speech, freedom of the press, just proclaimed by Russian democracy—all this was again *verboten*.

For years Communist propaganda has claimed that all national minority problems have been solved in the Soviet Union and that the Jews,

* Under the czarist regime only a few Jews who had special permission were allowed to reside outside the "Pale of Settlement" comprising the western provinces of Russia.

like other nationalities, are free to live in accordance with their cultural needs and aspirations. For years Communists have pointed to the "Autonomous Jewish Republic of Biro Bidjan" as a symbol of Jewish national freedom in the Soviet Union. But Soviet reality is very different from the Soviet myth. The ill-fated Biro Bidjan colony which the Soviet government had set up on the fringes of Mongolia some twenty-five years ago as a counterpoise to Zionism has never had a Jewish character. According to official sources there are at most 22,000 Jews in Biro Bidjan today. This means that the Jews constitute no more than 18 per cent of the inhabitants of Biro Bidjan, and, according to the Soviet press itself, they not only speak Russian but are forced to live a thoroughly Soviet-Russian life which in its brutality and disrespect for the human individual violates the whole of Jewish tradition.

In the spring of 1929, while in Moscow, I asked for permission to visit Biro Bidjan. This permission was refused, and I could only assume that the Soviet authorities did not want me to see for myself the conditions of the settlement. In the meantime, a number of reports have emanated from there, eyewitness accounts chiefly of Australian Jews who had gone to Biro Bidjan with the illusion of finding there a Jewish and socialist republic. According to their testimony the standard of living is even lower than in European Russia. While Soviet Russia through Ambijan, an American Biro Bidjan Committee, received millions of dollars from private citizens in the United States, the Soviet government itself appears to have lost interest in the project except as a dumping ground for some Jewish refugees from recent anti-Semitic outbursts in Soviet Ukraine.

Soviet protagonists never tire of pointing to the official record of the Soviet government in suppressing anti-Semitism. But in 1936 and 1937 during the famous trials staged by the Politburo against Kamenev, Radek, Sinoviev, and other "deviationists," the Soviet authorities and newspapers never failed to mention the Jewish background of these intellectuals who apparently menaced the psychological security of the mediocre Stalinist bureaucracy, the new ruling class of Soviet Russia, just as the Jewish intelligentsia of Germany used to cause sleepless nights to Hitler and his gangster clique.

Similar signs of anti-Semitism in the highest Soviet circles became apparent after the creation of the State of Israel. When in the fall of 1948 Golda Myerson arrived in Moscow as head of the Israeli legation, the Jews who for thirty years had not dared to visit the one Moscow synagogue that had been allowed for purposes of show made the first unauthorized popular demonstration held in the capital of bolshevism since Stalin took power. On Rosh Hashanah, the Jewish New Year, they thronged the streets leading to the synagogue in order to greet Israel's ambassador on her way to the Jewish services. Joseph Newman, who represented the *New York Herald Tribune* in Moscow during that time, describes the event in these words: "There was an impassioned and almost hysterical outburst of feeling. Jewish men and women broke out in tears. They wept as they cheered and cried aloud: 'We have waited all our lives for this! For Israel! Tomorrow to Jerusalem! . . .' The throng was alive with emotion which could not be contained—an emotion which had been suppressed and thus accumulated over a period of many years. They pushed and shoved to get closer to the Israeli delegation, the symbol of the country to which they looked for salvation."

The Soviet leaders were not slow to punish the demonstrators and to terrify their fellow Jews all over Russia into abandoning the hope which had been so wildly demonstrated a few blocks from the Kremlin fortress.

> First [Newman writes], a group of Jews accused of having been the ringleaders of the demonstration was rounded up and imprisoned. . . . Next, the Soviet police raided and liquidated the only two Yiddish language printing plants in Moscow—the newspaper "Einheit" and "Emess," a house which published books, pamphlets and magazines in Yiddish, especially the works of Sholom Aleichem. At the same time they liquidated the offices of the Jewish Anti-Fascist Committee, which the Soviet leaders evidently felt had served its purpose in mobilizing support during the war but should not be permitted to continue as a center through which Jews could keep in touch with one another. . . . The next step in the campaign against the Jews was to cut them off and isolate them absolutely from the Israeli Legation. . . .

The final move to suppress the flame of freedom among the Jews of Soviet Russia was an anti-Zionist campaign which soon turned into full fledged anti-Semitism. In *My Three Years in Moscow,* Lieutenant General Walter Bedell Smith, our former ambassador to the Soviet Union, describes the anti-Jewish manifestations in the Soviet Union in these words:

> The campaign began on ideological lines with a slashing attack on January 28, 1949 in Pravda upon "cosmopolitanism," which was associated with international Jewry, with Zionism, with pan-Americanism and with Catholicism, all of whose followers were said to be "cosmopolites actively serving the interests of imperialist reaction." To this term the Soviet propagandists added the frequent use of such expressions as "people without kith or kin," "passportless wanderers" and "people without tribe." The first assault was upon certain Jewish theatre critics, but it rapidly was extended to the fields of literature, music, the cinema, philosophy, natural science, atomic energy and even sports. . . . Fuel was added to the campaign on March 14 by a

particularly vicious article published in the Vechernaya Moskva that clearly labeled the victims of its attack as Jews by publishing in brackets the Jewish names they had before they adopted Russian pseudonyms. . . .

Zionism is prohibited in Soviet Russia. Those Jews who long for information about Israel and Jewish life in other countries cannot satisfy their yearnings. The Hebrew language may not be cultivated. A genuine Jewish communal life has been made impossible. Just as Mussolini ordered the Jews of Italy to give up their belief in human equality and join instead an arrogant Fascist "elite," Stalin's regime coerces the Jews of Russia into the surrender of most Jewish values. Moreover, the fact that self-respecting Jews apparently never accept the verdict of any dictatorship, however ruthless it may be, tends to make even Communists of Jewish ancestry suspect in official Soviet circles.

Lazar Kaganovich is the only "Jew" left as a member of the Politburo. No "Jew" has held a high post in the Soviet government since Ivan Maisky and Maksim Litvinov were discharged from the Foreign Office. Many "Jews" have been purged as "Trotskyites" from the party membership. The strength of anti-Jewish sentiment in present-day Russia is indicated by the almost complete absence of Jews from the local administrative services and from the ranks of the managerial bureaucracy of the Soviet industries.

In all probability some of the younger Jews of Soviet Russia are Jews in name only. Nurtured in the aggressive atheism of the bolshevist regime they have never attended a synagogue or temple. Like the non-Jewish youth they have been so indoctrinated as to consider all religion, Judaism included, a dangerous "opiate" for the masses. Membership in an ethnic group comes through the family which transmits the culture of that group. Where, as in Soviet Russia, the social fabric imposes social, economic, and political uniformity on men and women of diverse cultural origins, where Jewish parents are prevented from bringing up their children with a consciousness of their cultural inheritance, the term "Jew" may have the meaning of a serial number, but it ceases to convey the idea of a cultural experience, of a special training in religion and social conduct.

The Moscow demonstration in the fall of 1948 proves that there are many Jews left in Soviet Russia who in spite of all official intimidation have preserved a strong sentiment of sympathy for the national and religious expressions of their people. But since the Soviet government does not allow its citizens to leave Russian territory, since the Iron Curtain virtually shuts them off from the rest of the world, the Zionistic elements in the Jewish population of the Soviet Union are prevented from the possibility of joining with Jews of other lands in the building of the Jewish Commonwealth.

In contrast to the situation in Soviet Russia itself, the satellite countries of eastern Europe permitted the Zionist organizations a few years of independent action. In view of the widespread destruction in all the countries of eastern Europe, it was obvious that even under the best of conditions there would be a difficult transition period before the Jews could be reintegrated into the economic life of these nations. Practically all Jewish survivors were destitute. The new governments, preoccupied with the rebuilding of wrecked industries and transportation systems, regarded the special problems of the Jews as something of an intrusion. Not a few of the local Nazi collaborationists had remained in possession of the stolen Jewish properties by the simple expedient of joining the Communist party. In many cases Jewish communal properties had been taken over by the state. Without the aid rendered by American Jewish organizations like the Joint Distribution Committee and ORT, the Jewish survivors of eastern Europe, penniless, propertyless, hungry, and often sick, would have faced a rather hopeless fate.

With the exception of Bulgaria anti-Semitism had been popular in eastern Europe long before Hitler's rise to power. The Nazi propaganda had done its utmost to keep the flame of hatred burning. While the new governments tried to combat anti-Semitism for fear of a resurrection of Nazi movements, they welcomed, at least temporarily, the Zionist groups which were actively engaged in facilitating the emigration of Eastern European Jews to Palestine. Moreover, Zionism fighting against the British mandatory power in the immediate postwar period seemed to weaken the Anglo-American position in the Middle East. Chiefly for this reason the Soviet Union and its satellites supported the Zionist cause in Lake Success.

With the end of the Arab-Jewish war and the increasing certainty that the State of Israel would refuse to become a tool of the Kremlin, the political reasons for the support of Zionism were gone. As the new "People's Democracies" emerged with American financial help from the postwar crisis and prepared for five-year plans of economic reconstruction and expansion, they began to realize the potential usefulness of the Jews in the local economies. By the fall of 1948 the eagerness of the satellites to rid themselves of the Jewish problem gave way to a desire to keep the Jews in the country.

It was Ilya Ehrenburg's sad privilege to turn against the fondest hopes of his own people in eastern Europe by launching, on October 21, 1948, in *Pravda* a scathing attack against all Zionist activities in the

Soviet orbit and by demanding, certainly not without orders from the Politburo, the immediate and ruthless suppression of all Jewish emigration from the satellite countries to the State of Israel. Early in December the offices of the Zionist organization in Rumania were occupied by Communists, and the Jewish officials were arrested. In February, 1949, Czechoslovakia and Hungary imprisoned most of the functionaries of the Zionist organizations and thousands of other Jews as "dangerous bourgeois nationalists." Poland sharply cut the number of emigration permits, especially for such categories as physicians and engineers. Only Bulgaria's Jews escaped the wrath of Soviet fascism. For when Ehrenburg's article appeared, only 2,000 Jews were left in that country. All the others had settled safely in the land of Israel.

In the Arab countries, as in the Soviet Union, the virtual ban on emigration has so far prevented a larger Jewish exodus. The leaders of the Iraqi Jewish community had told me in 1946 that practically all 90,000 Jews of Iraq were anxious to emigrate to the Jewish National Home. Before World War II members of the Iraqi government had evinced a keen interest in an exchange of Arab-Jewish populations because Iraq, a land of great fertility with an acute need for more population, could well absorb all Palestine Arabs. But during the Arab-Jewish war the Iraqi government, like the governments of the other Arab states, realized that the Arab refugees from the Jewish area of Palestine represented not only a springboard for an attack on Israel but also valuable pawns in the Arab dynastic rivalries in the Middle East, while the Iraqi Jews could be used as hostages. For this reason the government of Iraq clamped down on Jewish emigration and refused to accept Arab refugees into its borders.

Early in 1949 several thousand Jewish families from Libya, Morocco, Tunisia, and Algeria arrived in Israel, and in the summer over 35,000 Jews from the Yemen were flown to Israel in American-built C-54 Skymasters.

Jews have lived in the Yemen even before the second destruction of the Temple. Although they formed but a small minority within the Arab world, spoke Arabic, and resembled the Arabs in physical appearance, they had kept alive the knowledge of the Hebrew language and the Bible as had few Jewish groups. For over two thousand years, generation after generation of Yemenites had prayed the prayer of all Jews, "Next year, oh Lord, in Jerusalem." When in May, 1948, the Jewish State had officially come into existence, the elders of the Jewish community in the Yemen rushed to San'a, the capital of the Yemen and asked the Imam for permission to leave the country. This permission was granted on condition that all emigrating Jews, men, women, and children, would pay him a head tax of three silver dollars and leave behind them whatever little property they had.

As the wealthier paid for those who did not even have the three dollars, the entire Jewish community pulled up its stakes and left for the British protectorate of Aden. There Jewish physicians and social workers from Israel received the emigrees in a camp organized by the American Joint Distribution Committee. In the order in which they arrived, the Yemenites were given Israeli identity cards and new clothing, put in trucks, taken to the airport, and flown, 170 per plane, to the Israeli airport of Lydda. (At this time of writing some 15,000 Yemenite Jews are still traveling the roads of Yemen en route to the receiving center at the outskirts of Aden. With their departure there will end another chapter of enforced social inferiority and misery for a Jewish minority in an Arab land.)

Since the two million Jews of Soviet Russia are separated from the Jewish world by the same forces which separate all Soviet citizens from normal human relationships with the outside world, the five million Jews of the United States of America, representing half of today's Jewish population of the world, remain as the last great reservoir of strength for the development of the State of Israel and of Jewish life in general.

Among the five million Americans who consider themselves Jews, some feel more strongly about their identification as Jews than do others. There are Jews who feel no ties with fellow Jews and do not share Jewish religious, national, or cultural beliefs. They often identify themselves as Jews only because in an era of rampant anti-Semitism, they are too proud and sensitive to abandon a minority group whose sole crime consists of the fact that it maintains and preserves a civilization different from that of the majority.

There are Jews who emphasize their nationality to the exclusion of religious beliefs. Again, there are Jews who believe in the religious universalism of Judaism but hate to be reminded of its ties with a Jewish folk entity and with the national origin of Israel. There used to be descendants of German Jews who looked with disdain on the "Eastern" habits and the jargon of Polish and Russian Jews, until the Nazis condemned both Western and Eastern European Jews to the gas furnaces of their infernal concentration camps. There are Park Avenue Jews who have no traffic with the Jews of the slums. And there are Jews without money who will battle forever against Jews with money. There are Jewish Republicans, Jewish Democrats, and Jewish radicals.

There are orthodox Jews who consider the Torah a divine document miraculously transmitted by God to Moses and the ancient Jews on Mount Sinai. They conceive of the Jews as a priest-people, separated from the rest of the peoples as a priest or monk is separated from the layman. They dedicate themselves deliberately to a conduct in daily life which they feel is the only safeguard protecting God's revelation against the forces of disintegration. They, therefore, insist on the strictest observance of all the laws which are codified in the five books of Moses and the Commentaries of the great rabbis.

There are conservative Jews who subject the Mosaic laws to interpretation in an attempt to bring them into harmony with contemporary conditions. They honor the scriptural commands; they see in them a sort of collective memory of valuable experiences. But they do not regard them as infallible. They demand of the Jew an ethical personality and remind him that he should not cause *Hillul Ha-Shem,* the profanation of God's name, by immoral and vulgar behavior on earth. Judaism, they believe, must strengthen in the Jew his devotion to the fundamental ideal, the Kingdom of God on earth. It must seek to prevent the always possible reversion of mankind to the law of the jungle, to the doctrine that might makes right. With the help of the laws of the Torah, Judaism must therefore endeavor to make Jewish life contribute toward human welfare generally.

There are reformed Jews who in their effort to separate the eternal from the temporal, the spirit from the form, at first cast aside much that gave Judaism its distinctiveness. In the age of "emancipation" following the French Revolution, the founders of the Reform Movement saw Judaism scorned by hosts of Jewish men and women who sought the rights and responsibilities of citizens on equal terms with all other citizens and who resented what they considered an outlandish and outmoded tradition. Abraham Geiger in Germany, Isaac Wise in the United States, met the challenge of the time by minimizing Hebrew as a language of prayer, by discarding the traditional ceremonials, by exchanging a Sunday service for the Sabbath, and by repudiating all Zionist aspirations for the restoration of the Jewish center in Palestine. But in recent years most of the reformed congregations in this country and abroad have reintroduced a number of the traditional rituals, and probably the majority of reformed Jews have come to realize that in Judaism religious universalism and Jewish peoplehood are entwined and intermingled.

American Jews of all walks of life, orthodox, conservative, and reformed, have made their contribution to the restoration of the Jewish homeland, and the overwhelming majority of American Jews will doubtless continue to support the Jewish Commonwealth morally as well as financially. Mordecai Kaplan, in his thought-provoking book *The Future of the American Jew,* compares the role of American Jewry in its relation to the State of Israel to the role of the American home front in relation to the battle front during the recent World War.

> Should the morale of the American Jewish front deteriorate [Kaplan writes], should American Jewry grow listless and disheartened, or should it lose faith in the significance of its struggle for existence, after the manner of our faint-hearted escapists and assimilationists, what would become of a Jewish Eretz Yisrael? Would the little Yishuv alone be able to withstand British imperialism, Arab intransigence and ubiquitous anti-Semitism? What it has already achieved with the aid and support of world Jewry is miracle enough, but to expect it to perform similar miracles in the future, without such aid, is to ask the impossible. We dare not let our home front crumble, and thus betray those who are fighting our battle and holding the line on its most crucial sector, Eretz Yisrael.

Those Jews whom Professor Kaplan of the Jewish Theological Seminary calls "escapists and assimilationists" have at times been worried by the thought that the establishment of the State of Israel might lead to a "dual political allegiance" of American Jewry. As Daniel Frisch, the President of the Zionist Organization of America, stated on November 13, 1949, in his address before the National Administrative Council of the Zionist Organization, this fear has no roots in reality. "American Jews," Frisch said, "are an integral part of the American community. To them the establishment of the State of Israel represents the realization of the historic aspirations of the Jewish people. In no way is their political allegiance affected by the emergence of the State of Israel. American Jews owe their political allegiance to the government of the United States, while the citizens of Israel owe theirs to the government of the State of Israel. The bogey of dual allegiance conjured up by some who should know better is just pure invention. It is a figment of the imagination."

It is important to remember that such political separation does not imply any severance of the close cultural ties existing between the American Jewish community and the Jewish community of Israel. These bonds which existed long before the establishment of the Jewish State, will probably continue to exist as long as Jews acknowledge their tradition and consider themselves as part of a living people.

This does not mean, however, that there are no peripheral Jews. Throughout the history of the dispersion there have been individual Jews who reacted to the conditions of their environment by assimilating themselves to the non-Jewish cultures and religions until they or their children disappeared as Jews. This is the distinction between the Jews who have no quarrel with their Jewishness and the "escapists and assimilationists"; while the latter regard the world as culturally atomistic and attempt to drown themselves in the culture of their non-Jewish environment, the former assimilate all foreign cultures to themselves and preserve their Jewish personality.

I, for one, believe that a Jew is a person who wants to be identified as a Jew. Anyone who cherishes his democratic convictions will realize that each person should have the right to follow his inclinations and make his own choice as to his religious, national, or cultural affiliations.

It should be remembered, too, that the overwhelming majority of American Jews, with complete justification, see no incompatibility whatsoever between their Americanism and their profound interest in the fate and future of the new State of Israel. Jewish civilization, as exemplified in Jewish history and tradition identifies the destiny of the Jews with the destiny of democracy the world over. Jewish ethics, the Jewish ideal of the brotherhood of man, are one with the American declaration that "all men are created equal." The Jewish State can be built only on democratic foundations, or it will not be Jewish. In 1915 an outstanding American and Jew, the late Supreme Court Justice Louis D. Brandeis wrote:

> Let no American imagine that Zionism is inconsistent with Patriotism. Multiple loyalties are objectionable only if they are inconsistent. A man is a better citizen of the United States for being also a loyal citizen of his State, and of his city; for being loyal to his family, and to his profession or trade; for being loyal to his college or his lodge. Every Irish American who contributed towards advancing home rule was a better man and a better American for the sacrifice he made. Every American Jew who aids in the advancing of the Jewish settlement in Palestine, though he feels that neither he nor his descendants will ever live there, will likewise be a better Jew and a better American for doing so.

The creation of the Jewish State is in complete consonance with the best American interests in the Middle East. In fact, if there is one outpost beyond the continental United States which conforms to the "American dream" with its rise of the common man, its faith in self-government and individual freedom, it is the new Jewish Commonwealth.

Throughout the centuries pious Jews, turning their faces toward Jerusalem, could do little more than pray for the restoration of Zion as the center of Jewish life. From now on, American Jews will have the rare privilege of forming a living bridge between the United States and the Republic of Israel. Americans—Jewish and otherwise—will have a chance to serve Israel as many other Americans served the various peoples in the Far East—as engineers, as educators, as doctors, and as missionaries. The United Jewish Appeal, the Zionist Organization, Hadassah, B'nai B'rith, in full accord with the humanitarian principles of Americanism, will be able to concentrate their efforts in behalf of the ingathering of all those Jews who need a home; and at last the multitude of Jewish orphans roaming the highways and byways of Europe and North Africa will no longer be without shelter and without loving care. There is no antithesis between America and Israel. But a fundamental conflict does exist between loyalty and lack of character. He who remains true to his tradition, he who cares for the homeless of his people will also be loyal to the state of which he is a citizen. He who is faithless to the one will usually be faithless to both.

Those who insinuate that Zionists are incapable of wholehearted allegiance to the United States, those who cast reflections on the patriotism of millions of American Jews, have never really understood the spirit of America. The United States is neither Hitlerian Germany nor Soviet Russia. America stands for democracy which provides for the full expression of all socially legitimate human interests and integrates the many loyalties arising from the varied human relationships within the framework of the larger association of all citizens, the state. America stands for cultural pluralism and not the totalitarian strait jacket.

Americanism does not require the suppression of culture, however originated. It is the greatness of America that it encourages the release of all potential abilities of the individual and of the group of which he is a member. There is nothing disloyal or un-American in a Catholic who sends his financial contributions to Rome and who receives his religious inspiration from the Vatican. There is nothing disloyal in an American of French descent sending CARE packages abroad and helping French democrats build a new, respected France. Within the framework of American democracy there is ample room for the Jewish group, too, to alleviate the pressing burdens assumed by the fledgling State of Israel to absorb the Jewish homeless and to develop, along with other cultural and ethnic groups, a heritage which can only enrich our American civilization.

It was Voltaire who said that every cultured person should have two fatherlands, his own and France. In a similar, equally nonpolitical sense, the Jews of the world, and perhaps quite a few non-Jews, will look upon Israel.

The bridge between the outside Jewish world and the State of Israel will be a two-way passage. New works on ethical and religious themes can be expected to emanate from Israel. American-Jewish community life, which has so often been devoid of intellectual and cultural substance, will receive new stimulus. The Hebrew University will contribute to a betterment of Jewish education everywhere. It would be folly to assume that American Jewry can live by a culture imported wholesale from the State of Israel. Its own needs will by necessity continue to create its own patterns of life. But the fraternal interchange with Israel, the two-way passage, will be of great and new significance.

I have not spoken of the 700,000 Jews of the British Commonwealth of Nations, the 350,000 Jews of the European Continent west of the Iron Curtain, and the 600,000 Jews in the countries of Latin America. Their problems are essentially the same as the problems of American Jewry. A few of them will want to settle in the Jewish Commonwealth and accept Israeli citizenship. Most of them will stay in the countries of their birth and present citizenship, feeling about the State of Israel as the American of British descent feels whose parents migrated to the United States to become American citizens but bequeathed to their children their own sentimental attachment for "the old country."

Appreciative of the wonderful freedom of this country, Jews have always been among the most loyal and most devoted citizens of the United States. American Jews owe no allegiance to the State of Israel, but they share with Jews everywhere a common heritage of history, religion, and culture which justifiably commands their respect and devotion. They have therefore a genuine interest in the flowering of Jewish civilization, in the security and happiness of the Jews in Israel. Because they cherish America as their home, they consider it a sacred duty to secure the blessings of a home for those of their fellow Jews who are homeless. Their love of Zion rests on the firm knowledge that a strong democratic commonwealth in the Middle East serves the best interests of the United States.

EPILOGUE

Our times have seen the emergence of several new free commonwealths. Oppressed peoples have risen up and freed their cultures from the shackles that bound them in the past. Large and small nations have striven into equality with those whose political and economic life has been firmly established for centuries. Among them were the Jews of Palestine.

In a sense, they had been under their own government for years. For it was the Jewish national institutions and not the apathetic mandatory administration which were doing the work of state building. They organized schools and health services. Through local councils they administered cities, towns, and villages. Though taxes were levied by the British Government, the Jews imposed on themselves a system of self-taxation for the Jewish National Fund, for industrial reconstruction, for Haganah—which, though voluntary, no Jew evaded. Their military units joined the Allies during the last World War. Their young men and women served in the Palestine defense forces. And so when the mandate ended, the Jewish community marched onward to the threshold of statehood.

It was at the moment of utmost peril that Israel proclaimed its national independence. Well-organized Arab armies stood within a few miles of its main centers ready to strike, while the troops of the mandatory power made their last effort to dislodge the Haganah from its defense posts. The new republic passed through a time of which books will tell as they tell of the Maccabees, of the beginnings of the Swiss Confederacy, and the union of the thirteen states of North America. It was a time of blood and toil and real sacrifices. Israel strained every nerve, mobilized all resources for survival, and she won her way through the crucial first stage.

It is no gratifying task to look ahead in order to discern how the pattern of the future will be shaped. Real peace and understanding between Israel and her Arab neighbors are still to come. There is still the problem of Jerusalem. While the Holy Places are rightfully the concern of religious mankind, the Jews of Jerusalem will decide their political fate as all other Jews of Israel have decided theirs.

There is still the problem of the resettlement of the Arab refugees from Palestine. When the appointment of a United Nations Economic Mission to the Middle East under the chairmanship of Gordon Clapp of TVA was announced in August, 1949, there was hope that projects on the TVA pattern would make a living reality of President Truman's new Point Four Program and allow the rehabilitation of the refugees in the vast underdeveloped regions of the Arab world. But because of the intransigence of most of the Arab States, the Clapp Mission has bogged down in minor relief projects which, important as they may be for the beneficiaries among the refugees, are no proper substitute for the original scheme.

If the Arab States should persist in demanding the return of all those Arabs who lived in or near the Jewish area of Palestine to the State of Israel, the government of Israel would be well-advised to follow Bartley Crum's suggestions in the *Jewish National Monthly* of November, 1949, and demand the extension of its sovereignty over the whole of Palestine territory as it existed under the British Mandate and as it was promised to the Jews by the League of Nations. For only in a larger, economically viable and militarily defensible area, could Israel dare to attempt the reintegration of all those Arabs who fled the country under the goad of the ex-Mufti of Jerusalem and the Arab Higher Committee.

Israel is still on a war footing and cannot afford to relax her watchfulness. Yet she must plan ahead. Israel is the homeland, not only for those Jews who are already there, but also for the hundreds of thousands who look to Israel as their country and the goal of a long journey. Zionism, the creation of a commonwealth for the homeless members of the Jewish people, motivated the struggle and the sacrifice. Now that the Commonwealth has been achieved, it recognizes as its foremost obligation the gathering in of all those Jews who want to live within its borders and in an atmosphere of democratic freedom.

The government of Israel, planning for the increase of the country's absorptive capacity to the very maximum, cannot in fairness be expected to carry the double load of defending and resettling the country, of solving a problem which fundamentally is a task not only for the Jewish people as a whole but also for the international community.

Literally the future of the State of Israel will depend upon the Jews of the world, especially upon the Jews of America and their willingness to come to the aid of the young Jewish Commonwealth. This time is not only a test for Israel. For the Jews of America this is also "their finest hour."

The day of peace and unhindered development is, I hope, not far ahead. Yet the fact remains that Israel, in spite of a further rapid growth of her population, will always be a Jewish island in a turbulent Arab sea. It would be lighthearted to assume that the Arab countries will never again try to reconquer the Jewish land and absorb it in the Arab domain. The struggle between France and Germany over Alsace-Lorraine and many other analogous struggles should warn us that such an urge may persist for centuries to come.

It would not be wise to count upon the backwardness of the Arab countries as compared with the progressive Jewish Commonwealth. Azzam Pasha came close to the truth when he remarked, "The difference between ignorance and knowledge is ten years in school." The rise of Israel will have an immense influence on the whole of the Middle East and spur the Arabs to unprecedented efforts. But quite apart from the pace of their own growth, as Emanuel Neumann has pointed out in the *New Palestine* of November 22, 1949: "There will always be the danger of their deriving from outside sources and interested powers the resources, the equipment, the instruction and technical forces to effect a revolutionary change in their military potential. Left to itself, Israel may therefore be repeatedly exposed to mortal danger on its several fronts, or forced to carry the staggering burden of a large and permanent military establishment, with all that it implies."

For a great many years to come the State of Israel will need the help of the Jews the world over who are not its citizens but have a legitimate and vital stake in its welfare. For a great many years to come the Jews of America and with them the hundreds of thousands of American Christians who have already demonstrated their sympathy for Israel will have to continue their vigilance lest the geographical and numerical inferiority of the young state might bring it disaster.

Israel and the truly progressive and liberal forces the world over are partners in a great and wonderful enterprise. As British statesmen in their long-term planning take the support of the whole English speaking world into account, Israel must be enabled to base her plans for the future on a powerful Zionist movement and the loyal backing of all truly democratic men and women.

The Republic of Israel is a firm reality. But there is more in store for the people of the Bible. The mandates of the Sinaitic message remain valid in the future as they have been valid in the past. They have their significance for Jews as well as non-Jews. The battle for the removal of all barriers which bar the way of man to his divine patrimony has just begun. In this battle men and women of good will, irrespective of race, color, religion, and nationality, must join.

SELECTED REFERENCES

BOOKSTABER, PHILIP D., *Judaism and the American Mind,* Bloch Publishing Co., New York, 1939.

BOROCHOV, BER, *Nationalism and the Class Struggle,* Young Poale Zion Alliance of America, New York, 1937.

COHEN, ISRAEL, *The Zionist Movement,* Zionist Organization of America, New York, 1947.

CROSSMAN, RICHARD, *Palestine Mission,* Harper & Brothers, New York, 1947.

FRIEDRICH, CARL J., *American Policy Toward Palestine,* Public Affairs Press, Washington, D.C., 1944.

GOLDMAN, SOLOMON, *Crisis and Decision,* Harper & Brothers, New York, 1938.

DE HAAS, JACOB, *Theodor Herzl,* The Leonard Company, Chicago–New York, 1927.

HOURANI, A. H., *Minorities in the Arab World,* Oxford University Press, New York, 1947.

KAPLAN, MORDECAI, *The Future of the American Jew,* The Macmillan Company, New York, 1948.

LOWDERMILK, W. C., *Palestine, Land of Promise,* Harper & Brothers, New York, 1944.

The Middle East, Europa Publications, London, 1948.

Palestine Affairs, A Monthly Bulletin on Palestine and the Middle East, vols. 1–4, American Zionist Emergency Council.

"Palestine Royal Commission Report," Cmd. 5479, London, 1937.

SACHAR, ABRAM LEON, *A History of the Jews,* Alfred A. Knopf., Inc., New York, 1948.

WEIZMANN, CHAIM, *Trial and Error,* Harper & Brothers, New York, 1949.

WELLES, SUMNER, *We Need Not Fail,* Houghton Mifflin Company, Boston, 1948.

APPENDIXES

THE MANDATE FOR PALESTINE

The Council of the League of Nations:

Whereas the Principal Allied Powers have agreed, for the purpose of giving effect to the provisions of Article 22 of the Covenant of the League of Nations, to entrust to a Mandatory selected by the said Powers the administration of the territory of Palestine, which formerly belonged to the Turkish Empire, within such boundaries as may be fixed by them; and

Whereas the Principal Allied Powers have also agreed that the Mandatory should be responsible for putting into effect the declaration originally made on November 2nd, 1917, by the Government of His Britannic Majesty, and adopted by the said Powers, in favour of this establishment in Palestine of a national home for the Jewish people, it being clearly understood that nothing should be done which might prejudice the civil and religious rights of existing non-Jewish communities in Palestine, or the rights and political status enjoyed by Jews in any other country; and

Whereas recognition has thereby been given to the historical connection of the Jewish people with Palestine and to the grounds for reconstituting their national home in that country; and

Whereas the Principal Allied Powers have selected His Britannic Majesty as the Mandatory for Palestine; and

Whereas the mandate in respect of Palestine has been formulated in the following terms and submitted to the Council of the League for approval; and

Whereas His Britannic Majesty has accepted the mandate in respect of Palestine and undertaken to exercise it on behalf of the League of Nations in conformity with the following provisions; and

Whereas by the fore-mentioned Article 22 (paragraph 8), it is provided that the degree of authority, control or administration to be exercised by the Mandatory, not having been previously agreed upon by the Members of the League, shall be explicitly defined by the Council of the League of Nations;

Confirming the said mandate, defines its terms as follows:

Article 1

The Mandatory shall have full powers of legislation and of administration, save as they may be limited by the terms of this mandate.

Article 2

The Mandatory shall be responsible for placing the country under such political, administrative and economic conditions as will secure the establishment of the Jewish national home, as laid down in the preamble, and the development of self-governing institutions, and also for safeguarding the civil and religious rights of all the inhabitants of Palestine, irrespective of race and religion.

Article 3

The Mandatory shall, so far as circumstances permit, encourage local autonomy.

Article 4

An appropriate Jewish agency shall be recognised as a public body for the purpose of advising and co-operating with the Administration of Palestine in such economic, social and other matters as may affect the establishment of the Jewish national home and the interests of the Jewish population in Palestine, and, subject always to the control of the Administration, to assist and take part in the development of the country.

The Zionist organisation, so long as its organisation and constitution are in the opinion of the Mandatory appropriate, shall be recognised as such agency. It shall take steps in consultation with His Britannic Majesty's Government to secure the co-operation of all Jews who are willing to assist in the establishment of the Jewish national home.

Article 5

The Mandatory shall be responsible for seeing that no Palestine territory shall be ceded or leased to, or in any way placed under the control of, the Government of any foreign Power.

Article 6

The Administration of Palestine, while ensuring that the rights and position of other sections of the population are not prejudiced, shall facilitate Jewish immigration under suitable conditions and shall encourage, in co-operation with the Jewish agency referred to in Article 4, close settlement by Jews on the land, including State lands and waste lands not required for public purposes.

Article 7

The Administration of Palestine shall be responsible for enacting a nationality law. There shall be included in this law provisions framed so as to facilitate the acquisition of Palestine citizenship by Jews who take up their permanent residence in Palestine.

Article 8

The privileges and immunities of foreigners, including the benefits of consular jurisdiction and protection as formerly enjoyed by Capitulation or usage in the Ottoman Empire, shall not be applicable in Palestine.

Unless the Powers whose nationals enjoyed the aforementioned privileges and immunities on August 1st, 1914, shall have previously renounced the right to their re-establishment, or shall have agreed to their non-application for a specified period, these privileges and immunities shall, at the expiration of the mandate, be immediately re-established in their entirety or with such modifications as may have been agreed upon between the Powers concerned.

Article 9

The Mandatory shall be responsible for seeing that the judicial system established in Palestine shall assure to foreigners, as well as to natives, a complete guarantee of their rights.

Respect for the personal status of the various peoples and communities and for their religious interests shall be fully guaranteed. In particular, the control and administration of Wakfs shall be exercised in accordance with religious law and the dispositions of the founders.

Article 10

Pending the making of special extradition agreements relating to Palestine, the extradition treaties in force between the Mandatory and other foreign Powers shall apply to Palestine.

Article 11

The Administration of Palestine shall take all necessary measures to safeguard the interests of the community in connection with the development of the country, and, subject to any international obligations accepted by the Mandatory, shall have full power to provide for public ownership or control of any of the natural resources of the country or of the public works, services and utilities established or to be established therein. It shall introduce a land system appropriate to the needs of the country, having regard, among other things, to the desirability of promoting the close settlement and intensive cultivation of the land.

The Administration may arrange with the Jewish agency mentioned in Article 4 to construct or operate, upon fair and equitable terms, any public works, services and utilities, and to develop any of the natural resources of the country, in so far as these matters are not directly undertaken by the Administration. Any such arrangements shall provide that no profits distributed by such agency, directly or indirectly, shall exceed a reasonable rate of interest on the capital, and any further profits shall be utilised by it for the benefit of the country in a manner approved by the Administration.

Article 12

The Mandatory shall be entrusted with the control of the foreign relations of Palestine and the right to issue exequaturs to consuls appointed by foreign Powers. He shall also be entitled to afford diplomatic and consular protection to citizens of Palestine when outside its territorial limits.

Article 13

All responsibility in connection with the Holy Places and religious buildings or sites in Palestine, including that of preserving existing rights and of securing free access to the Holy Places, religious buildings and sites and the free exercise of worship, while ensuring the requirements of public order and decorum, is assumed by the Mandatory who shall be responsible solely to the League of Nations in all matters connected herewith, provided that nothing in this article shall prevent the Mandatory from entering into such arrangements as he may deem reasonable with the Administration for the purpose of carrying the provisions of this article into effect; and provided also that nothing in this mandate shall be construed as conferring upon the Mandatory authority to interfere with the fabric or the management of purely Moslem sacred shrines, the immunities of which are guaranteed.

Article 14

A special Commission shall be appointed by the Mandatory to study, define and determine the rights and claims in connection with the Holy Places and the rights and claims relating to the different religious communities in Palestine. The method of nomination, the composition and functions of this Commission shall be submitted to the Council of the League for its approval, and the Commission shall not be appointed or enter upon its functions without the approval of the Council.

Article 15

The Mandatory shall see that complete freedom of conscience and the free exercise of all forms of worship, subject only to the maintenance of public order and morals, are ensured to all. No discrimination of any kind shall be made between the inhabitants of Palestine on the ground of race, religion or language. No person shall be excluded from Palestine on the sole ground of his religious belief.

The right of each community to maintain its own schools for the education of its own members in its own language, while conforming to such educational requirements of a general nature as the Administration may impose, shall not be denied or impaired.

Article 16

The Mandatory shall be responsible for exercising such supervision over religious and eleemosynary bodies of all faiths in Palestine as may be required for the maintenance of public order and good government. Subject to such supervision, no measures shall be taken in Palestine to obstruct or interfere with the enterprise of such bodies or to discriminate against any representative or member of them on the ground of his religion or nationality.

Article 17

The Administration of Palestine may organise on a voluntary basis the forces necessary for the preservation of peace and order, and also for the defence of the country, subject however, to the supervision of the Mandatory, but shall not use them for purposes other than those above specified save with the consent of the Mandatory. Except for such purposes, no military, naval or air forces shall be raised or maintained by the Administration of Palestine.

Nothing in this article shall preclude the Administration of Palestine from contributing to the cost of the maintenance of the forces of the Mandatory in Palestine.

The Mandatory shall be entitled at all times to use the roads, railways and ports of Palestine for the movement of armed forces and the carriage of fuel and supplies.

Article 18

The Mandatory shall see that there is no discrimination in Palestine against the nationals of any State Member of the League of Nations (including companies incorporated under its laws) as compared with those of the Mandatory or of any foreign State in matters concerning taxation, commerce or navigation, the exercise of industries or professions, or in the treatment of merchant vessels or civil aircraft. Similarly, there shall be no discrimination in Palestine against goods originating in or destined for any of the said States, and there shall be freedom of transit under equitable conditions across the mandated area.

Subject as aforesaid and to the other provisions of this mandate, the Administration of Palestine may, on the advice of the Mandatory, impose such taxes and customs duties as it may consider necessary, and take such steps as it may think best to promote the development of the natural resources of the country and to safeguard the interests of the population. It may also, on the advice of the Mandatory, conclude a special customs agreement with any State the territory of which in 1914 was wholly included in Asiatic Turkey or Arabia.

Article 19

The Mandatory shall adhere on behalf of the Administration of Palestine to any general international convention already existing, or which may be concluded hereafter with the approval of the League of Nations, respecting the slave traffic, the traffic in arms and ammunition, or the traffic in drugs, or relating to commercial equality, freedom of transit and navigation, aerial navigation and postal, telegraphic and wireless communication or literary, artistic or industrial property.

Article 20

The Mandatory shall co-operate on behalf of the Administration of Palestine, so far as religious, social or other conditions may permit, in the execution of any common policy adopted by the League of Nations for preventing and combating disease, including disease of plants and animals.

Article 21

The Mandatory shall secure the enactment within twelve months from this date, and shall ensure the execution of a Law of Antiquities based on the following rules. This law shall ensure equality of treatment in the matter of excavations and archaeological research to the nationals of all States Members of the League of Nations.

(Rules 1–8 omitted.)

Article 22

English, Arabic and Hebrew shall be the official languages of Palestine. Any statement or inscription in Arabic on stamps or money in Palestine shall be repeated in Hebrew and any statement or inscription in Hebrew shall be repeated in Arabic.

Article 23

The Administration of Palestine shall recognise the holy days of the respective communities in Palestine as legal days of rest for the members of such communities.

Article 24

The Mandatory shall make to the Council of the League of Nations an annual report to the satisfaction of the Council as to the measures taken during the year to carry out the provisions of the mandate. Copies of all laws and regulations promulgated or issued during the year shall be communicated with the report.

Article 25

In the territories lying between the Jordan and the eastern boundary of Palestine as ultimately determined, the Mandatory shall be entitled, with the consent of the Council of the League of Nations, to postpone or withhold application of such provisions of this mandate as he may consider inapplicable to the existing local conditions and to make such provision for the administration of the territories as he may consider suitable to those conditions, provided that no action shall be taken which is inconsistent with the provisions of Articles 15, 16 and 18.

Article 26

The Mandatory agrees that if any dispute whatever should arise between the Mandatory and another Member of the League of Nations relating to the interpretation or the application of the provision of the mandate, such dispute, if it cannot be settled by negotiation, shall be submitted to the Permanent Court of International Justice provided for by Article 14 of the Covenant of the League of Nations.

Article 27

The consent of the Council of the League of Nations is required for any modification of the terms of this mandate.

Article 28

In the event of the termination of the mandate hereby conferred upon the Mandatory, the Council of the League of Nations shall make such arrangements as may be deemed necessary for safeguarding in perpetuity, under the guarantee of the League, the rights secured by Articles 13 and 14, and shall use its influence for securing, under the guarantee of the League, that the Government of Palestine will fully honour the financial obligations legitimately incurred by the Administration of Palestine during the period of the mandate, including the rights of public servants to pensions or gratuities.

The present instrument shall be deposited in original in the archives of the League of Nations and certified copies shall be forwarded by the Secretary-General of the League of Nations to all Members of the League.

Done at London the twenty-fourth day of July, one thousand nine hundred and twenty-two.

RESOLUTION ADOPTED BY THE GENERAL ASSEMBLY, NOVEMBER 29, 1947

THE GENERAL ASSEMBLY, HAVING MET in special session at the request of the Mandatory Power to constitute and instruct a Special Committee to prepare for the consideration of the question of the future government of Palestine at the second regular session;

HAVING CONSTITUTED a Special Committee and instructed it to investigate all questions and issues relevant to the problem of Palestine, and to prepare proposals for the solution of the problem; and

HAVING RECEIVED AND EXAMINED the report of the Special Committee, including a number of unanimous recommendations and a plan of partition with economic union approved by the majority of the Special Committee;

CONSIDERS that the present situation in Palestine is one which is likely to impair the general welfare and friendly relations among nations;

TAKES NOTE of the declaration by the Mandatory Power that it plans to complete its evacuation of Palestine by August 1, 1948;

RECOMMENDS to the United Kingdom, as the Mandatory Power for Palestine, and to all other Members of the United Nations the adoption and implementation, with regard to the future government of Palestine, of the Plan of Partition with Economic Union set out below;

REQUESTS THAT

THE SECURITY COUNCIL take the necessary measures as provided for in the Plan for its implementation;

The Security Council consider if circumstances during the transitional period require such consideration, whether the situation in Palestine constitutes a threat to the peace. If it decides that such a threat exists, and in order to maintain international peace and security, the Security Council should supplement the authorization of the General Assembly by taking measures, under Articles 39 and 41 of the Charter, to empower the United Nations Commission, as provided in this resolution, to exercise in Palestine the functions which are assigned to it by this resolution;

The Security Council determine as a threat to the peace, breach of the peace or act of aggression, in accordance with Article 39 of the Charter, any attempt to alter by force the settlement envisaged by this resolution;

The Trusteeship Council be informed of the responsibilities envisaged for it in this Plan;

CALLS UPON the inhabitants of Palestine to take such steps as may be necessary on their part to put this Plan into effect;

APPEALS to all Governments and all peoples to refrain from taking any action which might hamper or delay the carrying out of these recommendations; and

AUTHORIZES the Secretary-General to reimburse travel and subsistence expenses of the members of the Commission, on such basis and in such form as he may determine most appropriate in the circumstances, and to provide to the Commission the necessary staff to assist in carrying out the functions assigned to the Commission by the General Assembly.

PLAN OF PARTITION WITH ECONOMIC UNION

FUTURE CONSTITUTION AND GOVERNMENT OF PALESTINE

The Mandate for Palestine shall terminate as soon as possible but in any case not later than August 1, 1948.

The armed forces of the Mandatory Power shall be progressively withdrawn from Palestine, the withdrawal to be completed as soon as possible but in any case not later than August 1, 1948.

The Mandatory Power shall advise the Commission, as far in advance as possible, of its intention to terminate the Mandate and to evacuate each area.

The Mandatory Power shall use its best endeavors to ensure that an area situated in the territory of the Jewish State, including a seaport and hinterland adequate to provide facilities for a substantial immigration, shall be evacuated at the earliest possible date and in any event not later than February 1, 1948.

Independent Arab and Jewish States and the Special International Regime for the City of Jerusalem, set forth in this Plan, shall come into existence in Palestine two months after the evacuation of the armed forces of the Mandatory Power has been completed but in any case not later than October 1, 1948. The boundaries of the Arab State, the Jewish State, and the City of Jerusalem shall be as described below.

The period between the adoption by the General Assembly of its recommendation on the question of Palestine and the establishment of the independence of the Arab and Jewish States shall be a transitional period.

Steps Preparatory to Independence

A Commission shall be set up consisting of one representative of each of five Member States. The Members represented on the Commission shall be elected by the General Assembly on as broad a basis, geographically and otherwise, as possible.

The administration of Palestine shall, as the Mandatory Power withdraws its armed forces, be progressively turned over to the Commission, which shall act in conformity with the recommendations of the General Assembly, under the guidance of the Security Council. The Mandatory Power shall to the fullest possible extent coordinate its plans for withdrawal with the plans of the Commission to take over and administer areas which have been evacuated.

In the discharge of this administrative responsibility the Commission shall have authority to issue necessary regulations and take other measures as required.

The Mandatory Power shall not take any action to prevent, obstruct or delay the implementation by the Commission of the measures recommended by the General Assembly.

On its arrival in Palestine the Commission shall proceed to carry out measures for the establishment of the frontiers of the Arab and Jewish States and the City of Jerusalem in accordance with the general lines of the recommendations of the General Assembly on the partition of Palestine. Nevertheless, the boundaries as described in this Plan are to be modified in such a way that village areas as a rule will not be divided by state boundaries unless pressing reasons make that necessary.

The Commission, after consultation with the democratic parties and other public organizations of the Arab and Jewish States, shall select and establish in each State as rapidly as possible a Provisional Council of Government. The activities of both the Arab and Jewish Provisional Councils of Government shall be carried out under the general direction of the Commission.

If by April 1, 1948 a Provisional Council of Government cannot be selected for either of the States, or, if selected, cannot carry out its functions, the Commission shall communicate that fact to the Security Council for such action with respect to that State as the Security Council may deem proper, and to the Secretary-General for communication to the Members of the United Nations.

Subject to the provisions of these recommendations, during the transitional period the Provisional Councils of Government, acting under the Commission, shall have full authority in the areas under their control, including authority over matters of immigration and land regulation.

The Provisional Council of Government of each State, acting under the Commission, shall progressively receive from the Commission full responsibility for the administration of that State in the period between the termination of the Mandate and the establishment of the States' independence.

The Commission shall instruct the Provisional Councils of Government of both the Arab and Jewish States, after their formation, to proceed to the establishment of administrative organs of government, central and local.

The Provisional Council of Government of each State shall, within the shortest time possible, recruit an armed militia from the residents of that State, sufficient in number to maintain internal order and to prevent frontier clashes.

This armed militia in each State shall, for operational purposes, be under the command of Jewish or Arab officers resident in that State, but general political and military control, including the choice of the militia's High Command, shall be exercised by the Commission.

The Provisional Council of Government of each State shall, not later than two months after the withdrawal of the armed forces of the Mandatory Power, hold elections to the Constituent Assembly which shall be conducted on democratic lines.

The election regulations in each State shall be drawn up by the Provisional Council of Government and approved by the Commission. Qualified voters for each State for this election shall be persons over eighteen years of age who are: (a) Palestinian citizens residing in that State and (b) Arabs and Jews residing in the State, although not Palestinian citizens, who, before voting, have signed a notice of intention to become citizens of such State.

Arabs and Jews residing in the City of Jerusalem who have signed a notice of intention to become citizens, the Arabs of the Arab State and the Jews of the Jewish State, shall be entitled to vote in the Arab and Jewish States respectively.

Women may vote and be elected to the Constituent Assemblies.

During the transitional period no Jew shall be permitted to establish residence in the area of the proposed Arab State, and no Arab shall be permitted to establish residence in the area of the proposed Jewish State, except by special leave of the Commission.

The Constituent Assembly of each State shall draft a democratic Constitution for its State and choose a provisional government to succeed the Provisional Council of Government appointed by the Commission. The Constitutions of the States shall embody the first two major subsections of the Declaration provided for below and include *inter alia* provisions for:

Establishing in each State a legislative body elected by universal suffrage and by secret ballot on the basis of proportional representation, and an executive body responsible to the legislature.

Settling all international disputes in which the State may be involved by peaceful means in such a manner that international peace and security, and justice, are not endangered.

Accepting the obligation of the State to refrain in its international relations from the threat or use of force against the territorial integrity or political independence of any State, or in any other manner inconsistent with the purposes of the United Nations.

Guaranteeing to all persons equal and non-discriminatory rights in civil, political, economic and religious matters and the enjoyment of human rights and fundamental freedoms, including freedom of religion, language, speech and publication, education, assembly and association.

Preserving freedom of transit and visit for all residents and citizens of the other State in Palestine and the City of Jerusalem, subject to considerations of national security, provided that each State shall control residence within its borders.

The Commission shall appoint a Preparatory Economic Commission of three members to make whatever arrangements are possible for economic cooperation, with a view to establishing, as soon as practicable, the Economic Union and the Joint Economic Board, as provided below.

During the period between the adoption of the recommendations on the question of Palestine by the General Assembly and the termination of the Mandate, the Mandatory Power in Palestine shall maintain full responsibility for administration in areas from which it has not withdrawn its armed forces. The Commission shall assist the Mandatory Power in the carrying out of these functions. Similarly the Mandatory Power shall cooperate with the Commission in the execution of its functions.

With a view to ensuring that there shall be continuity in the functioning of administrative services and that, on the withdrawal of the armed forces of the Mandatory Power, the whole administration shall be in the charge of the Provisional Councils and the Joint Economic Board, respectively, acting under the Commission, there shall be a progressive transfer, from the Mandatory Power to the Commission, of responsibility for all the functions of government, including that of maintaining law and order in the areas from which the forces of the Mandatory Power have been withdrawn.

The Commission shall be guided in its activities by the recommendations of the General Assembly and by such instructions as the Security Council may consider necessary to issue.

The measures taken by the Commission, within the recommendations of the General Assembly, shall become immediately effective unless the Commission has previously received contrary instructions from the Security Council.

The Commission shall render periodic monthly progress reports, or more frequently if desirable, to the Security Council.

The Commission shall make its final report to the next regular session of the General Assembly and to the Security Council simultaneously.

DECLARATION

A Declaration shall be made to the United Nations by the Provisional Government of each proposed State before independence. It shall contain *inter alia* the following clauses:

General Provision

The stipulations contained in the Declaration are recognized as fundamental laws of the State and no law, regulation or official action shall conflict or interfere with these stipulations, nor shall any law, regulation or official action prevail over them.

Holy Places, Religious Buildings and Sites

Existing rights in respect of Holy Places and religious buildings or sites shall not be denied or impaired.

In so far as Holy Places are concerned, the liberty of access, visit and transit shall be guaranteed, in conformity with existing rights, to all residents and citizens of the other State and of the City of Jerusalem, as well as to aliens, without distinction as to nationality, subject to requirements of national security, public order and decorum.

Similarly, freedom of worship shall be guaranteed in conformity with existing rights, subject to the maintenance of public order and decorum.

Holy Places and religious buildings or sites shall be preserved. No act shall be permitted which may in any way impair their sacred character. If at any time it appears to the Government that any particular Holy Place, religious building or site is in need of urgent repair, the Government may call upon the community or communities concerned to carry out such repair. The Government may carry it out itself at the expense of the community or communities concerned if no action is taken within a reasonable time.

No taxation shall be levied in respect of any Holy Place, religious building or site which was exempt from taxation on the date of the creation of the State.

No change in the incidence of such taxation shall be made which would either discriminate between the owners or occupiers of Holy Places, religious buildings or sites, or would place such owners or occupiers in a position less favorable in relation to the general incidence of taxation than existed at the time of the adoption of the Assembly's recommendations.

The Governor of the City of Jerusalem shall have the right to determine whether the provisions of the Constitution of the State in relation to Holy Places, religious buildings and sites within the borders of the State and the religious rights appertaining thereto, are being properly applied and respected, and to make decisions on the basis of existing rights in cases of disputes which may arise between the different religious communities or the rites of a religious community with respect to such Places, buildings and sites. He shall receive full cooperation and such privileges and immunities as are necessary for the exercise of his functions in the State.

Religious and Minority Rights

Freedom of conscience and the free exercise of all forms of worship, subject only to the maintenance of public order and morals, shall be ensured to all.

No discrimination of any kind shall be made between the inhabitants on the ground of race, religion, language or sex.

All persons within the jurisdiction of the State shall be entitled to equal protection of the laws.

The family law and personal status of the various minorities and their religious interests, including endowments, shall be respected.

Except as may be required for the maintenance of public order and good government, no measure shall be taken to obstruct or interfere with the enterprise of religious or charitable bodies of all faiths or to discriminate against any representative or member of these bodies on the ground of his religion or nationality.

The State shall ensure adequate primary and secondary education for the Arab and Jewish minority respectively, in its own language and its cultural traditions.

The right of each community to maintain its own schools for the education of its own members in its own language, while conforming to such educational requirements of a general nature as the State may impose, shall not be denied or impaired. Foreign educational establishments shall continue their activity on the basis of their existing rights.

No restriction shall be imposed on the free use by any citizen of the State of any language in private intercourse, in commerce, in religion, in the press or in publications of any kind, or at public meetings.*

No expropriation of land owned by an Arab in the Jewish State (by a Jew in the Arab State) ** shall be allowed except for public purposes. In all cases of

* The following stipulation shall be added to the Declaration concerning the Jewish State: "In the Jewish State adequate facilities shall be given to Arabic-speaking citizens for the use of their language, either orally or in writing, in the legislature, before the Courts and in the administration."

** In the Declaration concerning the Arab State, the words "by an Arab in the Jewish State" should be replaced by the words "by a Jew in the Arab State."

expropriation full compensation as fixed by the Supreme Court shall be paid previous to dispossession.

Citizenship

Palestinian citizens residing in Palestine outside the City of Jerusalem, as well as Arabs and Jews who, not holding Palestinian citizenship, reside in Palestine outside the City of Jerusalem shall, upon the recognition of independence, become citizens of the State in which they are resident and enjoy full civil and political rights. Persons over the age of eighteen years may opt within one year from the date of recognition of independence of the State in which they reside for citizenship of the other State, providing that no Arab residing in the area of the proposed Arab State shall have the right to opt for citizenship in the proposed Jewish State and no Jew residing in the proposed Jewish State shall have the right to opt for citizenship in the proposed Arab State. The exercise of this right of option will be taken to include the wives and children under eighteen years of age of persons so opting.

Arabs residing in the area of the proposed Jewish State and Jews residing in the area of the proposed Arab State who have signed a notice of intention to opt for citizenship of the other State shall be eligible to vote in the elections to the Constituent Assembly of that State, but not in the elections to the Constituent Assembly of the State in which they reside.

International Conventions

The State shall be bound by all the international agreements and conventions, both general and special, to which Palestine has become a party. Subject to any right of denunciation provided for therein, such agreements and conventions shall be respected by the State throughout the period for which they were concluded.

Any dispute about the applicability and continued validity of international conventions or treaties signed or adhered to by the Mandatory Power on behalf of Palestine shall be referred to the International Court of Justice in accordance with the provisions of the Statute of the Court.

Financial Obligations

The State shall respect and fulfil all financial obligations of whatever nature assumed on behalf of Palestine by the Mandatory Power during the exercise of the Mandate and recognized by the State. This provision includes the right of public servants to pensions, compensation or gratuities.

These obligations shall be fulfilled through participation in the Joint Economic Board in respect of those obligations applicable to Palestine as a whole, and individually in respect of those applicable to, and fairly apportionable between, the States.

A Court of Claims, affiliated with the Joint Economic Board, and composed of one member appointed by the United Nations, one representative of the United Kingdom and one representative of the State concerned, should be established. Any dispute between the United Kingdom and the State respecting claims not recognized by the latter should be referred to that Court.

Commercial concessions granted in respect of any part of Palestine prior to the adoption of the resolution by the General Assembly shall continue to be valid according to their terms, unless modified by agreement between the concessionholder and the State.

Miscellaneous Provisions

The provisions of the first two major subsections of the Declaration shall be under the guarantee of the United Nations, and no modifications shall be made in them without the assent of the General Assembly of the United Nations. Any Member of the United Nations shall have the right to bring to the attention of the General Assembly any infraction or danger of infraction of any of these stipulations, and the General Assembly may thereupon make such recommendations as it may deem proper in the circumstances.

Any dispute relating to the application or the interpretation of this Declaration shall be referred, at the request of either party, to the International Court of Justice, unless the parties agree to another mode of settlement.

ECONOMIC UNION AND TRANSIT

The Provisional Council of Government of each State shall enter into an Undertaking with respect to Economic Union and Transit. This Undertaking shall be drafted by the Commission, utilizing to the greatest possible extent the advice and cooperation of representative organizations and bodies from each of the proposed States. It shall contain provisions to establish the Economic Union of Palestine and provide for other matters of common interest. If by April 1, 1948 the Provisional Councils of Government have not entered into the Undertaking, the Undertaking shall be put into force by the Commission.

The objectives of the Economic Union of Palestine shall be: a customs union; a joint currency system providing for a single foreign exchange rate; operation in the common interest on a non-discriminatory basis of railways, interstate highways, postal, telephone and telegraphic services, and ports and airports involved in international trade and commerce; joint economic development, especially in respect of irrigation, land reclamation and soil conservation; access for both States and for the City of Jerusalem on a non-discriminatory basis to water and power facilities.

There shall be established a Joint Economic Board, which shall consist of three representatives of each of the two States and three foreign members appointed by the Economic and Social Council of the United Nations. The foreign members shall be appointed in the first instance for a term of three years; they shall serve as individuals and not as representatives of States.

The functions of the Joint Economic Board shall be to implement either directly or by delegation the measures necessary to realize the objectives of the Economic Union. It shall have all powers of organization and administration necessary to fulfil its functions.

The States shall bind themselves to put into effect the decisions of the Joint Economic Board. The Board's decisions shall be taken by a majority vote.

In the event of failure of a State to take the necessary action the Board may, by a vote of six members, decide to withhold an appropriate portion of that part of the customs revenue to which the State in question is entitled under the Economic Union. Should the State persist in its failure to cooperate, the Board may decide by a simple majority vote upon such further sanctions, including disposition of funds which it has withheld, as it may deem appropriate.

In relation to economic development, the functions of the Board shall be the planning, investigation and encouragement of joint development projects, but it shall not undertake such projects except with the assent of both States and the City of Jerusalem, in the event that Jerusalem is directly involved in the development project.

In regard to the joint currency system the currencies circulating in the two States and the City of Jerusalem shall be issued under the authority of the Joint Economic Board, which shall be the sole issuing authority and which shall determine the reserves to be held against such currencies.

So far as is consistent with the above provision for a common currency, each State may operate its own central bank, control its own fiscal and credit policy, its foreign exchange receipts and expenditures, the grant of import licenses, and may conduct international financial operations on its own faith and credit. During the first two years after the termination of the Mandate, the Joint Economic Board shall have the authority to take such measures as may be necessary to ensure that, to the extent that the total foreign exchange revenues of the two States from the export of goods and services permit, and provided that each State takes appropriate measures to conserve its own foreign exchange resources, each State shall have available, in any twelve months' period, foreign exchange sufficient to assure the supply of quantities of imported goods and services for consumption in its territory equivalent to the quantities of such goods and services consumed in that territory in the twelve months' period ending December 31, 1947.

All economic authority not specifically vested in the Joint Economic Board is reserved to each State.

There shall be a common customs tariff with complete freedom of trade between the States, and between the States and the City of Jerusalem.

The tariff schedules shall be drawn up by a Tariff Commission, consisting of representatives of each of the States in equal numbers, and shall be submitted to the Joint Economic Board for approval by a majority vote. In case of disagreement in the Tariff Commission, the Joint Economic Board shall arbitrate the points of difference. In the event that the Tariff Commission fails to draw up any schedule by a date to be fixed, the Joint Economic Board shall determine the tariff schedule.

The following items shall be a first charge on the customs and other common revenue of the Joint Economic Board: the expenses of the customs service and of the operation of the joint services; the administrative expenses of the Joint Economic Board; the financial obligations of the Administration of Palestine consisting of: the service of the outstanding public debt; the cost of superannuation benefits, now being paid or falling due in the future, in accordance with the rules and to the extent established by the section on "Financial Obligations" above.

After these obligations have been met in full, the surplus revenue from the customs and other common services shall be divided in the following manner: not less than five per cent and not more than ten per cent to the City of Jerusalem; the residue shall be allocated to each State by the Joint Economic Board equitably, with the objective of maintaining a sufficient and suitable level of government and social services in each State, except that the share of either State shall not exceed the amount of that State's contribution to the revenues of the Economic Union by more than approximately four million pounds in any year. The amount granted may be adjusted by the Board according to the price level in relation to the prices prevailing at the time of the establishment of the Union. After five years, the principles of the distribution of the joint revenues may be revised by the Joint Economic Board on a basis of equity.

All international conventions and treaties affecting customs tariffs rates and those communications services under the jurisdiction of the Joint Economic Board shall be entered into by both States. In these matters, the two States shall be bound to act in accordance with the majority vote of the Joint Economic Board.

The Joint Economic Board shall endeavor to secure for Palestine's exports fair and equal access to world markets.

All enterprises operated by the Joint Economic Board shall pay fair wages on a uniform basis.

Freedom of Transit and Visit

The Undertaking shall contain provisions preserving freedom of transit and visit for all residents or citizens of both States and of the City of Jerusalem, subject to security considerations; provided that each State and the City shall control residence within their borders.

Termination, Modification and Interpretation of the Undertaking

The Undertaking and any treaty issuing therefrom shall remain in force for a period of ten years. It shall continue in force until notice of termination, to take effect two years thereafter, is given by either of the Parties.

During the initial ten-year period, the Undertaking and any treaty issuing therefrom may not be modified except by consent of both Parties and with the approval of the General Assembly.

Any dispute relating to the application or the interpretation of the Undertaking and any treaty issuing therefrom shall be referred, at the request of either Party, to the International Court of Justice, unless the Parties agree to another mode of settlement.

ASSETS

The movable assets of the Administration of Palestine shall be allocated to the Arab and Jewish States and the City of Jerusalem on an equitable basis. Allocations should be made by the United Nations Commission referred to above. Immovable assets shall become the property of the government of the territory in which they are situated.

During the period between the appointment of the United Nations Commission and the termination of the Mandate, the Mandatory Power shall, except in respect of ordinary operations, consult with the Commission on any measure which it may contemplate involving the liquidation, disposal or encumbering of the assets of the Palestine Government, such as the accumulated treasury surplus, the proceeds of Government bond issues, State lands or any other asset.

ADMISSION TO MEMBERSHIP IN THE UNITED NATIONS

When the independence of either the Arab or the Jewish State as envisaged in this Plan has become effective and the Declaration and Undertaking, as envisaged in this Plan, have been signed by either of them, sympathetic consideration should be given to its application for admission to membership in the United Nations in accordance with Article 4 of the Charter of the United Nations.

BOUNDARIES

The Arab State

The area of the Arab State in Western Galilee is bounded on the west by the Mediterranean and on the north by the frontier of the Lebanon from Ras en Naqura to a point north of Saliha. From there the boundary proceeds southwards, leaving the built-up area of Saliha in the Arab State, to join the southernmost point of this village. Thence it follows the western boundary line of the villages of 'Alma, Rihaniya and Teitaba, thence following the northern boundary line of Meirun village to join the Acre-Safad sub-district boundary line. It follows this line to a point west of Es Sammu'i village and joins it again at the northernmost point of Farradiya. Thence it follows the sub-district boundary line to the Acre-Safad main road. From here it follows the western boundary of Kafr I'nan village until it reaches the Tiberias-Acre sub-district boundary line, passing to the west of the junction of the Acre-Safad and Lubiya-Kafr I'nan roads. From the southwest corner of Kafr I'nan village the boundary line follows the western boundary of the Tiberias sub-district to a point close to the boundary line between the villages of Maghar and Eilabun, thence bulging out to the west to include as much of the eastern part of the plain of Battuf as is necessary for the reservoir proposed by the Jewish Agency for the irrigation of lands to the south and east.

The boundary rejoins the Tiberias sub-district boundary at a point on the Nazareth-Tiberias road southeast of the built-up area of Tur'an; thence it runs southwards at first following the sub-district boundary and then passing between the Kadoorie Agricultural School and Mt. Tabor, to a point due south at the base of Mt. Tabor. From here it runs due west, parallel to the horizontal grid line 230, to the northeast corner of the village lands of Tel Adashim. It then runs to the northwest corner of these lands, whence it turns south and west so as to include in the Arab State the sources of the Nazareth water supply in Yafa village. On reaching Ginneiger it follows the eastern, northern and western boundaries of the lands of this village to their southwest corner, whence it proceeds in a straight line to a point on the Haifa-Afula railway on the boundary between the villages of Sarid and El Mujeidil. This is the point of intersection.

The southwestern boundary of the area of the Arab State in Galilee takes a line from this point, passing northwards along the eastern boundaries of Sarid and Gavat to the northeastern corner of Nahalal, proceeding thence across the land of Kefar ha Horesh to a central point on the southern boundary of the village of 'Ilut, thence westwards along that village boundary to the eastern boundary at Beit Lahm, thence northwards and northeastwards along its western boundary to the northeastern corner of Waldheim and thence northwestwards across the village lands of Shafa 'Amr to the southeastern corner of Ramat Yohanan. From here it runs due north-northeast to a point on the Shafa 'Amr-Haifa road, west of its junction with the road to I'Billin. From there it proceeds northeast to a point on the southern boundary of I'Billin situated to the west of the I'Billin-Birwa road. Thence along that boundary to its westernmost point, whence it turns to the north, follows across the village land of Tamra to the northwesternmost corner and along the western boundary of Julis until it reaches the Acre-Safad road. It then runs westwards along the southern side of the Safad-Acre road to the Galilee-Haifa District boundary, from which point it follows that boundary to the sea.

The boundary of the hill country of Samaria and Judea starts on the Jordan River at the Wadi Malih southeast of Beisan and runs due west to meet the Beisan-

Jericho road and then follows the western side of that road in a northwesterly direction to the junction of the boundaries of the sub-districts of Beisan, Nablus, and Jenin. From that point it follows the Nablus-Jenin sub-district boundary westwards for a distance of about three kilometres and then turns northwestwards, passing to the east of the built-up areas of the villages of Jalbun and Faqqu'a, to the boundary of the sub-districts of Jenin and Beisan at a point northeast of Nuris. Thence it proceeds first northwestwards to a point due north of the built-up area of Zir'in and then westwards to the Afula-Jenin railway, thence northwestwards along the district boundary line to the point of intersection on the Hejaz railway. From here the boundary runs southwestwards, including the built-up area and some of the land of the village of Kh.Lid in the Arab State to cross the Haifa-Jenin road at a point on the district boundary between Haifa and Samaria west of El Mansi. It follows this boundary to the southernmost point of the village of El Buteimat. From here it follows the northern and eastern boundaries of the village of Ar'ara, rejoining the Haifa-Samaria district boundary at Wadi'Ara, and thence proceeding south-southwestwards in an approximately straight line joining up with the western boundary of Qaqun to a point east of the railway line on the eastern boundary of Qaqun village. From here it runs along the railway line some distance to the east of it to a point just east of the Tulkarm railway station. Thence the boundary follows a line half-way between the railway and the Tulkarm-Qalqiliya-Jaljuliya and Ras el Ein road to a point just east of Ras el Ein station, whence it proceeds along the railway some distance to the east of it to the point on the railway line south of the junction of the Haifa-Lydda and Beit Nabala lines, whence it proceeds along the southern border of Lydda airport to its southwest corner, thence in a southwesterly direction to a point just west of the built-up area of Sarafand el'Amar, whence it turns south passing just to the west of the built-up area of Abu el Fadil to the northeast corner of the lands of Beer Ya'Aqov. (The boundary line should be so demarcated as to allow direct access from the Arab State to the airport). Thence the boundary line follows the western and southern boundaries of Ramle village, to the northeast corner of El Na'ana village, thence in a straight line to the southernmost point of El Barriya, along the eastern boundary of that village and the southern boundary of 'Innaba village. Thence it turns north to follow the southern side of the Jaffa-Jerusalem road until El Qubab, whence it follows the road to the boundary of Abu Shusha. It runs along the eastern boundaries of Abu Shusha, Seidun, Hulda to the southernmost point of Hulda, thence westwards in a straight line to the northeastern corner of Umm Kalkha, thence following the northern boundaries of Umm Kalkha, Qazaza and the northern and western boundaries of Mukhezin to the Gaza District boundary and thence runs across the village lands of El Mismiya El Kabira and Yasur to the southern point of intersection, which is midway between the built-up areas of Yasur and Batani Sharqi.

From the southern point of intersection the boundary lines run northwestwards between the villages of Gan Yavne and Barqa to the sea at a point half way between Nabi Yunis and Minat el Qila, and southeastwards to a point west of Qastina, whence it turns in a southwesterly direction, passing to the east of the built-up areas of Es Sawafir Esh Sharqiya and Ibdis. From the southeast corner of Ibdis village it runs to a point southwest of the built-up area of Beit 'Affa, crossing the Hebron-El Majdal road just to the west of the built-up area of Iraq Suweidan. Thence it proceeds southwards along the western village boundary of El Faluja to the Beersheba sub-district boundary. It then runs across the tribal lands of 'Arab el Jubarat to a point on the boundary between the sub-districts of Beersheba and Hebron north of

Kh. Khuweilifa, whence it proceeds in a southwesterly direction to a point on the Beersheba-Gaza main road two kilometres to the northwest of the town. It then turns southeastwards to reach Wadi Sab' at a point situated one kilometre to the west of it. From here it turns northeastwards and proceeds along Wadi Sab' and along the Beersheba-Hebron road for a distance of one kilometre whence it turns eastwards and runs in a straight line to Kh. Kuseifa to join the Beersheba-Hebron sub-district boundary. It then follows the Hebron-Beersheba boundary eastwards to a point north of Ras Ez Zuweira, only departing from it so as to cut across the base of the indentation between vertical grid lines 150 and 160.

About five kilometres northeast of Ras Ez Zuweira it turns north, excluding from the Arab State a strip along the coast of the Dead Sea not more than seven kilometres in depth, as far as Ein Geddi, whence it turns due east to join the Trans-Jordan frontier in the Dead Sea.

The northern boundary of the Arab section of the coastal plain runs from a point between Minat el Qila and Nabi Yunis, passing between the built-up areas of Gan Yavne and Barqa to the point of intersection. From here it turns southwestwards, running across the lands of Batani Sharqi, along the eastern boundary of the lands of Beit Daras and across the lands of Julis, leaving the built-up areas of Batani Sharqi and Julis to the westwards, as far as the northwest corner of the lands of Beit Tima. Thence it runs east of El Jiya across the village lands of El Barbara along the eastern boundaries of the villages of Beit Jirja, Deir Suneid and Dimra. From the southeast corner of Dimra the boundary passes across the lands of Beit Hanun, leaving the Jewish lands of Nir-Am to the eastwards. From the southeast corner of Beit Hanun the line runs southwest to a point south of the parallel grid line 100, then turns northwest for two kilometres, turning again in a southwesterly direction and continuing in an almost straight line to the northwest corner of the village lands of Kirbet Ikhza'a. From there it follows the boundary line of this village to its southernmost point. It then runs in a southerly direction along the vertical grid line 90 to its junction with the horizontal grid line 70. It then turns southeastwards to Kh. El Ruheiba and then proceeds in a southerly direction to a point known as El Baha, beyond which it crosses the Beersheba-El 'Auja main road to the west of Kh. el Mushrifa. From there it joins Wadi El Zaiyatin just to the west of El Subeita. From there it turns to the northeast and then to the southeast following this Wadi and passes to the east of 'Abda to join Wadi Nafkh. It then bulges to the southwest along Wadi Nafkh, Wadi Ajrim and Wadi Lassan to the point where Wadi Lassan crosses the Egyptian frontier.

The area of the Arab enclave of Jaffa consists of that part of the town-planning area of Jaffa which lies to the west of the Jewish quarters lying south of Tel-Aviv, to the west of the continuation of Herzl street up to its junction with the Jaffa-Jerusalem road, to the southwest of the section of the Jaffa-Jerusalem road lying southeast of that junction, to the west of Miqve Yisrael lands, to the northwest of Holon local council, to the north of the line linking up the northwest corner of Holon with the northeast corner of Bat Yam local council area and to the north of Bat Yam local council area. The question of Karton quarter will be decided by the Boundary Commission bearing in mind among other considerations the desirability of including the smallest possible number of its Arab inhabitants and the largest possible number of its Jewish inhabitants in the Jewish State.

The Jewish State

The northeastern sector of the Jewish State (Eastern Galilee) is bounded on the north and west by the Lebanese frontier and on the east by the frontiers of Syria and Trans-Jordan. It includes the whole of the Huleh Basin, Lake Tiberias, the whole of the Beisan sub-district, the boundary line being extended to the crest of the Gilboa mountains and the Wadi Malih. From there the Jewish State extends northwest following the boundary described in respect of the Arab State.

The Jewish section of the coastal plain extends from a point between Minat el Qila and Nabi Yunis in the Gaza sub-district and includes the towns of Haifa and Tel-Aviv, leaving Jaffa as an enclave of the Arab State. The eastern frontier of the Jewish State follows the boundary described in respect of the Arab State.

The Beersheba area comprises the whole of the Beersheba sub-district, including the Negev and the eastern part of the Gaza sub-district, but excluding the town of Beersheba and those areas described in respect of the Arab State. It includes also a strip of land along the Dead Sea stretching from the Hebron-Beersheba sub-district boundary line to Ein Geddi, as described in respect of the Arab State.

THE CITY OF JERUSALEM

The City of Jerusalem shall be established as a *corpus separatum* under a Special International Regime and shall be administered by the United Nations. The Trusteeship Council shall be designated to discharge the responsibilities of the Administering Authority on behalf of the United Nations.

The City of Jerusalem shall include the present municipality of Jerusalem plus the surrounding villages and towns, the most eastern of which shall be Abu Dis; the most southern Bethlehem; the most western Ein Karim (including also the built-up area of Motsa) and the most northern Shu'fat.

The Trusteeship Council shall within five months from the approval of the present plan elaborate and approve a detailed Statute of the City which shall contain *inter alia* the substance of the following provisions:

Government Machinery: Special Objectives

The Administering Authority in discharging its administrative obligations shall pursue the following special objectives: to protect and to preserve the unique spiritual and religious interests located in the City of the three great monotheistic faiths throughout the world, Christian, Jewish and Moslem; to this end to ensure that order and peace, and especially religious peace, reign in Jerusalem; to foster cooperation among all the inhabitants of the City in their own interests as well as in order to encourage and support the peaceful development of the mutual relations between the two Palestinian peoples throughout the Holy Land; to promote the security, well-being and any constructive measures of development of the residents, having regard to the special circumstances and customs of the various peoples and communities.

Governor and Administrative Staff

A Governor of the City of Jerusalem shall be appointed by the Trusteeship Council and shall be responsible to it. He shall be selected on the basis of special qualifications and without regard to nationality. He shall not, however, be a citizen of either State in Palestine.

The Governor shall represent the United Nations in the City and shall exercise on their behalf all powers of administration including the conduct of external affairs. He shall be assisted by an administrative staff classed as international officers in the meaning of Article 100 of the Charter and chosen whenever practicable from the residents of the City and of the rest of Palestine on a non-discriminatory basis. A detailed plan for the organization of the administration of the City shall be submitted by the Governor to the Trusteeship Council and duly approved by it.

Local Autonomy

The existing local autonomous units in the territory of the City (villages, townships and municipalities) shall enjoy wide powers of local government and administration.

The Governor shall study and submit for the consideration and decision of the Trusteeship Council a plan for the establishment of special town units consisting, respectively, of the Jewish and Arab sections of new Jerusalem. The new town units shall continue to form part of the present municipality of Jerusalem.

Security Measures

The City of Jerusalem shall be demilitarized, its neutrality shall be declared and preserved, and no para-military formations, exercises or activities shall be permitted within its borders.

Should the administration of the City of Jerusalem be seriously obstructed or prevented by the non-cooperation or interference of one or more sections of the population, the Governor shall have authority to take such measures as may be necessary to restore the effective functioning of the administration.

To assist in the maintenance of internal law and order and especially for the protection of the Holy Places and religious buildings and sites in the City, the Governor shall organize a special police force of adequate strength, the members of which shall be recruited outside of Palestine. The Governor shall be empowered to direct such budgetary provision as may be necessary for the maintenance of this force.

Legislative Organization

A legislative council, elected by adult residents of the City irrespective of nationality on the basis of universal and secret suffrage and proportional representation, shall have powers of legislation and taxation. No legislative measures shall, however, conflict or interfere with the provisions which will be set forth in the Statute of the City, nor shall any law, regulation, or official action prevail over them. The Statute shall grant to the Governor a right of vetoing the bills inconsistent with the provisions referred to in the preceding sentence. It shall also empower him to promulgate temporary ordinances in case the Council fails to adopt in time a bill deemed essential to the normal functioning of the administration.

Administration of Justice

The Statute shall provide for the establishment of an independent judiciary system including a court of appeal. All the inhabitants of the City shall be subject to it.

Economic Union and Economic Regime

The City of Jerusalem shall be included in the Economic Union of Palestine and be bound by all stipulations of the undertaking and of any treaties issued therefrom, as well as by the decisions of the Joint Economic Board. The headquarters of the Economic Board shall be established in the territory of the City.

The Statute shall provide for the regulation of economic matters not falling within the regime of the Economic Union, on the basis of equal treatment and non-discrimination for all Members of the United Nations and their nationals.

Freedom of Transit and Visit; Control of Residents

Subject to considerations of security, and of economic welfare as determined by the Governor under the directions of the Trusteeship Council, freedom of entry into, and residence within, the borders of the City shall be guaranteed for the residents or citizens of the Arab and Jewish States. Immigration into, and residence within, the borders of the City for nationals of other States shall be controlled by the Governor under the directions of the Trusteeship Council.

Relations with the Arab and Jewish States

Representatives of the Arab and Jewish States shall be accredited to the Governor of the City and charged with the protection of the interests of their States and nationals in connection with the international administration of the City.

Official Languages

Arabic and Hebrew shall be the official languages of the City. This will not preclude the adoption of one or more additional working languages, as may be required.

Citizenship

All the residents shall become *ipso facto* citizens of the City of Jerusalem unless they opt for citizenship of the State of which they have been citizens or, if Arabs or Jews, have filed the notice of intention to become citizens of the Arab or Jewish State respectively.

The Trusteeship Council shall make arrangements for Consular protection of the citizens of the City outside its territory.

Freedoms of Citizens

Subject only to the requirements of public order and morals, the inhabitants of the City shall be ensured the enjoyment of human rights and fundamental freedoms, including freedom of conscience, religion and worship, language, education, speech and press, assembly and association, and petition.

No discrimination of any kind shall be made between the inhabitants on the grounds of race, religion, language or sex.

All persons within the City shall be entitled to equal protection of the laws.

The family law and personal status of the various persons and communities and their religious interests, including endowments, shall be respected.

Except as may be required for the maintenance of public order and good government, no measure shall be taken to obstruct or interfere with the enterprise of religious or charitable bodies of all faiths or to discriminate against any representative or member of these bodies on the ground of his religion or nationality.

The City shall ensure adequate primary and secondary education for the Arab and Jewish community respectively, in its own language and its cultural traditions.

The right of each community to maintain its own schools for the education of its own members in its own language, while conforming to such educational requirements of a general nature as the City may impose, shall not be denied or impaired. Foreign educational establishments shall continue their activity on the basis of their existing rights.

No restriction shall be imposed on the free use by any inhabitant of the City of any language in private intercourse, in commerce, in religion, in the press or in publications of any kind, or at public meetings.

Holy Places

Existing rights in respect of Holy Places and religious buildings or sites shall not be denied or impaired.

Free access to the Holy Places and religious buildings or sites and the free exercise of worship shall be secured in conformity with existing rights and subject to the requirements of public order and decorum.

Holy Places and religious buildings or sites shall be preserved. No act shall be permitted which may in any way impair their sacred character. If at any time it appears to the Governor that any particular Holy Place, religious building or site is in need of urgent repair, the Governor may call upon the community or communities concerned to carry out such repair. The Governor may carry it out himself at the expense of the community or communities concerned if no action is taken within a reasonable time.

No taxation shall be levied in respect of any Holy Places, religious building or site which was exempt from taxation on the date of the creation of the City. No change in the incidence of such taxation shall be made which would either discriminate between the owners or occupiers of Holy Places, religious buildings or sites, or would place such owners or occupiers in a position less favorable in relation to the general incidence of taxation than existed at the time of the adoption of the Assembly's recommendations.

Powers of the Governor in Respect of the Holy Places

The protection of the Holy Places, religious buildings and sites located in the City of Jerusalem shall be a special concern of the Governor.

With relation to such Places, buildings and sites in Palestine outside the City, the Governor shall determine on the ground of powers granted to him by the Constitutions of both States whether the provisions of the Constitutions of the Arab and Jewish States in Palestine dealing therewith and the religious rights appertaining thereto are being properly applied and respected.

The Governor shall also be empowered to make decisions on the basis of existing rights in cases of disputes which may arise between the different religious communities or the rites of a religious community in respect of the Holy Places, religious buildings and sites in any part of Palestine.

In this task he may be assisted by a consultative council of representatives of different denominations acting in an advisory capacity.

Duration of the Special Regime

The Statute elaborated by the Trusteeship Council on the aforementioned principles shall come into force not later than October 1, 1948. It shall remain in force in the first instance for a period of ten years, unless the Trusteeship Council finds it necessary to undertake a re-examination of these provisions at an earlier date. After the expiration of this period the whole scheme shall be subject to reexamination by the Trusteeship Council in the light of the experience acquired with its functioning. The residents of the City shall be then free to express by means of a referendum their wishes as to possible modifications of the regime of the City.

CAPITULATIONS

States whose nationals have in the past enjoyed in Palestine the privileges and immunities of foreigners, including the benefits of Consular jurisdiction and protection as formerly enjoyed by capitulation or usage in the Ottoman Empire, are invited to renounce any right pertaining to them to the re-establishment of such privileges and immunities in the proposed Arab and Jewish States and the City of Jerusalem.

TEXT OF DRAFT CONSTITUTION

I. General Provisions

Article 1

The name of the State is ISRAEL.

Article 2

The State of Israel is a sovereign, independent, democratic republic.

Article 3

The State of Israel is designed to be the National Home of the Jewish People and shall admit every Jew who desires to settle within its territory subject to such regulative provisions as may from time to time be enacted by the Chamber of Deputies.

Article 4

(1) All persons within the jurisdiction of the State of Israel shall be entitled in equal measure to the protection of the law. No discrimination of any kind shall be made by the State between the inhabitants of the State on the grounds of race, religion, language or sex.

(2) All citizens of the State shall enjoy equal civic and political rights. No citizen shall be at a disadvantage as a candidate for public office or employment or in the matter of promotion, on account of his race, religion, language or sex.

(3) No land, buildings or other property may be expropriated except for public purposes. In all cases of expropriation full compensation, as prescribed by law, shall be paid.

Article 5

The official language of the State of Israel is Hebrew. Adequate facilities shall be given to Arabic-speaking citizens for the use of their language, either orally or in writing, in the legislature, before the courts and before the executive and administrative authorities.

Article 6

(1) The following persons shall be citizens of Israel and shall enjoy the rights and privileges and be subject to the obligations of such citizenship:

(a) All Jews who were resident in the area of the State at the time of the enactment of this Constitution.

(b) All Jews over the age of 18 years resident in that part of Palestine which is not included in the State of Israel who, within one year, opt for citizenship of Israel. The exercise of this right of option shall include the wife and children under 18 years of age of the person so opting.

(c) All residents of Israel other than Jews who were citizens of Palestine at the time of the termination of the Mandate, provided that any such person being over the age of 18 may, within one year, elect not to accept the citizenship of Israel. The exercise of this right of option includes the wife and children under 18 years of age of the persons so opting.

(2) The conditions governing the future acquisition and termination of citizenship in the State of Israel shall be determined by a Nationality Law.

Article 7

The flag of the State of Israel is a white banner with two horizontal blue stripes and the Shield of David in the centre.

Article 8

All natural resources within the jurisdiction of the State of Israel shall belong to the State subject to any rights therein vested in any person or body, and shall be controlled and administered by the Government of Israel in accordance with such regulations and provisions as shall from time to time be approved by legislation.

Article 9

The State shall enact legislation to ensure the proper conservation and economic utilisation of the soil and water for the benefit of the people.

Article 10

The Antiquities of Israel, being a precious heritage of the past, shall be considered as a trust to be conserved by the State for future generations, and the State shall enact legislation to this end.

Article 11

The State of Israel shall seek to settle all international disputes of whatever nature or origin in which it may be involved by pacific means only. The generally recognised rules of international law shall form part of the municipal law of Israel.

II. Fundamental Rights

Article 12

The State shall ensure the sanctity of human life and uphold the dignity of man. There shall be no penalty of death, nor shall anyone be subjected to torture, flogging or humiliating punishment. The application of moral pressure or physical violence in the course of police interrogations is prohibited: evidence obtained by such methods shall not be admissible in Court.

Article 13

(1) The liberty of the person is inviolable. No one shall be detained except pursuant to an order or judgment of a Court of Law, or when apprehended in flagrante delicto, or for the purpose of bringing him before a Court on a charge of having committed a crime.

(2) Preventive detention by executive order shall be unlawful except when authorised by specific legislation in time of war or national emergency and subject to continuous parliamentary control.

(3) Any person arrested shall be informed in writing within twenty-four hours by what authority and on what grounds he is being detained, and shall be brought up for trial not later than two days from the date of his arrest. Upon complaint being lodged by or on behalf of any person to the High Court or any Judge thereof, that any such person is being unlawfully detained, the High Court or the Judge to whom such complaint is made shall require the officer in whose custody such person is detained, to produce him without delay and certify in writing the grounds of his detention. If satisfied that the detention is not in accordance with the law, the Judge shall order the immediate release of the detainee.

(4) No person under arrest shall be held incommunicado.

(5) No person shall be deprived of his liberty on account of a debt or other contractual obligation except for fraud.

(6) No one shall be tried save by due process of law. Extraordinary courts shall not be established. No person other than members of the Armed Forces of the State on active service, shall, at any time, be subjected to the jurisdiction of military tribunals.

(7) No one shall be convicted of any infringement of the law which did not constitute an offence when it was committed, nor shall any amendment of the law increasing the penalty for any offence or altering the rules of evidence to the detriment of the accused, have retroactive effect.

(8) Anyone wrongfully arrested, convicted or punished shall have an enforceable claim for compensation against the State.

Article 14

The dwelling of every person is inviolable and shall not be entered or searched except in accordance with the law and in the manner therein prescribed. Private correspondence as well as telegraphic and telephonic communications shall not be intercepted. Any temporary suspension of these guarantees in time of war or national emergency shall require specific legislative authorisation and shall be subject to parliamentary control.

Article 15

(1) Freedom of conscience and the free exercise of all forms of worship, subject only to the maintenance of public order and morals, shall be ensured to all.

(2) Existing rights in respect of Holy Places and religious buildings or sites shall not be denied or impaired. The liberty of access, visit and transit to Holy Places shall be guaranteed, in conformity with existing rights, to all without distinction, subject to the requirements of national security, public order and decorum.

(3) No taxation shall be levied in respect of any Holy Place, religious building or site which was exempt from taxation on the date of the establishment of the State. No change in the incidence of such taxation shall be made which would either discriminate between the owners or occupiers of Holy Places, religious buildings or sites, or would place such owners or occupiers in a position less favourable in relation to the general incidence of taxation than existed prior to the establishment of the State.

(4) The Sabbath and the Jewish Holy Days shall be days of rest and spiritual elevation and shall be recognised as such in the laws of the country. The Holy Days of other religious denominations shall equally be recognised as legal days of rest for the members of such denominations.

Article 16

Freedom of speech and the free expression of opinion in writing or in any other form, are guaranteed. This constitutional guarantee shall not extend to utterances or publications which are libellous, slanderous or obscene, or which are designed to stir up racial or religious hatred, or to incite to violence or crime, or which advocate the suppression of human rights, or of the democratic system of government or which reveal secrets of national defence. The institution of a preventive censorship shall be unlawful save in time of war or national emergency and shall require specific legislative authorisation and be subject to continuous parliamentary control and review.

Article 17

All citizens of the State of Israel shall have the right to assemble peaceably without arms and to form associations, subject to such regulative provisions as may be enacted from time to time by the Chamber of Deputies. Such enactments shall contain no discrimination on grounds of race, religion, language or political belief.

This constitutional guarantee shall not extend to assemblies or associations aiming at the suppression of human rights or of the democratic form of government.

Article 18

Any officer of the State of Israel who, contrary to the provisions of this Constitution, knowingly violates the rights and liberties of any person, shall be liable to proceedings under the civil and criminal law.

Article 19

Every citizen of the State of Israel has the right, either individually or in association with others, to petition the President, the Government, the Chamber of Deputies, or any other public authority for the redress of grievances or for the enactment of legislation.

Article 20

No one may be extradited to any foreign country where he is liable to be deprived of such fundamental personal and political rights as are guaranteed by this Constitution. The Government of Israel may in its absolute discretion refuse to deliver up any of its subjects to a foreign government for prosecution or punishment.

Article 21

The economic order of the State of Israel shall be based on the principles of social justice. Every citizen shall have an equitable share in the national income and a right to social security. The State shall encourage and aid every form of cooperative effort.

Article 22

Every one has the right to work. The State of Israel shall endeavour to ensure to all its citizens without distinction a decent standard of living and a fair and equal opportunity of earning a livelihood. Legislation shall be enacted making provision for reasonable wages, working hours and conditions of work and for the provision of state insurance against the risks of accident, sickness, disablement, unemployment, old age and other causes of undeserved want. Special protective measures shall be enacted for the benefit of working mothers and children, and of widows and orphans.

Article 23

The right of workers to form trade union associations, to enter into collective bargaining contracts and to strike in defence of their economic rights and interests is guaranteed by the Constitution. Any provision embodied in a contract of employment which involves renunciation or diminution of these rights shall be null and void.

Article 24

Care for the health of the population is a primary duty of the State. Legislation shall be enacted providing for the establishment of a national health service, the protection of motherhood and child life, the promotion of public and personal hygiene, and the grant of state aid towards the construction of hygienic workers' dwellings.

Article 25

(1) The State shall provide adequate facilities for primary and secondary education to be given to Jews and Arabs in their own language and cultural traditions.

(2) The right of each community to maintain its own schools for the education of its own members in its own language, while conforming to such educational requirements of a general nature as the State may impose, shall not be denied or impaired.

(3) Foreign educational establishments shall be allowed to continue their activity on the basis of their existing rights.

III. The Legislature

Article 26

The legislative power in the State of Israel shall be vested in the Chamber of Deputies.

Article 27

All citizens of the State who have reached the age of twenty-one and are not subject to any legal disability or incapacity under the electoral law shall be entitled to vote in the elections to the Chamber.

Article 28

All citizens of the State who have reached the age of twenty-five and are not subject to any legal disability or incapacity under the electoral law, shall be eligible to the Chamber. Judges, civil servants, members of the Armed Forces of the State of Israel serving with the colours, and persons who are also citizens of a foreign state shall not be eligible.

Article 29

The Chamber of Deputies shall be elected by equal, direct and universal suffrage and by secret ballot on the basis of proportional representation. The mode of election shall be determined by an electoral law. The country shall be divided into a number of electoral districts, each 10,000 of the population approximately to be represented by one deputy. The electoral districts shall be revised once in three years, having regard to intervening changes in the numbers and distribution of the population. Vacancies caused by the death, resignation, or disqualification of any deputy shall be filled in accordance with the provisions of the electoral law.

Article 30

Elections shall be held within two months from the expiration of the term or the dissolution of the preceding Chamber. They shall be held on the same date throughout the country.

Article 31

The Chamber shall meet within one month of its election. It shall hold two sessions every year, beginning in the first week of Cheshvan and Iyar, respectively. The sessions shall be convened by the Chairman on the day fixed by the Chamber upon its adjournment. At the request of one-third of the deputies, an extraordinary session shall be called.

Article 32

On taking their seats, deputies shall make the following solemn declaration: "I pledge myself to be faithful to the State of Israel and to uphold its Constitution and its laws."

Article 33

The Chamber shall be elected for a period of four years, but it may extend its term in case of war or emergency, but for not more than one additional term.

Article 34

The President of the Republic may dissolve the Chamber of Deputies prior to the expiration of its term if the Executive Council in office has resigned and no alternative Executive Council can be formed commanding the support of a stable majority in the Chamber.

Article 35

No legal action shall be taken against any deputy in respect of any statements made or votes taken in the Chamber or in respect of any opinions expressed by him outside the Chamber in his official capacity. No deputy may be required, even after having ceased to be a deputy, to give evidence in any court of law in regard to matters confided to him in that capacity. This provision shall not apply to any investigation conducted by a committee of enquiry appointed by the Chamber.

Article 36

No criminal proceedings may be taken against any deputy except with the consent of the Chamber. No deputy may be arrested except if apprehended in flagrante delicto.

If any deputy is so arrested, the Chairman shall be immediately informed and shall bring the matter to the notice of the Chamber. Unless the Chamber within a fortnight approves of the detention and authorises the institution of legal proceedings against the deputy, he shall be released.

Article 37

Deputies shall receive a remuneration to be fixed by the Chamber.

Article 38

Official reports of proceedings in the Chamber and its Committees, as well as true reports of such proceedings wherever published, shall be privileged.

Article 39

The Chamber shall adopt Standing Orders for regulating its procedure, maintaining internal discipline and protecting its members from any molestation, interference or attempt at corruption. It shall elect a Chairman and Vice-Chairmen and fix their powers and remuneration.

Article 40

The proceedings of the Chamber shall be held in public. Upon a motion supported by two-thirds of the deputies present, the public may be excluded.

Article 41

Save as otherwise prescribed in this Constitution or in the Standing Orders, decisions shall be by a majority of those present. In case of any equality of votes the presiding officer shall exercise a casting vote.

Article 42

The initiative in introducing legislation shall rest with the Executive Council. Deputies may propose legislative measures, but such proposals shall be referred to a Select Committee of the Chamber. They shall be introduced by the Executive Council if recommended by a majority of the Select Committee and in the form recommended by that Committee.

Article 43

All revenues of the State, from whatever source arising, shall form one Consolidated Revenue Fund and shall be appropriated by the Chamber of Deputies for the purposes of the State in the manner and subject to the charges and liabilities imposed by this Constitution.

Article 44

The Chamber shall consider the estimates of income and expenditure for the current financial year submitted to it by the Executive Council, and shall enact the Finance Act prior to the end of the financial year. No resolution for the appropriation of funds or for the increase of any grant or charge may be moved except by a member of the Executive Council.

Article 45

After a Bill has been passed by the Chamber, two copies of it shall be transmitted by the Chairman to the President of the Republic for his signature. One copy shall be deposited in the Record Office of the Chamber and the other shall be transmitted to the Registrar of the High Court to be enrolled for record in his office. It shall come into force upon its publication in the Official Gazette.

Article 46

The recruiting and maintenance of the Armed Forces shall be subject to the control of the Chamber of Deputies.

Article 47

Treaties and other agreements with foreign countries shall not be binding on the State unless approved by the Chamber of Deputies. By such approval these treaties and agreements shall become part of the municipal law of Israel. All such treaties and agreements shall be published in the Official Gazette.

IV. The Executive Power

Article 48

The executive power in the State of Israel shall be vested in the President of the Republic and in the Executive Council.

(1) *The President of the Republic.*

Article 49

Any citizen of Israel, who is eligible to the Chamber of Deputies and has reached the age of 35, may be elected to the office of President.

Article 50

The President of the Republic shall be elected by the Chamber of Deputies by secret ballot. If, in two successive ballots, no candidate receives an absolute majority of votes, the candidate for whom, in the third ballot, a relative majority of votes is cast, shall be deemed to have been elected.

Article 51

The term of office of the President shall be five years. He may be re-elected on the expiry of his term or at any subsequent election, but only for one additional term of office.

Article 52

The election of the President shall take place not later than one month prior to the expiration of the term of the President in office. If the latter dies, resigns, is removed from office or becomes permanently incapacitated, such incapacity being established by a decision of the Supreme Court, the election of a new President shall take place within one month therefrom.

Article 53

If the office of the President becomes vacant as a result of the death, resignation, removal, or permanent incapacity of the holder, the Chairman of the Chamber of Deputies shall exercise the functions of the President until the election of a new President.

Article 54

The President, upon entering his office, shall make the following declaration in the presence of members of the Executive Council, the Chamber of Deputies and the Judges of the Supreme Court and the High Court: "I solemnly promise that I will maintain the Constitution and the laws of Israel, that I will dedicate myself to the service and welfare of the People of Israel and that I will act justly and rightly to all citizens of Israel."

Article 55

Every official act of the President shall be countersigned by the Prime Minister or a member of the Executive Council who shall thereby assume responsibility for it.

Article 56

The President shall, after consultation with the leaders of the parliamentary parties, appoint the Prime Minister and, upon his advice, the other members of the Executive Council. The President shall appoint the ambassadors and ministers of the State of Israel. The President shall appoint the Commander-in-Chief of the Armed Forces of Israel and issue commissions to the officers of these Forces.

Article 57

The President shall receive the diplomatic envoys accredited to the State of Israel and shall issue exequaturs to foreign consuls.

Article 58

The President shall promulgate the laws enacted by the Chamber within ten days from the date of such enactment. If the law was enacted as an urgent measure it shall be promulgated within three days.

Article 59

The President shall exercise the prerogative of mercy.

Article 60

The President shall, upon the advice of the Executive Council and with the assent of the Chamber of Deputies, conclude treaties with foreign states.

Article 61

The President shall be removed from office on impeachment by two-thirds of the Chamber of Deputies and on conviction by the Supreme Court of high treason, bribery or culpable violation of the Constitution.

(2) *The Executive Council.*

Article 62

The Executive Council shall consist of the Prime Minister, the heads of the Departments of State and such Ministers without Portfolio as may from time to time be appointed. The total number of Ministers shall not exceed fifteen. All Ministers shall be members of the Chamber of Deputies and shall be appointed in the manner prescribed in Article 56.

Article 63

The Prime Minister shall preside over the meetings of the Executive Council. He shall be responsible for the coordination of the activities of the Executive Council and for the execution by the Departments of State of the policies adopted by the Executive Council. He shall keep the President of the Republic informed on all major questions of domestic and foreign policy.

Article 64

The Executive Council shall be collectively responsible to the Chamber of Deputies. It shall resign if it ceases to retain the support of a majority in the Chamber of Deputies, but shall continue in office until its successors have been appointed. The resignation of the Prime Minister shall entail that of the Executive Council as a whole. Individual Ministers may resign from office by placing their resignation in the hands of the Prime Minister for submission to the President of the Republic.

Article 65

No Minister may be a member of the Board of Directors of any Joint Stock or Limited Liability Company carrying on business for profit.

Article 66

The organisation of the Departments of State, the designation of Ministers and their remuneration shall be regulated by law.

Article 67

The organisation of and admission to the Civil Service shall be regulated by law. After the enactment of this Constitution, all appointments to the Civil Service shall be by examination to be conducted by a Civil Service Commission. In exceptional cases the Civil Service Commission may authorise the appointment of senior officers without examination.

Article 68

The Executive Council and any of its members shall have power to make orders and regulations within the framework of existing laws. Such orders and regulations shall be tabled in the Chamber of Deputies and shall become inoperative if a motion to that effect is adopted by the Chamber within two weeks therefrom.

(3) *The Comptroller and Auditor General.*

Article 69

There shall be a Comptroller and Auditor General to control, on behalf of the State, all payments and to audit all accounts of monies administered by or under the authority of the Chamber of Deputies. He shall not be a member of the Chamber of Deputies nor hold any other office or position of emolument. The manner of his appointment and the length and conditions of his tenure of office shall be fixed by law.

V. The Judicial Power

Article 70

The judicial power shall be vested in and exercised by the Courts of Law established under this Constitution. They shall comprise:

(a) Magistrates' Courts;
(b) District Courts;
(c) A High Court with original and appellate jurisdiction in civil and criminal matters, and with exclusive original jurisdiction in all questions relating to validity of any law having regard to the terms of the Constitution;
(d) A court of final appeal to be called the Supreme Court;
(e) Religious courts of the Jewish, Moslem and Christian communities exercising jurisdiction in matters of personal status and of religious foundations and endowments.

Article 71

The organisation and jurisdiction of the courts, the remuneration, pensions and age of retirement of the judges, and all matters of procedure shall be regulated by law.

Article 72

All judges, other than the members of the Religious Courts, shall be appointed by the President of the Republic on the advice of the Minister of Justice who, in tendering such advice, shall be guided by the recommendations of a Selection Board consisting of a member of the Supreme Court, a High Court judge, two senior officers of the Department of Justice, three deputies chosen by the Chamber and three representatives of the Bar Association. The Selection Board shall be reconstituted annually. The judges of the Religious Courts shall be appointed by the President of the Republic acting on the advice of the Minister for Religious Affairs who, in tendering such advice, shall be guided by the recommendations of the Supreme Religious Council of the community concerned.

Article 73

No judge of the Civil Courts shall be removed from office except for stated misbehaviour or incapacity upon a resolution supported by two-thirds of the members of the Chamber of Deputies. No judge of the Religious Courts shall be removed from office except for stated misbehaviour or incapacity upon a motion of the Supreme Religious Council of the community concerned and upon a resolution supported by two-thirds of the members of the Chamber of Deputies. The removal shall be effected by an order of the President of the Republic.

Article 74

Where any action of personal status involves persons of different religious communities, the President of the Supreme Court shall decide which court shall exercise jurisdiction. In deciding such issue, he shall invite the assistance of assessors from the Religious Courts of the communities concerned. Whenever the question arises as to whether or not a case is one of personal status within the exclusive jurisdiction of a religious court, the matter shall be referred to a special tribunal, the constitution of which shall be prescribed by law.

VI. Amendment of the Constitution

Article 75

The Chamber of Deputies shall have power to amend the Constitution, but every such amendment shall require the assent of two-thirds of the total membership of the Chamber and shall not come into force unless passed by that majority in two successive sessions of the Chamber, and unless not less than six months have elapsed between the two successive enactments.

VII. Constitution and Legislation

Article 76

No law shall be enacted which is in any respect repugnant to any of the provisions of this Constitution. If the Courts pronounce any law or any provision thereof to be repugnant to the Constitution, such law or provision shall, to the extent of such repugnancy, be thenceforth absolutely void and inoperative.

VIII. The Law

Article 77

The laws in force in the State of Israel at the time of the enactment of this Constitution shall continue in force to the extent of which they are not inconsistent with the terms of this Constitution until the same or any of them shall have been repealed or amended by the Chamber of Deputies or under its authority. Future legislation in Israel shall be guided by the basic principles of Jewish Law. Wherever the existing law does not provide adequate guidance, the Courts-of-Law shall have recourse to these basic principles.

IX. Promulgation

Article 78

This Constitution shall come into force on the day of its publication in the Official Gazette.

INDEX

H

I

J

K

L

M

N

O

P

T

U

V

W

Y

Z